G

D

CONDITIONS OF PEACE

CONDITIONS OF PEACE

BY

EDWARD HALLETT CARR

PROFESSOR OF INTERNATIONAL POLITICS
IN THE UNIVERSITY COLLEGE OF WALES

"Shall we attain, as some prophets, perhaps as vain as
their predecessors, assure us, a social transformation more
complete and more profound than our fathers foresaw and
desired, or than we ourselves are able to foresee? Or are
we about to enter on intermittent anarchy—that chronic
and incurable malady well known to ancient peoples?"
—*Souvenirs de Alexis de Tocqueville*

NEW YORK
THE MACMILLAN COMPANY
1942

CONTENTS

PART I

SOME FUNDAMENTAL ISSUES

CHAPTER 1

CHAPTER 2

CHAPTER 3

CHAPTER 4

CHAPTER 5

PART II

SOME OUTLINES OF POLICY

CHAPTER 6

vi CONTENTS

NOTE

THE hazards of any study of international affairs made in the midst of the shifting fortunes of war will be apparent to every reader, as they have been apparent to the writer, of this book. The fundamental issues at stake in the war—and in any future peace—have not changed, and will not change, their character. But every fresh extension of the battlefield alters in some degree the perspectives through which they are viewed and the policies designed to meet them. It should therefore be said that the general shape of this book had been determined, and much of it had been written, before the entry of Soviet Russia into the war transformed some of the problems with which it attempts to deal; and that it was already in the press when Japan and the United States of America joined the ranks of the belligerents. These considerations reinforce the warning given on p. 167 of the tentative nature of the discussions of policy in the concluding chapters.

January 1942

INTRODUCTION

THE civilised world on which the war of 1914 broke so suddenly was on the whole a prosperous and orderly world. It was a world of contented and reasoned optimism—a world which, looking back on the past hundred years with pardonable self-satisfaction, believed in progress as a normal condition of civilised human existence. The war was regarded not as a symptom that mankind had got on to the wrong path (for that seemed almost inconceivable), but as a shocking and meaningless digression. "We were sure . . . in 1914", says Lord Halifax, "that once we had dealt with the matter in hand the world would return to old ways, which, in the main, we thought to be good ways."[1] Some grains of optimism could even be extracted from the awful experience. In the closing stages of the war the belief became current that the result of an Allied victory would be to create a still better world than had been known before, a world safe for democracy and fit for heroes to live in, a world in which a new international order would assure universal justice and perpetual peace. There was felt to be nothing revolutionary about this conception. A return to the old ways, which were also good ways, naturally meant a resumption of the orderly march of human progress. "There is no doubt", wrote General Smuts in 1918 in a much-quoted passage, "that mankind is once more on the move. . . . The tents have been struck, and the great caravan of humanity is once more on the march."[2]

[1] Viscount Halifax, *Speeches on Foreign Policy*, 1934-1939, p. 360.
[2] J. C. Smuts, *The League of Nations: A Practical Suggestion*, p. 18.

This vision of a resumption of the age-long march of mankind towards a better world did not last. It faded through the long months of the Peace Conference, and perished in the first post-war economic crisis of 1920. In laying aside their arms, the war-weary peoples of the victorious countries seemed to have abandoned their exalted ambitions for the future. Still obsessed with the idea of a return to the good old ways, they thought of it no longer as the return to an interrupted path of effort and progress, but as the return to a static condition of automatic and effortless prosperity. No longer expecting or demanding a key to paradise, they sank into a mood of comfortable resignation. Mr. Lloyd George, the restless innovator, was replaced by Mr. Baldwin smoking the pipe of peace and security. Woodrow Wilson, the prophet of the new order, was succeeded by Harding and Coolidge, the dispensers of "normalcy". Security and normalcy became the twin pillars of the temple. Both were interpreted in terms of the halcyon age before 1914. For twenty years, this unadventurous and backward-looking view was the characteristic attitude of the three Great Powers who were mainly responsible for the Versailles settlement.[1]

Far different was the psychological reaction of the so-called "dissatisfied" Powers. These included Germany, the only defeated Great Power; Soviet Russia, who was conducting a revolution against the whole political, social and economic system which the peace settlement was designed to perpetuate; Italy, driven into the rebel camp by disappointment with her share in the proceeds of victory; and Japan, whose successes in the past fifty years have imparted a strain of caution and conservatism to her policy, but whose jealousy of British and American influence in the Pacific range her on the side of the dissatisfied Powers. None of these countries was disposed to look back on the past with complacency. The satisfied Powers

[1] This statement requires qualification for the United States after 1933: the point will be discussed later.

continued to draw their inspiration from the conditions of the period which had witnessed their rise to power and their triumph, and too often failed to realise that those conditions had passed away. The dissatisfied Powers were in the position of revolutionaries renouncing and challenging the past in the name of new ideologies. [The psychological background of the twenty years between the two wars may be observed in the respective reactions of the satisfied and dissatisfied Powers to military, political and economic problems.]

The backward-looking view of the satisfied Powers is particularly well illustrated in the attitude of their military chiefs. Soldiers and sailors alike clung eagerly to the glorious traditions of nineteenth-century warfare. After the victorious struggle of 1914-18, security could best be assured by putting back the clock, or at any rate by seeing that it did not move on any further. The programme of the British and American General Staffs at the Peace Conference of 1919 contained two main desiderata: to abolish the submarine and to deprive Germany of military aviation. If only these two major innovations of the war could be somehow shuffled out of existence, we could return to the familiar and comfortable dispositions of nineteenth-century strategy. At the Disarmament Conference, Great Britain once more proposed the abolition of twentieth-century weapons: the submarine, the large tank, gas and bombing from the air. So reluctant were successive British Governments to recognise the potentialities of the air arm that Great Britain ranked at one time as the seventh air Power of the world. The Royal Air Force, being the youngest, was also the Cinderella of the services.[1] It was considered important that the British navy should be three times as strong as is the German. But in

---

[1] "The importance of this professional departmentalism in determining the actual allocation of our resources is greater than anyone who is not closely acquainted with the Government machine can well recognise. If we ask why, in the first allocation of the additional resources, the Air Ministry did not get more, the true answer is that it is the youngest of the fighting services" (A. Salter, *Security: Can We Retrieve It?* p. 183).

the air no more than equality with Germany was aimed at, and this was far from being achieved. "The sea gives us time", Campbell-Bannerman had exclaimed in 1871 arguing against an expansion of the army.[1] The same factor was felt to be valid more than sixty years later. If Britannia ruled the waves, then British supremacy was surely as secure in the twentieth century as in the nineteenth: British mentality was slow to adapt itself to any other view.

French strategy was still more retrograde. The two famous French memoranda on security submitted to the Peace Conference of 1919—the "Foch memorandum" of January 10 and the "Tardieu memorandum" of February 26—discussed military transport exclusively in terms of railways; and neither of them so much as mentioned air power. The one important French strategical conception of the inter-war period was the Maginot Line—an attempt to immobilise warfare and to freeze the *status quo*. Throughout this period, the French and British General Staffs appear to have assumed without question that immobile trench warfare would be the main form of land fighting in any future war—for no better reason than that this had been true of the last war. "Everything is being done", complained a prescient French critic in 1928, "as though the Versailles Treaty, which has compelled Germany to modernise her military ideas, permits us to go back to the military routine of 1914—and then fall asleep." [2] It is perhaps unfair to pass a similar stricture on the military policy of the smaller satisfied Powers, since their conservative outlook was dictated by lack of resources as well as by lack of imagination. Holland and Belgium failed to recognise that an army deprived of the assistance of air forces and mechanised units of appreciable strength is a negligible factor in modern warfare. Polish strategy

---

[1] J. A. Spender, *The Life of the Right Hon. Sir Henry Campbell-Bannerman*, i, p. 40.

[2] Quoted from *L'Œuvre* by M. Werner, *The Military Strength of the Powers*, p. 210.

assigned an important rôle to cavalry; and Switzerland based her plan of defence on a militia mounted on bicycles and renowned for its personal courage and for the accuracy of its marksmanship with the rifle.

While therefore the strategy of the satisfied Powers was dominated by an amalgam of nineteenth-century preconceptions and of the lessons of the war of 1914-18, the initiative passed to the rival group. The aeroplane was a French, the tank a British, invention. Yet in the period between the two wars, it was the German army which elaborated and perfected the tactics of aerial and mechanised warfare, while the British and French military mind was unable to clear itself of the precepts and habits of a bygone age. The parachutist landing behind enemy lines was a Russian device, studied and perfected by Germany and ignored by the satisfied Powers. It is difficult to exaggerate the advantage ultimately derived by Germany from the destruction of her armaments and of her whole military machine in 1919—a circumstance which obliged her not only to modernise her material but to think out again from the start every problem of equipment and organisation, while Britain and France remained embedded in the legacy of the past.[1] When war began, the enterprising nature of German tactics completely bewildered the British and French General Staffs. The German army, explained The Times, "is prepared to take risks of a character which, rightly or wrongly, has been condemned by French and British military doctrine." [2] "The truth

---

[1] It has been observed that German industry enjoyed an exactly similar advantage over British in the latter part of the nineteenth century: "The country being . . . not committed to antiquated sites and routes for its industrial plant, the men who exercised the discretion were free to choose with a single eye to the mechanical expediency of locations for the pursuit of industry. Having no obsolescent equipment and no out-of-date trade connexions to cloud the issue, they were also free to take over the processes of the new industry at their best and highest efficiency, rather than content themselves with compromises between the best equipment known and what used to be the best a few years or a few decades ago" (T. Veblen, *Imperial Germany*, pp. 187-8).

[2] *The Times* (leading article), May 14, 1940.

is", said the French Prime Minister a few days later, "that our classic conception of the conduct of war has come up against a new conception." [1] The significant fact about the first year of war was not so much that the Germans took the offensive throughout, but that every novelty in strategy or tactics, every new military invention of any importance, appeared on the German side.[2] Technically speaking, revolutionary conceptions of warfare were matched against pure conservatism.

The politicians of the satisfied Powers, no less than the soldiers and the sailors, had their eyes fixed on the past. "Our apparent inability to innovate or do any really original thinking", wrote an independent observer of British political life in 1934, "is the most exasperating feature of modern politics." [3] The democracy for which the world had been made safe in 1918 was understood to be the particular form of liberal democracy which had grown up in the special conditions of the nineteenth century. Conceived in these terms, it became one of those things which, being taken for granted, cease to be a living force. Democracy relied on the prestige of a glorious tradition and seemed to have nothing but its past achievements to offer as a contribution to the problems of the new world. It became the prerogative of the well-to-do and the privileged who could regard past and present with a substantial measure of satisfaction. In 1939 democratic governments survived in most of the ten or twelve countries of the world possessing the highest income per head of population—and hardly anywhere else. Prior to 1933, no attempt had been made to reinterpret democracy to meet the conditions of the post-war world; and in democratic countries few people recognised that it could not continue to function exactly as it had functioned before 1914. After 1933,

[1] Statement to French Senate of May 21, reported in *The Times*, May 22, 1940.

[2] The *Deutsche Allgemeine Zeitung* of August 24, 1940, tauntingly remarked that the one initiative taken by Great Britain in the first year of the war had been to declare it.

[3] E. Percy, *Government in Transition*, p. 99.

opinion in the United States began to move, in face of considerable opposition,[1] towards a radically new conception of democracy. But this movement had scarcely spread to Europe before the outbreak of war in 1939. In politics as in strategy, it was difficult to imagine that anything had happened to put an end for ever to the glorious and easy-going days of the nineteenth century.

Politically, too, therefore the initiative was left to the dissatisfied Powers. The first to take it was Soviet Russia. From 1921 onwards her example was followed by country after country which combined rebellion against the Versailles settlement with rejection of democracy, sometimes paying lip-service to democracy, as the Russians had done, by purporting to set up a new and more perfect form of it. The attraction of Bolshevism, Fascism and National Socialism lay not in their obscure, elastic and sometimes incoherent doctrines, but in the fact that they professedly had something new to offer and did not invite their followers to worship a political ideal enshrined in the past. Like the new strategy, the new political order had the merit of not having been tried before. A revolutionary frame of mind confronted an attitude of political complacency and nostalgia for the past.

In international affairs, the same confrontation appeared in a more overt and more dramatic form. Here there was a direct clash of interest between conservative Powers satisfied with the *status quo* and revolutionary Powers seeking to overthrow it. The League of Nations, more than any other institution, was overtaken by the reaction from the brief interlude of optimism of 1918-19 to the static complacency of the 'twenties. Created in a mood of burning faith in human progress, of which it was

[1] The backward-looking view was still firmly entrenched even in the United States. In 1937 a well-known American publicist prepared an "agenda of liberalism" which recommended a return to the point where "latter-day" liberals had gone off the rails somewhere about 1870 in order to complete "the unfinished mission of liberalism" (W. Lippmann, *The Good Society*, p. 225 and *passism*).

to be the principal instrument, it was quickly perverted into a tool of the satisfied Powers, who had been careful even at the Peace Conference to emasculate the only radical article in the Covenant. Every attempt to "strengthen" the Covenant meant another bulwark to uphold the *status quo*. The Geneva Protocol was the political counterpart of the Maginot Line. To make the Geneva trenches impregnable and wait for the enemy to attack was the summit of political wisdom. Like all privileged groups, the satisfied Powers insisted on the supreme importance of peace, and capitalised the fear of war in the same way in which conservatives at home capitalise the fear of revolution. "No special circumstances, no individual aspirations, however justifiable", said Briand to the Assembly in the palmiest days of the League, "can be allowed to transcend the interests of peace. Peace must prevail, must come before all. If any act of justice were proposed which would disturb world peace and renew the terrible disaster of yesterday, I should be the first to call on those promoting it to stop, to abandon it in the supreme interests of peace." [1] Let injustice persist rather than that the sacred rights of the existing order should be infringed. "The first purpose of the League", declared one of its English champions, "is the defence of its members—self-preservation which is the first law of life of any organisation." [2] The obsession of "security" hung like a millstone about the neck of the League and excluded every breath of life and freshness from its body. Politically, Geneva became the home of pure conservatism. "Govern and change nothing" had been Metternich's motto. The League changed nothing and failed only to govern.

Every movement for international change came therefore from the dissatisfied Powers, and was at once confronted by the vested interests of the *status quo*. It is true that some of the desired changes were destructive in character. But the absence

---

[1] League of Nations, *Ninth Assembly*, p. 83.
[2] N. Angell in *The Future of the League of Nations* (Royal Institute of International Affairs, 1936), p. 17.

of any proposals for constructive change, or indeed of any recognition of the need for change at all, from any other quarter left the field open to the challengers. The fund of prestige inherited by the League of Nations from its radical and idealistic origins was soon exhausted. The political offensive, like the strategic offensive, passed exclusively to the dissatisfied Powers.

In the economic field complacency was less easy to justify and a policy of inaction more difficult to maintain. Politically, the bankruptcy of the *status quo* was not fully revealed or recognised before the middle and later 'thirties. Strategically, the unmitigated conservatism of the satisfied Powers was exploded only by the military disasters of 1940. Economically, the break came far sooner. The first economic crisis of 1920 had created widespread disquiet, which was aggravated by the controversies over reparations and the Ruhr occupation. In the heyday of military predominance and political quiescence, the demon of economic insecurity was already raising its head. Even in 1924, amid the enthusiasm inspired by the Geneva Protocol, a French Delegate to the Assembly of the League sounded a warning note:

> If we are ever to rest secure in the edifice of peace, the great and grave problems of the distribution of raw materials, of markets, of emigration and immigration, will one day have to be taken in hand by the financial and economic organisations of the League and by its Assemblies. If they are left unsolved —let us make no mistake—they will cause internal disruption which will bring down in ruins the fabric we have reared.[1]

To dig oneself in might suffice as a guiding principle for soldiers or politicians. It was lamentably defective as an economic panacea. Economically, conservatism was not enough; for there was not even the semblance of a satisfactory *status quo* to conserve. The problem was urgent and inescapable. What remedy could be applied?

[1] League of Nations, *Fifth Assembly*, p. 219.

The answer given to this question was the completest expression of the backward-looking attitude of the satisfied Powers. Belief in progress was dead. If the *status quo* did not secure economic prosperity, if some change was unavoidable, then change could be conceived only in the form of a step backwards. If conservatism was not enough, the alternative was reaction. Economic man was no longer marching forward by new and untried paths towards hitherto unscaled heights. The aim was now to retrieve a false move, to undo what had been done, to erase from the fair page everything written on it since 1914. A return to the past meant a return to "normal" prosperity. "Lancashire is perfectly sanguine of success", wrote an observer in 1924, "once normal conditions have been restored."[1] "Business men", remarks another commentator, "wistfully awaited a return to 'normal', and convinced themselves that 'normal' meant the world of 1913."[2] In this fatal atmosphere even steps which were at the time hailed as landmarks of progress turned out on a longer view to be pure reaction. Thus the Dawes Plan, which seemed a highly enlightened way of disposing of reparations, was in essence a reactionary attempt to set up again the humpty-dumpty of nineteenth-century private international capitalism with its centre in New York instead of in London. When American financiers in 1929 found the burden too heavy, the world no longer had any shelter from the sweeping storm of economic revolution.

Yet nostalgia for the past still remained the dominant obsession. It is curious to reflect how many of the economic slogans of the period between the two wars began with the prefix *re*. We were successively concerned with reconstruction, retrenchment, reparations, repayment of war debts, revaluation of currencies, restoration of the gold standard, recovery and removal of trade barriers. Even inflation could be made respectable by calling it "reflation". In the 'thirties a leading British expert on

[1] A. Siegfried, *Post-War Britain*, p. 110.
[2] W. K. Hancock, *Survey of British Commonwealth Affairs*, ii, Pt. 1, p. 199.

international economic relations wrote two books of which the first was called *Recovery* and the second *Security: Can We Retrieve It?* [1] The collective wisdom of the economic world as expressed by the experts of the two international economic conferences of 1927 and 1933 taught that practically every trend of economic policy which had developed since 1914 was wrong and ought to be arrested or reversed.

It will not be pretended that those responsible for the economic policy of the satisfied Powers always listened to the pleas of their economic advisers for a return to nineteenth-century principles. Down to 1931, lip-service did indeed continue to be paid by the governments of almost all these countries to economic orthodoxy, though there were many derogations from it in practice. From 1931 onwards even the lip-service grew faint and perfunctory, and governments were driven before the economic hurricane into new and unprecedented courses. But the point is that this action was taken haphazard, under compulsion of circumstances, in defiance of accepted economic theory, yet without any understanding why that theory had broken down and what was being substituted for it. The statesmen who sponsored these new policies were on the defensive. The new course was represented as a temporary and distasteful necessity. It was adopted only to meet "unfair" competition. Appearances notwithstanding, it would expand not limit the volume of international trade. It was designed to pave the way for an eventual return to orthodoxy. These absurd and mutually contradictory explanations had only one significance. The statesmen who sponsored the policies neither understood nor believed in them. They had lost the initiative, and were being driven, hesitant, bewildered and apologetic, by forces too powerful for them to control.

In these conditions economic inventiveness, like military

[1] The "expert" is Sir Arthur Salter. The comment is intended not as a criticism of the books, but as an expression of admiration for titles so exactly calculated to appeal to the mood of the contemporary reader.

inventiveness, was honoured and practised only among the dissatisfied Powers. The innovations which, for good or evil, transformed the face of the economic world in the inter-war period
were developed and exploited by the revolutionary Powers
who challenged the existing order. "Planned economy"—the
regulation and organisation of national economic life by the
state for the needs of the community as a whole—may be said
to have made its first appearance in all the principal belligerent
countries (though predominantly in Germany, where the term
originated) in the war of 1914-18. But whereas Great Britain,
the United States and France, made haste at the end of the war
to cast off state control in the vain hope of returning to the
laissez-faire principles of the pre-war period, Soviet Russia, soon
to be followed by Fascist Italy and Nazi Germany, found in
"planned economy" the new twentieth-century concept which
was to replace nineteenth-century liberalism; and having gained
the initiative, these countries at length compelled the conservative Powers to follow slowly and reluctantly in their train.
State control of foreign trade and its use as a political weapon,
invented by Soviet Russia, were perfected by Nazi Germany;
and in 1938-39 Great Britain, under extreme German pressure,
had begun to take some faltering steps in the same direction.
The techniques of a managed currency and of foreign exchange
control were elaborately studied by the dissatisfied Powers
while these things were still regarded in Great Britain and the
United States with contemptuous horror. Necessity was, of
course, the mother of invention. But those on whom the necessity first descended scored an immense advantage through the
rapid development of the spirit of enterprise and innovation.
The fact that Soviet Russia and Nazi Germany had virtually
eliminated unemployment was slightingly dismissed with the
retort that this had been achieved only by methods, and at the
cost of sacrifices, which the satisfied countries would never
tolerate. The answer was clearly inadequate, so long as the satis-

fied Powers could find no answer of their own to a problem
whose acuteness could not be denied. If a considerable part of
the younger generation in many European countries came to
believe that either Soviet Russia or Nazi Germany held the
key to the future, this was because both these countries propounded new economic systems based on new principles and
therefore opening up a prospect of hope, whereas the political
and intellectual leaders of the satisfied countries appeared to
offer no solution of the economic problem but the return to a
past whose bankruptcy had been sufficiently demonstrated.
Nothing did more to discredit the satisfied Powers than the way
in which they allowed the effective initiative, in the critical
field of economic theory and practice, to pass to the rival group.
Only the United States began, after 1933, to move hesitatingly,
and with much lip-service to antiquated ideals, in the direction
of a new economic, as well as a new political, orientation.

If in the light of this outline, military, political and economic,
we now review the whole psychological background of the
past twenty years, we shall see that the attitude of the satisfied
Powers was stultified by two defects of outlook common to
almost all privileged and possessing groups. In the first place,
the privileged group tends to idealise the period in which it has
risen to the height of its power, and to see its highest good in
the maintenance of those conditions. Secondly, the privileged
group is preoccupied with the question of its own security
rather than with the need for reform or even for progress.
"Nothing is more certain", observed J. S. Mill eighty years ago,
"than that improvement in human affairs is wholly the work of
the uncontented characters." [1] In the satisfied countries, privileged groups have for a long time past been too powerful, and
"uncontented characters" not sufficiently numerous or influential. The widespread diffusion of privilege in the English-
speaking countries has been the foundation of the stability of

[1] J. S. Mill, *Considerations on Representative Government*, ch. iii.

their political institutions. But in revolutionary times the number of the privileged may present a positive danger by hindering the prompt recognition of new and vital needs.

⌐ The first moral for the victors in the present war is then not to look backwards in search of principles to guide the post-war settlement. This precept should be less difficult to follow than it was in 1919; for we are no longer blinded, as we were then, by the "old ways" of the pre-war world which we thought of as good ways. The most encouraging feature of the present situation is the prevalence, especially among the younger generation, of a deep-seated conviction that the world of the past decade has been a bad and mad world, and that almost everything in it needs to be uprooted and replanted. A revolutionary current is in the air. Nevertheless, there are many disquieting features, one of them being the very high average age of those who hold the key positions in the public life of Great Britain. Most men of sixty and over are more susceptible to impressions of the past than to future needs. The younger generation will hardly achieve its goal if it continues to rely, as exclusively as it appears to rely at present, on the leadership of veterans. France and Great Britain suffered military disaster in 1940 largely because they had prepared to fight the last war over again. Will it be said hereafter that we failed in peace-making because we had prepared only for the last peace?

⌐ The second moral, equally important and perhaps more easily forgotten, is the fatal consequence of undue preoccupation with security. This preoccupation is a constant pitfall of privileged groups. "The prosperous middle classes who ruled the nineteenth century", observes a distinguished scientist, "placed an excessive value on placidity of existence. . . . The middle-class pessimism over the future of the world comes from a confusion between civilisation and security. In the immediate future there will be less security than in the immediate past, less stability. . . . On the whole, the great ages have been unstable ages." [1] The quest for security inevitably becomes an instrument of reaction. "The clash of progress and security", which Professor Fisher has discussed in a stimulating book under that title, has a significance far beyond the specifically economic application which he has given to it. Everyone who followed the history of the League of Nations knows the stifling effect exercised at Geneva by the word "security" on any progressive movement. It is both shocking and alarming to learn from an American business man, a President of the International Chamber of Commerce, that "the thing that gives us most satisfaction in life is security".[2] If this is indeed true, our civilisation is doomed to perish.

It cannot be too often repeated—for it is still not widely understood—that neither security nor peace can properly be made the object of policy. "Personal security is like happiness", writes Professor Fisher, "in that it is likely to elude a direct search. In a progressive economy, stability and personal security are to be found only as a by-product of the search for something else." [3] International peace is another such by-product.[4] It cannot be achieved by the signing of pacts or covenants "outlawing" war any more than revolutions are prevented by making them illegal. A generation which makes peace and security its aim is doomed to frustration. The only stability attainable in human affairs is the stability of the spinning-top or the bicycle. If the victors in the present war are able to create the conditions for an orderly and progressive development of human society, peace and security will be added unto them. But they will have to learn the paradoxical lesson that the condition of security is

[1] Sir Alfred Whitehead, quoted in B. L. Richmond, *The Pattern of Freedom*, p. 68.

[2] *International Conciliation*, No. 362 (September 1940), p. 328.

[3] A. G. B. Fisher, *The Clash of Progress and Security*, p. 106.

[4] The thesis that peace is not, and never can be, a direct object of policy, is developed at greater length in E. H. Carr, *The Twenty Years' Crisis*, pp. 68-9. As Dorothy Sayers has wittily remarked, "we wooed peace as a valetudinarian woos health, by brooding over it until we became really ill" (*The Spectator*, November 24, 1939, p. 736).

continuous advance. The political, social and economic problems of the post-war world must be approached with the desire not to stabilise, but to revolutionise.

A further warning is necessary. We have seen how rapidly the idealistic urge generated at the end of the last war faded away into indolence and complacency. The perfectly natural phenomenon of war-weariness, coupled with the desire of the individual to return to "normal" life, completely eclipsed the vague inclination to play an effective part in the building of a new world. "The demand for 'demobilisation' in every sphere was so strong that even the victorious governments were carried along by the tide, and the statesmen at Paris had hardly begun to grapple with their task before they found their omnipotence ebbing away." [1] There is grave danger that war-weariness may play the same rôle at the end of the present war with still more disastrous results. "The true measure of nations", remarked Mr. Churchill in February 1919, "is what they can do when they are tired." [2] But much will depend on the existence of a government ready to give a clear and decisive lead; and this lead will not be forthcoming unless policy has been considered and plans carefully formulated in advance. This is one of several cogent answers to those who argue that reconstruction is an affair of the post-war period, and that it is premature or superfluous to examine such problems so long as hostilities continue.

[1] A. J. Toynbee, *The World After the Peace Conference*, p. 2.
[2] Speech at the English-Speaking Union, February 23, 1919, quoted in R. Sencourt, *Winston Churchill*, p. 169.

PART I

SOME FUNDAMENTAL ISSUES

CHAPTER I

WAR AND REVOLUTION

THE starting-point of our investigation into the underlying problems of the present war is the recognition that it is an episode in a revolution. "All great convulsions in the history of the world, and more particularly in modern Europe," writes a contemporary historian, "have been at the same time wars and revolutions."[1] This is most conspicuously true of wars which are both "total" and world-wide in their scope and effects. Local and limited wars like the Crimean War, the Franco-Prussian War or the Boer War, which have none of this revolutionary character, are contrasted with general upheavals like the Napoleonic wars or the contemporary war of which the first outbreak occurred in 1914 and the second in 1939. Wars of this latter kind break up and sweep away the half-rotted structure of an old social and political order, and lay the foundations of a new. New trends germinating unseen beneath the surface are brought to sudden maturity in the forcing-house of war. War begets new needs and new loyalties which help to determine social and political forms for the coming century. Social forms reflect the experience of war, and reconcile war-time mobilisation with peace-time reconstruction. . . . War is never the end, but always the beginning of a new social order.[2] So much justification can be found for the ancient aphorism that "war is the father of all things". Yet it is fair to add that wars are just as much the product as the

[1] E. Halévy, *The World Crisis, 1914-18*, p. 7.
[2] E. Rosenstock-Huessy, *Out of Revolution*, p. 672.

cause of revolution. War is produced by the conditions which have made revolution necessary, and in turn hastens the consummation of the revolution. It is part of a revolutionary process, and cannot be isolated from it either as cause or as effect.

The revolutionary character of the present war has become unusually obvious. The war of 1914 had, throughout the earlier part of its course, all the external aspects of a purely national war; and the fanning of national hatred was on all sides the principal stimulant to public morale. Not until 1918 did the British Government use the propaganda weapon to set Germans against Germans, invoking ideological divisions to split national unity, and building up the hypothesis of a "good" and a "bad" Germany. The actual merits of this propaganda have perhaps been exaggerated; for its success was achieved against a people already enervated by physical hardships and by the first rumblings of defeat. But its novelty was striking and impressive to those who, like Hitler, knew a revolutionary weapon when they saw it. In the present war, attempts to create divisions between the people and their "plutocratic" or "Jewish" rulers have been the staple of the Nazi propaganda campaign. Britain in her propaganda to Germany has been careful to make "Nazis" and not "Germans" the target of her denunciations. Nor has this been a mere official convention. The flight of hundreds of thousands of refugees from the persecution of their compatriots made it far more difficult than it was in the last war to treat Germans as a homogeneous mass, capable of being lumped together for purposes of favourable or unfavourable judgment. The presence in Great Britain of large numbers of Germans inspired by the keenest hatred of the Nazi régime kept alive the necessity of maintaining the distinction between "good" and "bad" Germans and of insisting that Britain was fighting not Germany, but Nazidom. In the last war, public opinion had angrily adjured the authorities to "intern the lot". In the present war, the spontaneous adoption of this policy by the authorities evoked equally angry protests. Those who still seek to fan national hatreds are survivors of the last war who have failed to understand the change of climate. The present war cannot be explained, and cannot be waged, purely in national terms. This is no local crisis whose origins are confined to a specific area of Europe: it is a major crisis going to the deepest roots of our civilisation.\

Revolution and Reaction

\Great wars are, then, commonly part of a revolutionary process whose fundamental causes may be quite different from the immediate causes of the war; and this explains why the ultimate results of such wars rarely correspond to the declared or conscious aims of any of the belligerents.\ This discrepancy is especially marked when war aims are conceived in a negative sense, *e.g.* to prevent the domination of the Continent by a single Power, to eradicate German militarism, or to destroy Hitlerism. No revolution can express its essence in mere negation or destruction.\Negative war aims are futile and deceptive; for, like other forms of "security", they can be achieved only as a by-product of some positive aim.\ In Great Britain, this simple truth has been obscured by the popular illusion, encouraged by the orthodoxy of the League of Nations, that the only object for which wars could properly be fought was to defend the existing order against attempts to disturb it. History shows that the one thing war never does is to maintain or restore the *status quo ante bellum*. It is not even true, as is sometimes suggested, that restoration at the end of a war is the first step towards reconstruction; on the contrary, restoration is often the greatest ob-

---

[1] "Our one agreed aim in 1914 was to break German militarism. It was no part of our original intention to break up the Hapsburg and Ottoman Empires, to create Czechoslovakia or resurrect Poland, to make a Russian revolution, to treble the size of Servia and double that of Roumania, to create Iraq and Estonia and Lithuania and a Jewish National Home, or to give the keys of the Brenner and the Adriatic to Italy. Yet, in the outcome, all these things—and much else—sprang from the war . . . while the one thing which we promised ourselves, the destruction of German militarism, we failed to achieve" (H. N. Fieldhouse, in *Fortnightly*, June 1940, pp. 580-81)

stacle to it. No sane person would propose that, as a first step towards the replanning and rebuilding of London, every bombed building should be restored to its original state. It is scarcely less fantastic to suggest that the first step towards the building of a new European order is to put back the frontier posts and restore the sovereignties of 1938 or 1939. It is an encouraging symptom that British opinion is becoming more and more alive to the necessity for a positive and constructive definition of war aims. Whether we like it or not, we are in the midst of a revolution. Any attempt to ignore it, or to stem it by a restoration of the past, is futile and disastrous. We need a policy which is both positive and revolutionary.

The fact that great historical upheavals commonly take on a character, and produce results, utterly remote from the conscious purposes of those who set them in motion and appear to direct them, has been attributed by some to the working of a God or a *Zeitgeist* and by others to an "inner dynamic" of history. These metaphysical explanations explain nothing It is safer to conclude that the men who are popularly said to "make history" are dealing with highly intractable material, that this material, which includes the wills of their fellow-men, can be moulded only in accordance with certain existing trends, and that the statesman who fails to understand, or refuses to comply with, these trends dooms himself to sterility. The stream can be harnessed to constructive purposes, but it cannot be made to turn back on its course. If we choose, we can lead and direct the revolution. But in order to achieve this we must first understand its nature and its aims.

The peace settlement of 1919 provides a classic example of failure to understand the revolutionary character of a world war or the nature of the revolution which had inspired it. The case is complicated and instructive. The original war aims of the Allies were negative: to resist "German militarism" and to defend small nations. But soon the need was felt for something more positive; and as early as 1915 we find a well-known British

154
13
98

MACKENZIE

CALL SLIP FOR BOOKS

REF ☐
CA ☐
STREF ☐

CALL # _____
(include letters)

AUTHOR _____

TITLE _____

_____

L3: 05/91

publicist, in words which a quarter of a century later sound grimly ironical, advocating "the dismemberment of the Hapsburg monarchy" as the indispensable condition of a policy "so to reconstitute Europe that a renewal of the struggle shall become impossible".[1] The liberation of subject nations under the banner of self-determination was proclaimed as a war aim by Woodrow Wilson after the entry of the United States into the war; and to it was added, rather less specifically, the extension of democratic government throughout Europe. The cause of democracy and the cause of nationalism—the rights of men and the rights of nations—were positive and revolutionary aims, and aroused an enthusiasm which merely negative aims could never have inspired. They had unfortunately one defect. They had been the aims of the French Revolution, and had been the directing ideas of Western civilisation throughout the nineteenth century. They were no longer adequate to meet the new revolutionary crisis, of which 1914 was the first and undiagnosed symptom. Woodrow Wilson and the enthusiasts for liberal democracy and national liberation were merely repeating the slogans of a bygone age. This explains the curious paradox that most of the idealists of the English-speaking world in the past twenty years have been, in the true sense of the word, reactionaries. They have allowed themselves to be carried away by the last expiring convulsions of a world revolution which set in 150 years ago, and put themselves in opposition to the new world revolution which first broke through the crust of the existing order in the Bolshevik Revolution of 1917.

The sterility of the peace settlement of 1919 was due to the failure of those who made it to understand the contemporary revolution. In retrospect, it is not difficult to see that the increasing strains of competitive capitalism were one of the most important underlying causes of the catastrophe of 1914. To multiply the number of competing units in the name of the ideals of the French Revolution was as sure and as mad a way as could

[1] H. Wickham Steed in *Edinburgh Review*, October 1915, p. 246.

well have been found of aggravating the crisis and of ensuring a repetition of the outbreak. The paradox which continues to puzzle students of the period between the two wars is that the victorious Allies "lost the peace". During those twenty years, the two great countries whose collapse in 1918 had been complete and spectacular made giant strides to recovery and were presently taking the political lead throughout Europe, while the victors of 1918 remained helpless spectators. (That the United States seceded from the settlement, that the Allies quarrelled among themselves, that Hitler was a gangster and that Great Britain disarmed and temporised, that the Versailles Treaty was too vindictive, that the Versailles Treaty was not vindictive enough—all these explanations are superficial and futile) The victors lost the peace, and Soviet Russia and Germany won it, because the former continued to preach, and in part to apply, the once valid, but now disruptive, ideals of the rights of nations and *laissez-faire* capitalism, whereas the latter, consciously or unconsciously borne forward on the tide of twentieth-century revolution, were striving to build up the world into larger units under centralised planning and control. (The Russians conceived this integration in cosmic terms, though in practice they soon began to limit their activities to the area of the Soviet Union. The Germans, whose outlook was from the first opportunistic and riddled with inconsistencies, conceived it in the more limited, but gradually expanding, framework of *Mittel-Europa*. But both were in their different ways looking forward to a new order based on new and revolutionary conceptions of social and economic organisation. Great Britain and France, embedded in the nineteenth-century tradition, forfeited the initiative through failure to understand the nature of the forces at work.

Napoleon and Hitler

The war of 1939 is the second stage in the twentieth-century revolution. France has fallen out of the race and is unlikely in the near future to regain her position as a leading Power. Great Britain, under the impulse of war, has experienced a marked revival of energy and power and has gone far to recover the initiative she had lost. Understanding may be assisted by the accidental, but remarkably close, parallel between the rôle of Napoleon and that of Hitler. Hitler's relation to the Bolshevik Revolution matches in many respects Napoleon's relation to the French Revolution. Just as Napoleon exploited the demand for liberty and equal political rights expressed in the French Revolution, so Hitler exploits for his purposes the demand for social equality and equal economic rights expressed in the Bolshevik Revolution. The processes of history are indirect and infinitely complicated. The whiff of grapeshot on the 18th Brumaire, and the burning of the Reichstag to dish the Communists, led contemporaries to suppose that Napoleon had set out to liquidate the French Revolution and Hitler to liquidate communism. Napoleon was supported by many Frenchmen in the belief that he was restoring the old order in a slightly different form; and Hitler proclaimed himself, and is still regarded by some people in many countries, as the leader of a counter-revolution against Bolshevism. Whether these were at any time the personal intentions of the two men is a point of trivial importance. Napoleon, who overthrew dynasties, abolished the Holy Roman Empire and swept away the millennial litter of the feudal system, carried the ideas of the French Revolution all over Europe. Hitler has consummated the work, which Marx and Lenin had begun, of overthrowing the nineteenth-century capitalist system.

It need therefore neither shock nor disconcert us that Hitler, like ourselves, announces as his war aim the creation of a new order. The same revolutionary forces are everywhere at work, and both sides are consciously or unconsciously impelled by them in the same direction. The point at issue is not the necessity for a new order, but the manner in which it shall be built. Hitler, like Napoleon, is the child of a revolution. He had succeeded, where Lenin failed, in spreading the destructive forces of revolution all over Europe; and in this sense his work, like that of Napoleon, cannot and will not be undone. The overthrow of Hitlerism will not restore the nineteenth-century capitalist system any more than the downfall of Napoleon restored feudalism. Indeed we meet here another paradox. It was the defeat not the victory of Napoleon which secured the ultimate triumph of the revolution whose ideas he had so effectively, though perhaps unwittingly, disseminated. Had he defeated Britain and reached the goal of his ambition, it would still have been necessary to overthrow him before these ideas could come to fruition. Hitler has succeeded, like Napoleon, only by methods of military domination and universal oppression which cannot endure. His work is primarily and essentially destructive. He is a revolutionary only in the negative sense; and the new order can come into being only through his defeat. It was not Napoleon himself, but those who had suffered most from his ambition, who ultimately had the largest share in the building of the nineteenth-century world. Hitler, like Napoleon, has performed the perhaps indispensable function of sweeping away the litter of the old order. The new order must be built by other hands and by other methods. One of the most valuable potential consequences of Soviet Russia's entry into the war is that Great Britain may thus regain, in the field of propaganda, something of the true and revolutionary initiative which Soviet Russia formerly held.

The Contemporary Revolution

What then is the fundamental character of the revolution which began in the last war, which has been the driving-force of every significant political movement of the last twenty years, and which is reaching its climax in the present war? If we fail to understand the nature of the forces at work, we shall be wholly unable to fashion any durable settlement after the war, and our efforts will be as sterile as those of 1919. It is not too early to attempt an analysis of our contemporary revolution. It is a revolution against the three predominant ideas of the nineteenth century: liberal democracy, national self-determination and *laissez-faire* economics.

The revolution against liberal democracy, though first preached by Marx in 1848, remained for seventy years beneath the surface and without visible influence on human affairs. In the latter part of the nineteenth century, few people contested the assumption that liberal democracy as practised in Western Europe and in the English-speaking world was an absolute good. Cases where democracy did not yet prevail were explained on the ground that the peoples concerned were still unripe for it, or were the unhappy victims of some kind of oppression or perversion which impeded the fulfilment of their natural democratic destiny. The mission of men of goodwill was therefore to "make the world safe for democracy". When Woodrow Wilson coined this famous phrase on April 2, 1917, he was felt to have given utterance to a universally recognised aspiration of humanity. Before that fateful year was out, the revolutionary government of a large and important country was loudly and impressively proclaiming, for the first time for many years, that liberal democracy was not a good thing at all, but a hollow sham. The revolt against liberal democracy, once set in motion by the Russian Revolution, spread rapidly, taking advantage of those anti-liberal and anti-democratic trends which had never been wholly absent from the Continental tradition. It was successively taken up by Mustapha Kemal, by Mussolini, by Pilsudski, by Salazar, before it was generalised by Hitler and extended all over the continent of Europe and over much of Latin America. A movement of these dimensions and of this extent is a major revolution. Nor does the attack come only from one side. Nazi propaganda against liberal democracy borrows familiar Marxist *clichés*, denouncing it as a synonym for plutocracy, exposing the hollowness of the liberty which it purports to confer, and appealing to the masses to rise against those who exploit them for their own advantage under the guise of democracy. But what is really under attack is not democracy as such, but liberal democracy in its specifically nineteenth-century form. The distinction should always be observed. The defence of democracy, like other negative aims, is dead and barren. The challenge of the revolution can only be met by re-defining and reinterpreting democracy in a new and revolutionary sense. The present crisis of democracy is the need for this re-definition.

The revolt against national self-determination as the constitutive principle of international society also finds its first substantial expression in the revolution of 1917. The anti-national character of the Bolshevik Revolution was apparent in its first manifestations. Borrowing from Marx the view that national aspirations represent only a transitory stage of social development, it claimed to override national in the name of social divisions. The process of de-nationalisation was carried to its highest point, the name of Russia disappearing from the official title of the country. Neither the use of national self-determination as a slogan for propaganda among colonial peoples nor the later revival of Russian nationalism under Stalin implied acceptance of an unrestricted right of national self-determination as the constitutional or ideological basis of the Soviet Union. The case of Germany is more striking. National Socialism began as a specifically nationalist movement, and even invoked the principle of national self-determination. But the "inner dynamic" of the revolution turned it into a supra-national movement for a European order in which the right of national self-determination would be subject to the limitations of a centralised military and economic dictatorship; and Hitler now contemplates "a Europe in which Nazi conquest has accomplished what democratic good intentions failed to achieve—the end of competing nations".[1] In 1928 Mussolini proclaimed that "Fascism is not an article for export". Two years later, he disowned this "banal" phrase, and

[1] F. Williams, *War by Revolution*, p. 111.

declared Fascism "universal".[1] Every modern revolutionary movement of any importance, whether its original ideology was national or international, is sooner or later impelled to turn away from nationalism as a self-sufficient principle of political action. There has even been a return to reactionary pre-democratic dynasticism in the form of nostalgia for the decayed glories of the Hapsburg Empire. But once more, the proper target of attack is not self-determination as such, but national self-determination in the form which it assumed in the later nineteenth century and which was taken as the basis of the peace settlement of 1919. The revolutionary challenge to self-determination, like the revolutionary challenge to democracy, must be met not by a purely negative defence, but by re-definition and reinterpretation.)

Lastly, the contemporary revolution is a revolt against economic *laissez-faire*. Here the revolution had already begun in a modest form with the movement for the "social service state"— a movement which first became conspicuous in Germany under Bismarck, spreading to Great Britain after 1906 and to the United States in 1933. "Planning" in the modern sense was no doubt a product of the war of 1914. But it is important to recognise that the demand for an omni-competent state was originally inspired by social, not by military motives, by the need, not of guns, but of a reasonably equitable distribution of butter. The introduction of "planned economy", not as a temporary expedient, but as a permanent instrument of policy, was the sequel of the Russian Revolution; and its spread has been rapid. In this field the revolution has made more effective progress than in any other. But Great Britain is still hampered by lingering regrets for the *laissez-faire* period which was that of her greatest prosperity, and has still to adapt her policy, consciously and deliberately, to the needs of the economic revolution. This is perhaps the most urgent of all the tasks which awaits her.

[1] *Scritti e Discorsi di Benito Mussolini*, vi, p. 151; vii, p. 230.

These then are the three headings under which the fundamental problems of the war—which are also the problems of our contemporary revolution—can be most conveniently discussed: the crisis of democracy, the crisis of national self-determination, and the economic crisis.

CHAPTER 2

THE CRISIS OF DEMOCRACY

THE crisis of democracy set in with dramatic suddenness at the moment when democracy seemed to have achieved its greatest triumph. The Allied victory of 1918 persuaded almost every country in Europe to accept the view of the victorious Powers that the world had been made safe for democracy. Hastily and obsequiously, politicians elaborated democratic constitutions and conferred political rights on their peoples. But this sudden conversion was artificial and struck no roots. Within three years, the retreat from democracy had begun; and in few cases did those on whom these rights had been bestowed show any interest in defending them. For masses of people all over the world, political rights had come to appear meaningless or irrelevant. While it has been common form to attribute the slump in democracy to the unscrupulous ambition of dictators, thoughtful democratic writers of all countries have been conscious of profounder causes. "While parliamentary government in 1920 was possibly receiving greater lip-service than ever before", wrote Professor Toynbee not long after that date, "there was a noticeable diminution in its actual prestige in almost every country where it was officially established." [1] In the Germany of 1930, notes a careful American observer, "the unemployed shook loose, fairly rapidly, from the conviction that the fight for labour rights and the democratic system had any real meaning for them. They began to move into the Communist Party and the National Socialist Party. The fight for labour rights and

[1] A. J. Toynbee, *The World After the Peace Conference*, p. 67.

democracy was no longer their fight." [1] "Democracy", said a distinguished publicist of the British Labour Party in 1935, ". . . has lost belief in itself and become an inert instead of a dynamic force in world affairs. . . . Unlike our opponents, we are uncertain what the democracy is for which we stand." [2] "The resistance of democracy in Western Europe", wrote an acute German *émigré* shortly before the present war, "depends . . . entirely upon the emotional and sentimental allegiance of the masses to the façade of democracy. This allegiance gives the façade some sort of independent existence even after the structure behind has broken down. . . . But . . . however strong such traditional resistance might be, it remains inert and purely negative." [3] Those responsible for British propaganda in Europe in the present war have found "the defence of democracy" a wholly inadequate rallying-cry. "Democracy is in its present plight", confessed a well-known British writer when the war was a year old, "because for years democrats have left the initiative entirely in the hands of their enemies." [4]

This inert and negative character of contemporary democracy, this uncertainty for what it stands, is well illustrated by the fluency and the vagueness with which the term is used by politicians of every complexion. Praise of democracy has served more often than not as an excuse for self-complacency and for doing nothing. Nobody in the past twenty years has spoken more eloquently or more sincerely of democracy than Calvin Coolidge and Mr. Hoover in the United States or Lord Baldwin in Great Britain. The word has been invoked so often and in so many contexts that it has lost much of its freshness; and while the attacks launched on democracy in the name of Marxism and of Fascism have been extremely precise, no defender of democracy had yet arisen to repel them in any but the vaguest and most

[1] S. Raushenbush, *The March of Fascism*, p. 242.
[2] R. H. S. Crossman, *Plato To-day*, p. 292.
[3] P. Drucker, *The End of Economic Man*, pp. 118-19.
[4] L. Woolf in *Political Quarterly*, October-December 1940, p. 340.

antiquated terms. During the same period, while books, essays and articles on Bolshevism, Fascism and National Socialism, laudatory, soberly critical or violently hostile, have poured from the presses of many countries, it is difficult to recall a single significant European exposition of democracy as a driving force in the modern world. The theme has become stale, unprofitable and "inert".

The picture becomes clearer if we compare these conditions with those of last century. In nineteenth-century Britain, though the word democracy was held in little honour, the struggle for political rights was the stuff of political life. The great political issues were by whom parliament should be elected and by what means parliament should make its voice decisive in the processes of government. The principles of democracy and the balance of power in the constitution were constant themes of the speeches of public men and the writings of men of letters: indeed the two rôles were not uncommonly combined. The political literature of the nineteenth century was varied, copious and brilliant. In 1832 the great Reform Act had conferred effective political rights on new strata of population, and thereby placed the control of the state machine in new hands. In 1867 the extension of the franchise, by broadening the basis of the ruling class, caused another perceptible shift in the distribution of power. These were milestones in British nineteenth-century history. The last important issues of this kind before 1914 were the demand for votes for women and the campaign to eliminate the non-representative House of Lords. Both raised popular feeling to a high pitch of excitement. Then after the war came an extraordinary reaction. Almost suddenly political rights appeared to lose their importance in the eyes of those formerly most concerned to possess them. The final abolition of plural voting and the extension of the franchise to those still excluded from it—measures which, fifty years earlier, would have seemed revolutionary—created hardly any stir and produced no visible effect. Women got the vote because it seemed fair and reasonable that they should get it if they wanted it, not because any-one—except a few fanatical partisans—imagined that it would have any important practical results. The same mood of sceptical indifference descended like an extinguisher on what had once been burning questions: the reform of the House of Lords, the introduction of the alternative vote, the establishment of par-liamentary commissions, devolution, and a dozen other current specifics for the improved working of our representative insti-tutions. It was not that such proposals were weighed and re-jected as bad. They were dismissed as irrelevant simply because it was impossible to excite any measure of public interest in them. The problem which we have to solve—the most crucial problem in contemporary life and thought—is why democracy in the interval between the two wars became "inert", and why political rights, once the subject of embittered dispute, seemed meaningless or unimportant to a multitude—perhaps even to a majority—of those who possessed them. The answer must be sought in a review of the conditions in which democ-racy first established itself.

The Historical Background

The word "democracy" is commonly used to cover two dif-ferent kinds of right which are historically linked but logically separate: the "passive" rights of citizenship such as freedom of opinion and association, or equality, or the assertion of the rule of law, and the "active" right to participate in the processes of government. "Democracy" may thus in ordinary parlance imply either the acceptance of certain ideals which are regarded as ends in themselves not requiring justification, or the establish-ment of a certain type of governmental machinery (*i.e.* repre-sentative government as being the nearest practicable modern equivalent to self-government), which is not an end in itself, but is justified as the most effective means of attaining demo-cratic ideals. The word is used in the former sense by those who say that the United States and some British Dominions are "more democratic" than Great Britain. The meaning is not that the representative system is more perfect, but that the social structure comes nearer to realising the democratic ideal of equality. Theoretically there is no reason why the "passive" rights of citizenship should not be enjoyed in full measure by the subjects of an autocrat. On the other hand it would be rash to pretend that full enjoyment of "active" rights in the form of universal suffrage is any guarantee that the "passive" rights implicit in the idea of democracy will never be infringed; and when we say that a country is not ripe for democracy, what we mean is that the establishment of democratic institutions there would not in fact promote the general enjoyment of the democratic rights of liberty, equality and so forth. When Woodrow Wilson urged that the world should be made safe for democracy, he was probably thinking of the universal realisation of these democratic ideals. But his words were afterwards interpreted, apparently by himself as well as by others, to imply the extension throughout the world of representative government based on universal suffrage—a different and more controversial proposition.

The confusion between these two ideas was promoted by the historical link between them. It is on the whole true to say that the "passive" rights of democracy have seldom been fully and securely enjoyed by peoples or classes not also possessing the "active" right of the franchise, and that this right has been sought not as an end in itself, but as a means to secure other rights. If therefore the term "political rights", like the word "democracy" itself, is commonly used to cover both "passive" and "active" rights, the reason is that the two kinds of right have commonly gone together. For three hundred years, and more especially since the French Revolution, Western civilisation has been gradually built up round the idea of political rights. The possession of political rights conferred power, and was eagerly sought after and fought for by individuals and classes who desired to control the state machine or use it to their advantage. At the same time, the "passive" democratic right of equality appeared to imply the extension of political rights to the greatest possible number of people. Democracy in its twofold sense meant the management of the state machine by, and in the interest of, this greatest number.

Both the theory and the practice of democracy were, however, evolved at a time when democracy in its contemporary sense did not exist. Until comparatively recent times most democratic societies consisted of groups of privileged persons enjoying equal rights among themselves, but not sharing those rights with other members of the community, who were disqualified on grounds of colour, sex, servile status or poverty. Of these disqualifications the last has been the most important during the period which saw the development of modern liberal democracy.[1] It was not until the latter part of the nineteenth century with the growth of large industrial populations that the progressive removal of this disqualification began. Mass democracy based on universal suffrage is a modern phenomenon, and is still on its trial. Most writers have too readily assumed as a matter of course that institutions appropriate to the limited liberal democracy of the eighteenth and nineteenth centuries are appropriate to the new mass democracy which gradually developed in the period 1870-1920. It can hardly be doubted that one of the reasons of the contemporary indifference to democratic institutions is that these institutions have not yet been fully adapted to the needs of mass democracy. It is therefore important to examine the fundamental nature of the changes inherent in the new phenomenon of mass democracy, and the measures necessary to meet them if democracy is to become once more effective.

[1] In the United States the virtual exclusion from the franchise of the negro and the recent immigrant was in effect a poverty disqualification, though the ground of exclusion was, in the one case, colour and, in the other, the time required to become naturalised.

Liberal democracy, which reached its culmination in the nineteenth century, was a democracy of property-owners. It interpreted "equality" as requiring the removal of all inequalities save those arising from the unequal distribution of wealth, and "liberty" as liberty to behave and to use one's property in any way not calculated to inflict physical damage on the person or property of others. The essential function of the liberal democratic state was to protect life, property and the freedom and sanctity of contract; and the enjoyment of the franchise by a gradually increasing number of property-owners assured the performance of this function. The struggle for democracy in this sense was carried on for nearly three centuries against the last remnants of feudalism represented by military power in the hands of hereditary rulers. Democracy was secure once the army transferred its allegiance from the king to the parliament, *i.e.* to the representatives of those who enjoyed political rights.

During the greater part of this long period, democratic thinkers were acutely conscious of a potential clash between political rights and military power. The possession of political rights conferred power only if their exercise was recognised and respected by the armed forces. "Wherein lies the real power?" wrote Hans Delbrück in a well-known passage. "In military strength. The question therefore by which to determine the essential character of a state is always the question 'whom does the army obey?' " [1] In imperial Germany, a fairly liberal extension of political rights was largely nullified by a system which in fact gave the army a controlling voice in ultimate decisions of policy; and the same was true of Japan. For this reason neither pre-1914 Germany nor Japan at any time can be said to have had a democratic form of government. Hence armies have commonly been regarded as the enemies of democracy (*gegen Demokraten helfen nur Soldaten*). Fear and distrust of the army were for centuries deeply ingrained in English political thought, and have

[1] H. Delbrück, *Regierung und Volkswille*, p. 133.

left their last quaint trace in the form of the annual Army Act. In France, the loyalty of the army to the Third Republic was frequently called in question. Conscription was thought of in many countries as a safeguard against the dangers of a standing army which would inevitably be a menace to democracy. This was the view taken, for example, by Jaurès. In Great Britain, during the Ulster dispute of 1914, an attempt was made to use the army as a decisive factor in a political issue; and the repercussions of this affair might have been more striking if war had not supervened. Nevertheless, in democratic countries it was true that the enjoyment of political rights was the effective basis of government, because these rights were not normally liable to be overridden by the military power. Democracy meant the abolition of the arbitrary rule of military power and the substitution of the rule of law as determined by a majority of members of the society for the agreed purpose of protecting the freedom of person and private property and the sanctity of private contract.

Liberal democracy in this sense was destroyed by two separate, though interconnected, factors which began to operate in the second half of the nineteenth century and had attained their full development in 1920. In the first place, the holders of economic power, instead of agreeing—as the theory of liberal democracy required—that the state should merely hold the ring while they competed against one another with economic weapons, now more and more openly descended into the political arena and used political weapons to secure economic benefits for themselves, thus making organised economic power for the first time the dominant factor in politics. Secondly, the acquisition of political power by the now enfranchised masses transformed democracy from a society of property-owners, maintaining the state at their own expense primarily for police purposes, into a society containing a high proportion of more or less specialised propertyless salary-earners who regard themselves as skilled technicians rather than as directors of policy, and a far higher proportion of propertyless non-taxpaying wage-earners whose relation to the state is primarily that of beneficiaries.[1] These two cardinal changes have clearly made contemporary democracy something quite different from nineteenth-century liberal democracy, which—since learning commonly lags at least a generation behind life—is still treated as the current form of democracy in most textbooks. If we wish to understand the crisis through which democracy is passing, we must first study these developments and the problems to which they have given rise.

The Twentieth-century Crisis

Before the end of the nineteenth century, organised groups of capitalists were exercising a predominant influence on the political life of all advanced countries. But the precise course of development varied considerably. In Germany, where *laissez-faire* doctrine never won more than half-hearted acceptance, where economic activity was never wholly immune from state patronage and control, and where military power had always ridden rough-shod over political rights, the equally matched forces of the army and of capitalism soon struck a close alliance; and this alliance, which goes far to explain the efficiency of the German military machine, became the source of effective political power. Japan followed later in Germany's wake, the economic arm being here very much the junior partner. In Great Britain and the United States, where the armed forces had long been excluded from any important political rôle, and where economic activity was almost wholly emancipated from state control, the new economic power had the field to itself and attained its maximum development. "Power in the form of money", as an American writer puts it, "took precedence over

[1] Most nineteenth-century thinkers, at any rate in Great Britain, would have been shocked at the mere idea that anyone receiving a direct financial benefaction from the state should have a voice in the control of policy. J. S. Mill regarded the receipt of relief as "a peremptory disqualification for the franchise" (*Considerations on Representative Government*, ch. viii).

power in the form of military weapons." [1] In the United States this transition was rendered particularly easy by the fact that the armed forces had never enjoyed great power and prestige, and that issues relating to political rights had been settled and disposed of far earlier than in Europe. Long before 1900 it was notorious that the two great American political parties represented no divergence of political creed or principle, but were cleverly constructed combinations of economic group interests, dependent for their financial maintenance on those interests and struggling on their behalf for the control of the political machine.

In Great Britain, the situation was more complicated. The growth of economic power and the declining importance of political rights were already becoming apparent in the last decades of the nineteenth century. But the process was retarded by two factors both peculiar to Great Britain. In the first place, the immensely powerful tradition of the landed aristocracy, outliving its practical importance, deprived economic power of the undisputed prestige which it enjoyed in the United States, and slowed down its advance. Secondly, capitalists in Great Britain were sharply divided between those primarily interested in the home market and those primarily interested in the export market. Although the Home Rule crisis of the 'eighties and 'nineties had been the excuse for a mass migration of capitalists and business men into the conservative camp, the free trade issue of the early nineteen-hundreds split them once more; and the interests primarily concerned in the defence of free trade were compelled to ally themselves with labour and progressive elements—the socially incongruous alliance which produced the unprecedentedly sweeping Liberal victory of 1906. It was not till after 1918, when British exporting interests were desperately menaced by the attacks both of British labour and of foreign competitors, that the rift in British capitalism was healed,

<hr>

[1] L. Mumford, *Faith for Living*, p. 28.

and economic power really came to dominate the state machine. But here too there was a peculiar feature which distinguished Great Britain from any other country. [Before the economic power of capital became supreme, the organisation of the trade unions had built up an economic power of its own, comparable with, though not equal to, that of captial. From the early nineteen-twenties onwards, the two principal political parties of Great Britain represented respectively the economic forces of capital and labour. The struggle between them turned on the possession, not of political rights, but of economic power. The situation in Great Britain more nearly resembled that foreseen by Marx than in any of the countries where Marxism had once been influential. The two really significant events in British domestic politics between the two wars were the general strike of 1926 and the general election of 1931. In both the issue was the same: [whether the economic system was to be controlled by organised captial or by organised labour.]

We should however be misled if we regarded this Marxist antithesis between capital and labour as the central factor in political life to-day. In Great Britain and the United States, it was clear from an early date that both capital and labour (at any rate the most highly paid and securely employed grades of labour which controlled the labour organisations) had a common interest in maintaining the profits of industry, however much they might dispute the proper distribution of those profits between themselves. "Anything that benefits the capitalist system as a whole", as Mr. Drucker says, "benefits by necessity this trade-unionist socialist movement, as it increases the total national income available for distribution between the classes. Socialism as an opposition from within is salutary and inevitable, but accepts necessarily the fundamentals of the capitalist social system."[1] This phenomenon, which had prevented the class struggle in both countries from taking on the catastrophic form

[1] P. Drucker, *The End of Economic Man*, p. 29.

predicted by Marx, became specially conspicuous during and after the economic crisis of 1930. In Great Britain (as also in the United States), both capital and labour turned to the Government to save them from the storm. Tariffs, subsidies and control schemes received the joint support of both. Measures which assisted industry by raising costs to the consumer were applauded by both. In no case did the enjoyment of political rights by the more numerous class of consumers affect the issue. No political opposition could be effective so long as both party machines were controlled respectively by organised capital and organised labour whose common interest united them against that of the consumer. Just as in the nineteen-twenties the two groups of British capitalists, by combining their forces, had obtained control over the state machine at the expense of labour, so now capital and labour, by combining in support of those producing enterprises in which both were interested, could dominate the political machine at the expense of the rest of the community. And whatever the character of these changing alignments, political rights had become irrelevant. Vital decisions were taken not by the electorate, and not by any body which could reasonably be considered to represent its views, but by a process of bargaining between party machines representing organised capital and organised labour.

The supremacy of the party machine dominated by economic interest has been a conspicuous feature of British democracy in the past twenty years. It has been exercised in the constituencies, where the party candidate for a promising seat is chosen, no longer—except on rare occasions—by representatives of the electors, but by the central party machine. It has been exercised still more effectively in the House of Commons, where individual members are subject to ever stronger pressure to obey the dictates of the party whip. The process thus becomes a double one. A member of Parliament is elected not on personal considerations or by the choice of his constituents, but as the agent and nominee of a party: except on increasingly rare occasions, he votes not as his conscience or as the supposed will of his constituents dictates, but as the party decides.[1] The fact is notorious. But two well-known illustrations may be given. In 1935 there is reason to suppose that a majority of voters, a majority of members of Parliament and even a majority of the Conservative Party would, on a free and secret vote, have endorsed the report of a Royal Commission which had by a majority advised the withdrawal of the sugar beet subsidy. The economic power of the agricultural interest speaking through the Conservative Party machine prevented the question coming up for a vote and, had a vote been taken, would have been strong enough to secure its rejection. At the present time, there is every reason to believe that a majority of voters, a majority of members of Parliament and even a majority of the Labour Party would, on a free and secret vote, support the introduction of a state system of family endowment. The economic power of the trade-union interest operating through the party machine vetoes the proposal and prevents its adoption by the Government. Under existing democratic institutions, the will of the unorganised majority is impotent to assert itself against the domination of organised economic power. It has come to be widely believed to-day, and with much plausibility, that the attitudes and policies of political parties in most democratic countries are determined only in a minor degree by the opinions of the electorate which they purport to represent, and in a major degree by the vested interests which supply the bulk of the party funds. In other words, national policy on vital issues is really settled, as Marx alleged, not

[1] A serious corollary of these developments is their effect on the quality of human material which enters Parliament and attains promotion to ministerial rank. Party machines concerned above all with the maintenance of party cohesion and party discipline exercise a continuous process of selection. Great wealth or a record of long and faithful party service are more desirable qualifications than strong and independent character or original thought. These conditions help to explain the notorious difficulty, experienced during the present war, of finding men even of minimum ministerial capacity in the ranks of Parliament and the necessity of recourse to "big business", where the same process of the survival of the unfittest has not been in operation.

by a democratic counting of votes, but by the result of a perpetual struggle for power between rival economic interests,
though the struggle has taken forms quite different from those
which Marx predicted.

We can thus diagnose the first and perhaps most fundamental
cause of the ailment which afflicts contemporary democracy.
Just as in pre-1914 Germany or Japan the forms of democracy
and the possession of political rights were rendered illusory, and
in large part nullified, by the overriding force of military power,
so during the past fifty years democratic forms and political
rights have been gradually emptied of their significance, even in
some of the most advanced democratic countries, by the overriding force of economic power.[1] Politicians and political
thinkers, obsessed by the traditional idea that the only threat
to democracy was from physical violence, were content to denounce the wickedness of gangsters and fascists, and were
amazed at the failure of the masses to rally to the defence of their
political rights. The masses, bewildered and leaderless as they
were, could not diagnose the nature of the disease, but were
prompt to discover its symptoms. They understood well enough
that democratic forms and the enjoyment of political rights no
longer automatically conferred the reality of power. When organised economic power became triumphant, the foundations of
nineteenth-century liberal democracy crumbled. Political rights
have come to seem irrelevant in so far as they no longer confer
control over those factors which determine the decisive issues
of national life. The foundations of twentieth-century democracy have still to be laid.

The second and cognate cause of the decline in the reality of
democratic rights has been the growth of bureaucracy. This is a
symptom and consequence of the assumption of new functions
by the state. To deplore or denounce it is futile; for the new
economic functions of the twentieth-century state cannot be

[1] The syndicalists, who advocated a boycott of politics and the use of economic weapons, were perhaps the first who dimly perceived this trend.

abandoned, and cannot be performed without a vast and complicated administrative machine. But it would be equally futile to ignore the grave problem presented by this new expansion of administration. As early as 1906 the German sociologist Max Weber wrote of this "new bondage",[1] which first began to attract attention in Great Britain more than twenty years later. The problem is twofold. In the first place, the House of Commons can no longer either discuss and criticise intelligently much of the highly technical legislation which it has to pass, or exercise even the most remote control over the processes of administration. Ministers are more dependent on their permanent civil servants than at any previous period; and unless they are exceptionally able or exceptionally industrious, they probably have little knowledge of what is done in their name and under their nominal responsibility. By force of circumstances, the bureaucrat and the specialist have very largely supplanted the minister and the member of Parliament as the managers of public affairs. Secondly—and as a corollary of this development—the ordinary voter is less able than ever before to feel that he is living under a system which makes him one of the governors as well as one of the governed. This alleged identity of ruler and ruled—one of the supposed criteria which distinguish democracy from dictatorship—is liable to become a hollow fiction as the processes of government grow more and more inaccessible and incomprehensible to ordinary men and women. The old democracy, under which property-owners valued political rights as the prerogative and instrument of a ruling class, is dead. The

[1] The whole passage is a striking prophecy which merits quotation in full: "Everywhere the framework of a new bondage is ready, waiting only for the slowing-down of technical 'progress', and for the victory of 'interest' over 'profit', in combination with the exhaustion of as yet 'free' territory and 'free' markets, to make the masses tractable to its compulsion. At the same time the increasing complexity of the economic system, its partial nationalisation or 'municipalisation', and the territorial magnitude of national organisms, is creating ever more clerical work, an increasing specialisation of labour and professional training in administration—and this means the creation of a bureaucratic caste" (quoted in J. P. Mayer, *Prophet of the Mass Age*, p. 157).

new democracy, which seeks to make the masses conscious of their rights and of their responsibilities as a ruling class, has not yet been born. The crisis of contemporary democracy is that it is suspended between these two stages, enmeshed in the obsolete traditions of the first and therefore unable to break its way through to the second.

The New Democracy

We are now perhaps in a position to examine the fundamental conditions of the birth of the new democracy towards which we are groping our way. There are three main conditions:

(1) The new democracy must achieve a reinterpretation, in predominantly economic terms, of the democratic ideals of "equality" and "liberty".

(2) Just as liberal democracy won the struggle to make political rights effective over military power, so the new democracy must win the struggle to make political rights effective over economic power.

(3) The new democracy must develop among its members a sense not only of common benefits to be derived from the state, but of common obligations to the state—in particular of a common responsibility to make democracy work.

(1) The nineteenth-century conception of a political world in which the rights of equality and liberty were valid, and a separate and independent economic world in which no right was recognised save that of the stronger has broken down. It is the task of the new democracy to make these political rights effective in the economic world. In the case of "equality", much progress has been made in theory, and some in practice. Marx long ago drove home the view that political equality—the equal right to vote or equal right of access to the court of law—was of little account in the presence of social and economic inequality. In recent years this truth has come to be widely ac-

cepted. The removal of economic inequalities is now commonly recognised as a democratic ideal, though its complete realisation may be regarded as utopian. But the distressing fact is that the practical application of this ideal has perhaps been carried furthest not in countries possessing representative government, but in countries which reject it. Democratic countries are only just beginning to take up the challenge implicit in this paradox. Democracy will be judged in the next few years partly by the extent to which it succeeds in carrying the democratic principle of equality from the political into the social and economic sphere.

The reinterpretation of "liberty" in economic terms is equally urgent and perhaps more difficult. Liberty is the noblest and loftiest of the democratic ideals. In one form or another it is recognised by most men as an absolute good, and its loss as an evil—though sometimes, no doubt, a necessary evil. But the word is to-day heavily overlaid with the exclusively political outlook of the nineteenth century. Liberty is still widely assumed to imply the enjoyment of certain civil and political rights established by law, and to have no concern with those economic compulsions of daily life which were outside the purview of the state. Hence it is that "persons acutely aware of the dangers of regimentation when it is imposed by government remain oblivious of the millions of persons whose behaviour is regimented by an economic system through whose intervention alone they can obtain a livelihood".[1] Liberty will no longer seem of paramount importance to the masses unless it raises the banner of liberation from the economic, as well as from the political, domination of the more fortunate. Even liberty of opinion and the liberty of the press lose some of their significance so long as the most powerful instruments of publicity are in the hands of economically predominant groups. In default of this reinterpretation in economic terms, the concep-

[1] John Dewey, *Freedom and Culture*, p. 167.

tion of liberty, like the conception of democracy, is in danger of becoming inert and lifeless. "The negative conception of freedom which expresses itself by 'let me alone' is characteristic of the comfortably situated. The others express their demand for freedom by 'give me a chance'." [1] If it is to regain its meaning, liberty must be re-defined as something like "maximum social and economic opportunity".

Nor is it enough to say that our previous view of liberty has been incomplete, that it requires extension to the economic sphere, and that all these different kinds of liberty are valuable and must be simultaneously maintained. As Abraham Lincoln once observed, "the sheep and the wolf are not agreed upon a definition of the word 'liberty' "; [2] and it would be rash to assume that their respective definitions could be equally and simultaneously applied. We are faced with what is in fact an irreconcilable opposition between a traditional interpretation of liberty, whose adherents claim an exclusive right to the term, and a new and hitherto largely unrecognised interpretation expressing itself in the "give me a chance" conception. "It is no longer possible to achieve true liberty for the mass of the people", writes Sir Stafford Cripps, "except by a very large measure of interference by law with the free action of all classes of individual members of our society." [3] But as the question-begging epithet "true" suggests, this kind of "liberty" is still not always recognised as such. Among the most vocal defenders of liberty to-day are representatives of big business, who wish to keep their operations free from the interference of state control, intellectuals in secure enjoyment of economic well-being, and politicians of all parties who are relieved to find a slogan which is assured of universal applause. In such hands liberty often degenerates into the watchword of reaction. "The cry for

[1] C, G. Vickers in *World Order Papers* (Royal Institute of International Affairs), p. 157.
[2] *Speeches and Letters of Abraham Lincoln* (Everyman ed.), p. 220.
[3] Stafford Cripps, *Democracy Up-to-Date*, pp. 32-3.

civil liberties to-day is not heard from the under-dogs but from the top-dogs." [1]

(2) The most crying need is, however, for a reinterpretation not merely of "equality" and "liberty", but of democracy itself, in terms which will take account of the modern development of economic power and which will have a meaning for those who, political rights notwithstanding, are conscious of their helpless subjection to that power. A twentieth-century malady cannot be cured by nineteenth-century specifics. The most serious attempt of recent years to reinterpret or refashion democracy has been made in the United States, where the domination of the political machine by economic power was first revealed in its most dramatic form. Theodore Roosevelt, Woodrow Wilson and Franklin Roosevelt in turn indicted capital and big business in the name of the "plain man" and the "little man". All of them attacked party machines dominated by economic interests. The Bolshevik Revolution in Russia took ownership and control of the "means of production" out of the hands of capital and vested them in the state. The Fascist and National Socialist Revolutions broke up the organised forces both of labour and of capital and subordinated them to the state. The appeal of these revolutions was against the producing interests to the "little man". The gravamen of the charge brought against nineteenth-century liberal democracy both by the American reformers and by the European revolutionaries was that it had left the little man helpless in the stranglehold of organised economic power. For non-democrats the moral of this widespread movement is that democracy is dead. For democrats outside the United States it scarcely appears to have had any moral; for they have buried their heads in the sand and refused to observe what is happening. In Europe the attempt to re-define democracy has hardly yet begun.

[1] L. Dennis, *The Dynamics of War and Revolution*, p. 128; cf. *ibid*. p. 166: "In 1940 America, the rich want liberty and the poor want ham and eggs".

The field has however now been cleared for the attempt. Democracy means the ultimate control of governmental power by, and in the interests of, those who enjoy political rights. The possession of political rights is important only where this condition is realised; and democracy becomes meaningless if the effective control is in fact exercised by some other form of organised power. The experience of several centuries has taught that this is true of organised military power. The experience of half a century now teaches that it is equally true of organised economic power. Democracy required that the holders of military power should be responsible to, and take their orders from, the community as represented by those exercising political rights. We now see that democracy, if it is to be effective, also requires that the holders of economic power should be responsible to, and take their orders from, the community in exactly the same way. Democracy will revive, and political rights will once more become important, when economic power has been brought under control in exactly the same way as military power was brought under control in democratic countries before the nineteenth century. The struggle for political rights has been fought in the past mainly as a struggle for emancipation from arbitrary military power. It has now to be reopened as a struggle for emancipation from arbitrary economic power. Democracy must be re-defined as a system of government based on political rights valid not merely against military, but against economic, power. The crisis of democracy is "the dilemma of how democracy is to evolve a system of government control of economic activity in the social interest—failing which economic chaos, unemployment and misery are now manifestly unavoidable—while retaining the recognition of the claims of the individual which is the soul of democracy".[1] The crisis of democracy is closely intertwined with the economic crisis; and the revolution against nineteenth-century liberal democracy

[1] F. Williams, *War by Revolution*, p. 85.

is part of the revolution against *laissez-faire* economics. The rebuilding of our political system and the rebuilding of our economic system are different aspects of the same problem.

(3) We shall presently see that the economic crisis is rooted in a moral crisis. The same is true of the crisis of democracy. For while it may be historically justifiable to call the recognition of the rights of the individual "the soul of democracy", it has become increasingly clear in recent years that democracy cannot subsist on that basis alone. It is necessary that the recognition of equally shared rights should be balanced by the same keen recognition of equally shared obligations.

This is another point on which the supposed identity between nineteenth-century liberal democracy and twentieth-century mass democracy leads to confused thinking. Liberal democracy limited the rights and benefits of the franchise to a restricted class; and their limitation was reconciled with current professions of universalism by the fact that the privileged class, in conditions of expanding prosperity and rapid economic development, took in a constant stream of new recruits, thereby fostering an atmosphere if not of equal, at any rate of widely diffused, opportunity. But the privileged class of liberal democracy was keenly aware—and inculcated this awareness on all who entered it—that, in order to justify and preserve the rights and benefits conferred on it by democratic institutions, it must perform services and make personal sacrifices to maintain these institutions. Unpaid public service was one of many forms in which this responsibility was recognised and accepted. A strong sense of duty was an essential part of the nineteenth-century liberal tradition; and duty to the community as a whole was subtly blended with the more intimate duty not to let one's class down. Hence liberal democracy provided the essential condition of a ruling class as profoundly conscious of its obligations as of its rights. In theory, there was much talk about the rights of man as the cornerstone of democracy. In practice, the important thing was that the privileged middle class as a whole thought of democracy as their affair and recognised a responsibility to make it work.

The twentieth-century problem is how to recreate this essential moral and psychological condition in terms of mass democracy. The doctrine of the rights of man is the theoretical foundation of universal suffrage. But the countervailing and equally essential doctrine of the responsibility of the ruling class for making democracy work even at the cost of personal sacrifice has had no such extension since the ruling class became —in so far as the franchise is effective—identical with the whole adult community. Whatever the causes of this failure, the fact is undoubted; and its recognition is vital to a full understanding of the present crisis of democracy. Probably a high proportion of those who now enjoy the franchise normally regard the democratic state not (except, perhaps, in time of war) as something which is their business and which they must keep going at personal sacrifice to themselves, but as an agency on which they have a claim for certain benefits and receipts, and which imposes on them certain more or less irksome obligations and restrictions. As a recent writer has said, "the L.C.C. officials, who insist that children's teeth shall be attended to and public-houses shut, seem as autocratic to many people as if they were appointed by a dictator".[1] There is no widely felt sense that those in authority are not "they" but "we", that "we" control "them" and that "they" represent "us". These basic presuppositions were accepted as real, and acted on, by the enfranchised classes of nineteenth-century liberal democracy. Twentieth-century mass democracy, at any rate in time of peace, has not yet incorporated them in its consciousness, or made them a basis of faith and action.

The failure to create in modern mass democracy this sense of common obligation to make democratic institutions work

[1] D. Spearman, *Modern Dictatorship*, p. 182.

is due mainly to circumstances which have already appeared in the course of our analysis. First of all, there is the failure to give adequate social and economic content to the concept of equality. Politics play a relatively small part in the life of the individual; and equality of political rights, however complete, will make little impression on his consciousness in the face of a social and economic inequality which is an ever-present factor in his ordinary affairs. The sense of shared obligation is likely to be strong only where there is a sense of equitably shared benefit. Secondly, there is the feeling that political rights have become largely a sham, since economic power exercises a predominant influence on political affairs by methods, and through channels, which the ordinary voter cannot control. Thirdly, there is the growing complication of the machinery of government, which unavoidably removes issues of great practical importance beyond the comprehension of the non-professional, and places the control of matters vitally affecting the everyday life of the citizen in the hands of bureaucrats and experts. The sense of identity between government and governed is particularly difficult to create where the process of government appears to consist largely of mysterious operations beyond the comprehension of the governed.

The remedy for this triple failure must likewise be threefold. We must supplement political equality by a progressive advance towards social and economic equality; we must make the will of the ordinary citizen prevail against the organised forces of economic power; and we must draw the ordinary citizen more and more into the processes of administration—in particular, into those processes which affect his daily life and interests. None of these things is easy. But they may be found easier if we regard them not as ways of conferring fresh rights on the individual, but as ways of kindling in him a fresh sense of obligation—an obligation to make democracy work because democracy will be regarded by him as his affair, because the antithesis of "we" and "they" will at last have been resolved.

The emphasis required is no longer on "the rights of man"—this was the slogan of the French Revolution—but on the truth, implicit in the new revolution, that the rights of the individual become effective only through the assumption of collective obligations. Nineteenth-century liberal democracy did in practice achieve for a privileged class this correlation of right and obligation. Twentieth-century mass democracy has not yet achieved it.

The crisis of democracy is, then, in the last resort a moral crisis, whose symptoms express themselves predominantly in economic terms. No analysis of it would be complete which did not involve an investigation of the economic crisis—the revolution against *laissez-faire* which is the economic aspect of the revolution against liberal democracy. But before we attempt this investigation, we must turn aside to consider the other major crisis of our times—the crisis of national self-determination, which is in some sense the counterpart of democracy in the international sphere.

CHAPTER 3

THE CRISIS OF SELF-DETERMINATION

From the time of the French Revolution onwards, it came to be accepted that nations like men have rights, above all, the right of freedom or, as it was afterwards called, self-determination. The liberation of "oppressed peoples" went on, amid the applause of radicals everywhere, throughout the nineteenth century. In this triumphal progress national self-determination and democracy went hand in hand. Self-determination might indeed be regarded as implicit in the idea of democracy; for if every man's right is recognised to be consulted about the affairs of the political unit to which he belongs, he may be assumed to have an equal right to be consulted about the form and extent of the unit. "The proclamation of the sovereignty of the people led undesignedly but inevitably to the question, What people? . . . . The abstract logic of democracy may tend towards cosmopolitanism, but the practical working of it had, and was bound to have, the psychological effect of intensifying nationalism."[1] The analogy between men and nations was regarded as complete. The community of nations, like the democratic community, was a community of members each enjoying certain indefeasible rights which other members of the community were under an obligation to respect. In nineteenth-century liberal philosophy, freedom was the cardinal right of the nation as of the individual.

The settlement of 1919 was the apogee of the right of national self-determination. The sequel has tarnished its splendour. Intelligent people can no longer believe that the break-

---

[1] William Temple, Archbishop of York, *Thoughts in War-Time*, pp. 112-13.

down has been due merely to failure to apply the principle of self-determination widely or impartially enough. The principle itself—far from providing, as Woodrow Wilson and others believed in 1919, the infallible short cut to a political paradise —has incurred discredit as the apparent cause of some of our most intractable political and economic problems. The crisis of national self-determination is parallel to the crisis of democracy. Self-determination, like democracy, has fallen on evil days because we have been content to keep it in the nineteenth-century setting of political rights. We have failed to adapt it to the twentieth-century context of military and economic problems; and we have failed to understand that the right of nations to self-determination, like every other right, is self-destructive unless it is placed in a framework of obligation. National self-determination requires to-day to be reinterpreted in this new light. There is no task which imposes itself more urgently on those engaged in formulating the outlines of the new world which must emerge out of the war.

Self-Determination and Nationality

The first stage in our investigation must be to clear up an important ambiguity as to the nature of the right itself—an ambiguity which arises from a common confusion between the subjective right of self-determination and the objective fact of nationality. The principle of self-determination, strictly defined, requires that a group of people of reasonable size desirous of constituting a state should be allowed to constitute a state. But this proposition, as enunciated in the nineteenth century, more often took the form that a "nation" had the right to constitute a state. The belief in self-determination as a natural corollary of democracy found concrete expression in an alliance between democracy and nationalism or, as it was commonly called, the "principle of nationality". This alliance, which identified self-determination with nationalism, and treated the nation as the natural basis of the state, continued to dominate political thought down to 1918.

The words "nation" and "state" carry with them a number of undefined and shifting implications which have led in the past, and still lead, to much confusion of thought. The state, whether we think of it as the apparatus of government or as the field in which that apparatus works, is the unit of political power. The nation is a community of men; and though modern usage restricts it to communities of a political character or having political aspirations, the nation is still a group of human beings, not a territory or an administrative machine. Hence the state may, in a loose way, be described as "artificial" or "conventional", the nation as "natural" or "organic". A state can be created, mutilated or destroyed overnight by a document drawn up in due form prescribed by international law. A nation grows or decays by a process which is independent of any single conscious act of the human will.

The French Revolution gave birth to the view, which in the nineteenth century came to prevail over a large part of Western Europe, and which was regarded merely as another way of defining the principle of self-determination, that "states" and "nations" ought to coincide, that states should be constituted on a national basis, and that nations ought to form states.[1] This appeared to be a natural corollary of the right of self-government which was as valid for nations as for individuals. This view leads, however, to an awkward dilemma. If we define a nation as a voluntary association of people who wish to live

[1] How deeply this idea has taken root is shown by the linguistic confusions to which it has given rise. Thus the English language, never having taken the trouble to evolve derivatives from the word "state", speaks of the "national debt" and the "nationalisation" of railways. The French language forms no adjective from État, but can speak of "Biens d'Etat" (though there are also "Domaines Nationaux") and has the useful if clumsy words étatisme and étatisation. In the United States of America, "state" is necessarily reserved for the component states of the Union, and "nation" is now frequently used to designate the Union as a whole. The "League of Nations" is a notable example of this confusion of terminology.

under a form of government uniting them, and distinguishing them from the rest of the world, on a basis of nationality, then the fundamental identity of self-determination and nationality, of democracy and nationalism, is saved, but the natural or organic quality of the nation is denied. If on the other hand this quality is asserted as something independent of the will of the individual, then the principle of nationality is, as Acton maintained, potentially incompatible with democracy since it "sets limits to the exercises of the popular will and substitutes for it a higher principle." [1] Most nineteenth-century thinkers had no doubt which horn of this dilemma to embrace. A nation was simply a group of people who wanted to be a nation. In Renan's famous phrase, the very existence of a nation was "un plébiscite de tous les jours". On this view, typical of nineteenth-century rationalism, a Frenchman differed from an Italian or a German simply because he wished to be a Frenchman. By an act of will, he could presumably transform himself into a German or an Italian. This theory had its application in the not uncommon practice, recognised by all states, of "naturalisation". In Western Europe, the assimilation of Jews went on apace and was approved by most enlightened Jews and non-Jews: the Jew, by an act of will, became a German, a Frenchman or an Englishman. In the Western hemisphere dissident Englishmen and voluntary migrants from other parts of Europe were creating a new American nation. Membership of a nation was an act of voluntary allegiance, and the right of a nation to self-determination was a corollary of the democratic principle.

It seems doubtful whether, outside a limited circle of intellectuals, this rationalistic estimate of the nature of nationality ever really carried conviction. Most Englishmen who chanted the Gilbertian chorus

---

[1] Acton, *History of Freedom*, p. 288. Cf. C. A. Macartney: "To claim . . . that every nation must form an independent state is to substitute for true self-determination a very different thing, which should rather be called national determinism" (*National States and National Minorities*, p. 100).

> In spite of all temptations
> To belong to other nations
> He remains an Englishman

probably treated as ironical not only the suggestion that an Englishman might prefer to be a Russian, a Frenchman or a Prussian, but the whole implication that nationality was decided by personal choice. Whether national distinctions were based on differences of physical type, or on differences of language, culture and tradition, it was apparent to most people that they had an objective character so far as the individual was concerned. Nationality was not simply a matter of political opinion or of voluntary allegiance. A Frenchman could not become an Englishman in the same way as a monarchist might become a republican or a free-trader a protectionist. In most countries, an increasing spirit of national exclusiveness made admission to membership a matter of difficulty even for the most eager recruits. Once nationality was recognised as an objective attribute, there was always a potential incongruity between it and self-determination. If the individual Frenchman or Italian was a Frenchman or an Italian for reasons independent of his own volition, it could not be assumed as a logical and necessary corollary of the existence of a French and an Italian nation that the members of these nations desired to create or maintain an independent French or Italian state.

This potential incongruity appears to have been ignored by the peacemakers of 1919, who were unconscious of any discrepancy, or indeed any distinction, between the principle of self-determination and the principle of nationality. Woodrow Wilson had emphatically insisted, prior to the entry of the United States into the war, on the right of self-determination: "Every people has a right to choose the sovereignty under which they shall live".[1] Yet when he came to elaborate the Fourteen Points, he spoke in terms not of self-determination,

---

[1] *Public Papers of Woodrow Wilson: The New Democracy*, ii, p. 187.

but of objectively ascertainable nationality: "A readjustment of the frontiers of Italy should be effected along clearly recognisable lines of nationality. . . . The relations of the several Balkan states to one another [should be] determined by friendly counsel along historically established lines of allegiance and nationality." Others concerned in the drafting of the peace settlement were equally blind to any inconsistency between the two principles. Some discussions took place as to the admissibility of derogations from the principle of nationality or self-determination on strategic and economic grounds. But it was assumed without more ado that nationality and self-determination meant the same thing and that, if a man had the objective distinguishing marks of a Pole or a Southern Slav, he wanted to be a citizen of a Polish or Southern Slav state. The confusion continued to prevail many years later. "The new political frontiers of Europe are Wilsonian", wrote Fisher in his *History of Europe*, "and so drawn that 3 per cent only of the total population of the Continent live under alien rule. Judged by the test of self-determination, no previous European frontiers had been so satisfactory." [1]

The failure to make any distinction between the principle of self-determination and the principle of nationality was due to one simple cause. In Western Europe, and in most of those overseas countries whose civilisation was derived from Western Europe, the distinction had ceased to have practical importance; and the political thought of the nineteenth century, which was still unchallenged in 1919, was the product of Western civilisation. It was characteristic of these countries that national feeling had grown up with, and within the framework of, an existing state. Nationalism meant loyalty to the state; and though it would not have been true to say that men were Frenchmen or Dutchmen simply because they wanted to be Frenchmen or Dutchmen, it was true on the whole that French-

[1] H. A. L. Fisher, *A History of Europe*, iii, p. 1161.

men and Dutchmen did in fact want to be citizens of independent states called France and Holland. In Germany and Italy, the historical background was different. German and Italian nationalism came into being before the German Reich and the Italian Kingdom existed, and helped to create them. But between 1870 and 1914 it became, within the frontiers of both countries, indistinguishable from loyalty to the state (though it left a problem, virtually unknown in Western Europe, of German and Italian irredentism outside those frontiers). Most Germans and Italians wanted to be citizens of Germany and Italy. Across the Atlantic it could be assumed with even greater certainty that the people of the United States wanted to be American citizens. Throughout the area occupied by the most advanced and progressive peoples of the world, the principle of nationality and the principle of self-determination were in substance identical. Advanced and progressive thinkers, such as those whose teachings inspired the peace settlement of 1919, assumed therefore that the two principles were identical elsewhere.

This assumption was a symptom of the profound ignorance prevailing in Western Europe about conditions east of Berlin and Vienna. In Eastern Europe, as well as in many parts of Asia, national feeling was rife. But except perhaps in the Far East, there were hardly any of those nation-states which were the characteristic feature of Western civilisation. In some cases national feeling held together a ruling group exercising sway over an alien population. In others national feeling united a subject population struggling to throw off alien rule. In these cases, social issues complicated national issues and tended to overshadow them. Elsewhere national differences were intertwined with religious differences and were scarcely distinguishable from them. In all these countries national feeling was far less widely disseminated than in Western Europe and affected a far smaller proportion of the population. If a peasant of what used to be the eastern marches of Poland were invited to express his view of self-determination, he would probably think of his desire to use his own particular forms of speech, to maintain the local customs of his village, to receive the ministrations of the Catholic or the Orthodox Church according to his own choice, to exchange a bad landlord for a good one, or perhaps—if he were capable of so daring a flight of imagination—to own his own land. It is unlikely that membership of a Polish or Russian national state would enter into his calculations at all. The conception, applicable in the Western world of closely integrated communities held together by the joint principle of nationality and self-determination, was almost wholly irrelevant elsewhere.

Before they had finished their work, the peacemakers of 1919 had some inkling of the complications of the problem. They fully understood that the territorial intermingling of different peoples made the drawing of frontiers in Eastern Europe on the basis of nationality a matter of extreme difficulty. They understood in part that the objective marks of nationality were not always clearly defined, so that it was impossible to say dogmatically whether the Ukrainians were a separate nation or merely Russians speaking a variant dialect, and whether Slav-speaking Macedonians were Serbs, Bulgars, or just Macedonians.[1] What they hardly understood at all was that, even where the objective marks of nationality were perfectly clear, the possession of these marks did not necessarily give the clue to the state of mind of their possessor. Mesmerised by the assumption that the principle of nationality and the principle of self-determination were indistinguishable in their results, and

[1] It was confidently assumed that the principal objective mark of nationality was language. "In Central and Eastern Europe", wrote Professor Toynbee, reflecting the assumptions of Peace Conference, "the growing consciousness of nationality had attached itself neither to traditional frontiers nor to new geographical associations, but almost exclusively to mother tongues" (*The World After the Peace Conference*, p. 18). Mr. C. A. Macartney traces back to Schlegel and Fichte the recognition of language as the essential criterion "both as constituting the spiritual link between the members of a nation and as offering proof of common origin" (*National States and National Minorities*, p. 99).

by the fact that this assumption on the whole worked in Western Europe, politicians and propagandists alike were content to believe that the man whose mother-tongue was Polish or Serb or Lithuanian wanted to be a citizen of a Polish or Serb or Lithuanian state. Only where the "lines of nationality" were not "clearly recognisable", or where for some other reason the fate of an area was especially debatable, was the expedient of a plebiscite adopted. To ascertain the will of the people was a method of applying the principle of nationality, only necessary where simpler methods of determining nationality were for some special reason inadequate.

The result of these plebiscites, which were conducted with sufficient fairness to ensure that all, or virtually all, the voters recorded their political preference without interference or intimidation, was most illuminating. Two were held within the confines of Western Europe: in Slesvig and in the Saar. In both the results showed no appreciable divergence from the language statistics. It was, broadly speaking, true that people who spoke German or Danish or French wanted to be citizens of a German or Danish or French state. The results of the remaining plebiscites—in Allenstein, in Marienwerder, in Upper Silesia and in Klagenfurt [1]—were equally conclusive in the opposite sense. In Allenstein, the 1910 census showed, by the test of mother-tongue, 46 per cent of Poles; in the plebiscite just over 2 per cent of the votes were cast for Poland. In Marienwerder, the corresponding figures were 15 and 7.5 per cent; in Upper Silesia 65 and 40 per cent. In Klagenfurt, census figures showed 68 per cent of Slovenes, the plebiscite figures just under 40 per cent. The expert who has surveyed these results observes that "language statistics gave little indication of national sympathies". Indeed, "in certain sections in Upper Silesia, Allenstein and

---

[1] A plebiscite at Sopron was conducted in markedly different conditions from the other plebiscites, and its results could scarcely be regarded as a safe guide.

Klagenfurt the results of the voting were the exact opposite of what the language figures seemed to portend".[1] One positive conclusion may however perhaps be drawn. The divergences, though variable in extent, were all in one direction. It seems justifiable to infer from these figures that, whereas people speaking German as their mother-tongue did as a rule desire to be citizens of a German state, only a proportion of people speaking Polish or Southern Slav as their mother-tongue (in one of these cases, a negligible proportion, in none of them a proportion exceeding two-thirds) preferred to be citizens of a Polish or Southern Slav rather than of a German state. This inference tallies with the conclusion already reached on other grounds that the supposed coincidence between the principle of nationality and the principle of self-determination is, generally speaking, valid for the peoples of Western Europe, but not elsewhere.

This conclusion is obviously one of considerable importance. In a sense all government rests on the consent of the governed. No political unit will be strong or durable which cannot count on the more or less spontaneous loyalty of a considerable part of its component population. The most effective unit will tend to be one made up of people who want to form a unit and are prepared for the necessary amount of self-sacrifice to maintain it. There is therefore much to be said for the principle of self-determination. But there is hardly anything to be said for the principle of including people in a particular political unit merely because they speak a particular language. In future, when we seek to apply the principle of self-determination outside the limits of Western Europe, we should be careful to disentangle it from those misleading associations with nationalism which nineteenth-century Western thought fastened on it.

The recognition of a right of self-determination for nations

---

[1] S. Wambaugh, *Plebiscites Since the World War*, i, pp. 202, 493. The figures cited above are taken from this monumental work (i, pp. 133-4, 198, 350).

thus involves the question, What nations? And this question requires not a theoretical general answer, but particular answers based on the facts of particular cases. In the last resort the only rights are the rights of men. In order to assert the right of a nation to self-determination, we must first enquire whether the men on whose behalf the claim is made want to be a nation, and what kind of rights they want to claim. The problem is one of great difficulty and of immense practical importance. The peacemakers of 1919, obsessed with the belief that nations were clearly defined entities possessing clearly defined rights, sometimes uncritically accepted self-appointed groups of men, many of whom had long been exiles from their native country, as repositories of these national rights, and shirked the admittedly thorny question how far the claims made corresponded to the wishes or interests of the "nation" in whose name they were made. This mistake must not be repeated. It can be avoided by keeping constantly in mind the truth that self-determination is not a right of certain recognised and pre-determined nations, but a right of individual men and women, which includes the right within certain limitations to form national groups. It will probably conduce to clear thinking on this subject if we speak less than we are at present in the habit of doing of the rights and claims of Ruritania as such and more of the rights and claims of individual Ruritarians.

The Limits of Self-Determination

Apart from the Wilsonian confusion between national self-determination and nationality, it is now clear to most observers that the peacemakers of 1919 attached too absolute a value to self-determination as a key to all political problems. Woodrow Wilson described it as "an imperative principle of action";[1] and even those who remembered the importance of other criteria for the fixing of state boundaries almost apologised for

[1] *Public Papers of Woodrow Wilson: War and Peace*, i, p. 180.

mentioning them.[1] Self-determination is one important principle which should be taken into account in deciding the form and extent of the political unit. But it cannot be safely treated as the sole or overriding principle to which all other considerations must be subordinated. There can be no absolute right of self-determination any more than there can be an absolute right to do as one pleases in a democracy. A group of individuals living in the middle of Great Britain or Germany cannot claim, in virtue of the principle of self-determination, an inherent right to establish an independent self-governing unit. In the same way, it would be difficult to claim for Wales, Catalonia and Uzbekistan an absolute and inherent right to independence, even if a majority of their inhabitants should desire it; such a claim to exercise self-determination would have to be weighed in the light of the interests, reasonably interpreted, of Great Britain, Spain and Soviet Russia. The same consideration of what is reasonable in the interest of others is also applicable to units which already enjoy an independent existence.

In these circumstances, a certain amount of fluctuation and inconsistency is inevitable in the meaning given to the right of self-determination. There can be no fixed standard of number or size establishing a right to form an independent unit; for the limit of what is possible and reasonable varies from one place to another and from one period of history to another. In classical Greece, 100,000 people could easily form an independent unit. Nobody would pretend that this is possible to-day. Hence every country tends to be inconsistent in affirming or denying the right of self-determination. The American colonists claimed and exercised it against Great Britain in 1787. Three-quarters

[1] For example Balfour wrote to House in the following terms: "Strong frontiers make for peace; and though great crimes against the principle of nationality have been committed in the name of 'strategic necessity', still if a particular boundary adds to the stability of international relations, and if the populations concerned be numerically insignificant, I would not reject it in deference to some *a priori* principle" (*Intimate Papers of Colonel House*, ed. C. Seymour, iv, pp. 52-3).

of a century later the descendants of some of them refused it to the descendants of others. This did not deter a Democratic President of the United States, half a century later still, from maintaining, in the phrase already quoted, that "every people has a right to choose the sovereignty under which they shall live". Lansing's cogent, though belated, comment is well known: "When the President talks of 'self-determination', what unit has he in mind? Does he mean a race, a territorial unit, or a community? Without a definite unit which is practical, application of this principle is dangerous to peace and stability."[1] Even Lansing, however, does not seem to have realised that this uncertainty was not a quality of Wilson's mind, but was inherent in the principle itself. Though the inconsistency with which the principle of self-determination was applied in the peace settlement of 1919 has been frequently censured, few of the critics have grasped that the principle is one which in the nature of things does not admit of consistent application.

If then we ask why "the liberation of oppressed peoples", which had rightly been regarded as a progressive principle in the nineteenth century, came to appear a reactionary and retrogressive principle which helped to put the clock back after 1919, the simplest answer is that Woodrow Wilson and his associates failed to recognise that the principle was a variable one requiring constant modification in the light of political and economic conditions, and that the extension given to it at Versailles was utterly at variance with twentieth-century trends of political and economic organisation. By treating the principle of national self-determination as absolute and by carrying it further than it had ever been carried before, they fostered the disintegration of existing political units, and favoured the creation of a multiplicity of smaller units, at a moment when strategic and economic factors were demanding increased integration and the grouping of the world into fewer and larger

[1] R. Lansing, *The Peace Negotiations: a Personal Narrative*, p. 86.

units of power. The makers of the 1919 settlement did indeed recognise that the effective self-determination of small nations was incompatible with unbridled military power and with complete independence in the military sphere. But they had no inkling of the developments of modern military technique; and the safeguards which they provided in the Covenant of the League of Nations were inappropriate as well as inadequate. What proved, moreover, equally serious was that they altogether failed to recognise that the self-determination of small nations was incompatible with unbridled economic power and complete economic independence. "You cannot create a large number of new states", said Stresemann towards the end of his life, "and wholly neglect to adapt them to the European economic system."[1] But the peacemakers of 1919 understood nothing of the European economic system or of the need of adaptation to it; and they were content with a pious, and not wholly sincere, aspiration in favour of "the equitable treatment of the commerce of all members of the League". Thus national self-determination, as applied in 1919, came more and more into conflict with the realities of military and economic power. The future of self-determination must be studied primarily in its relationship to power in these two forms.

Self-Determination and Military Power

The crisis of self-determination in relation to military power lies in the fact that the principle of self-determination has been invoked to justify the creation of an ever larger number of small independent states at a time when the survival of the small independent state as a political unit has been rendered problematical by developments of military technique.

The problem of the small independent state first emerged at the Congress of Vienna, where the affairs of the small Powers

[1] G. *Stresemann: His Diaries, Letters and Papers,* ed. and transl. E. Sutton, iii, p. 619.

were settled over their heads by decisions of the Great Powers. The system then pursued, unsatisfactory on paper but tolerable in practice, was that of the nineteenth-century "Concert of Europe". Small Powers were encouraged to conduct their own affairs on the assumption that they had no voice in the affairs of Europe as a whole. In wars between Great Powers, their status was one of neutrality. During the nineteenth century, the practice of states and the zeal of international lawyers built up a substantial code of rules for neutrality in time of war; and these rules were on the whole tolerably well observed in the spacious period of local and limited wars. In these conditions a real though limited right of independence could be enjoyed by small states.

The first serious blow to this conception of an honourable and ordered status of neutrality and independence for small states was struck by the war of 1914-18. Two small countries, Belgium and Greece, were directly forced into the war by military action. Others were induced to participate by extensive promises or by various forms of military or economic pressure. Others felt that, as their interests were bound up with the victory of one side, it was both profitable and honourable for them to fight on that side and hasten the victory. Those which remained neutral found that the exigencies of the blockade strained almost to breaking-point many of the rights which neutrals had hitherto enjoyed, and that they were hardly more immune from the consequences of war than the belligerents themselves. A considerable number of small countries did succeed, even in close proximity to the principal war zones, in upholding their neutrality throughout the war and in avoiding at any rate the direct ravages of military operations. Nevertheless there was no doubt that the neutrality, and therefore the effective independence, of small states had received a severe shock.

At the close of the war, there was a vague realisation in many quarters that the concept of the neutrality and independence of small states had somehow been destroyed or modified. At the same time, the peacemakers were committed, in virtue of the principle of self-determination, to the creation of more and more small states. A supposed solution of this dilemma was found in the League of Nations, whose Covenant declared that any war was "a matter of concern to the whole League" and that any member of the League resorting to war in defiance of its obligations under the Covenant "shall *ipso facto* be deemed to have committed an act of war against all other members of the League". "Between members of the League", declared the British Government on one occasion, "there can be no neutral rights, because there can be no neutrals." [1] The small states, no longer assured of independence by the maintenance of a strict neutrality, were to take sides in any future war between Great Powers, fighting in alliance with the "victim of aggression" against the "aggressor". This was the system which came to be known as "collective security".

There were several fallacies in this system. The first was the illusion that an arrangement whose basis was necessarily the preservation of the *status quo* could ever be universal: in fact there was never a time when the League of Nations included more than five of the seven Great Powers, and even this maximum was achieved only for a short period. The second fallacy was to suppose that the criterion of "aggression" was either equitably applicable or morally valid. The third and most important fallacy lay in the fact that modern warfare requires months or years of preparation, that if states are to collaborate effectively in war they must concert their preparations in advance, and that it is impossible, especially for a small country situated in proximity to one of the belligerents, to wait until an "act of aggression" has brought about a state of war before deciding on which side to fight. The only conception of collective security which was not hopelessly unrealistic was the French conception of a European alliance against a specific enemy

---

[1] *Memorandum on the Signature of His Majesty's Government in the United Kingdom of the Optional Clause*, Cmd. 3452, p. 10.

under French leadership; and this conception was unacceptable to the small Powers. The doctrine current in the 'twenties that neutrality was obsolete, though in substance true, was discredited by the only alternative doctrine offered as a substitute for neutrality. Recognition of the hollowness of this substitute, combined with natural conservatism, led small states to cling fervently to the shadow of their nineteenth-century independence. In the 'twenties, when the prospect of war seemed mainly academic, Switzerland and Germany—then a weak state —cautiously contracted out of any League obligation which might involve them in a breach of neutrality. In the 'thirties, when the prospect of war became real, the small Powers emphatically proclaimed their intention to remain neutral.[1] The doctrine of collective security embodied in the League Covenant was already bankrupt. It required the experience of 1940 to demonstrate that a return to the nineteenth-century conception of neutrality and independence for small states was equally impracticable.

Two factors in modern warfare have combined to destroy the independence of small states based on the principle of self-determination. The first of these factors has been the rapid growth of military disparity between strong and weak Powers. In the days when the rifle was the main weapon of offence and a fortress an impregnable barrier, a resolute small Power could offer serious resistance to a much stronger attacker, particularly if the main forces of the attacker were occupied elsewhere. In such conditions the strongest Power would have an inducement to respect the independence of small neutral countries

[1] A typical pronouncement was one made by the Netherlands Foreign Minister in the Lower House on November 24, 1934: "Holland will never surrender her traditional policy, and it is a mistake to believe that Dutch territory can be disposed of by other parties for the defence of another state. . . . Our country has no desire to follow in the wake of any one European state or group of states." In July 1940, when the unreality of such a position had been conclusively and dramatically demonstrated, Mr. De Valera was still assuring the world that his Government was "resolved to maintain and defend the country's neutrality in all circumstances" (*The Times*, July 5, 1940).

and not add more of them than he could help to the list of his enemies. In 1914 these conditions were already passing away. But even then the gallant delaying actions of the Belgian army were an important factor in the campaign which ended with the Battle of the Marne. In 1940 the resistance of small Powers had no more than a nuisance value. By this time the conduct of war depended primarily on the accumulation and marshalling of a vast mechanical equipment far beyond the industrial resources of a small country. Denmark did not attempt to defend herself; and the defences of Norway, Holland and Belgium, even with such hastily improvised assistance as could reach them from outside, did not delay the German forces long enough, or exact sufficient sacrifices from them, to affect in any material way the course of events. Henceforth the only way in which a small country could hope to defend itself against Great Power A would be to hand over the charge of its defences well in advance to Great Power B. But such action would not only be resented as a breach of neutrality by Great Power A,[1] but would constitute a virtual surrender of independence to Great Power B, since the Power which is responsible for the defence of a territory must necessarily control its policy in essentials. "Absolute neutrality", wrote the *Izvestia* in April 1940, "is a fantasy unless real power is present capable of sustaining

---

[1] In a note of May 10, 1940, to the Netherlands and Belgian Governments, the German Government made it a ground of complaint that they had concerted plans of defence with Great Britain and France and had thus forfeited their neutral status. This charge was unfortunately ill-founded. The Netherlands Minister for Foreign Affairs has since revealed that, in the week preceding May 10, the Netherlands Government received from its intelligence service information about the impending invasion "enough to cause the most serious alarm". But "even then the Government did not warn the Allies; we wanted to be absolutely certain that a founded accusation could never be made against us for having secretly abandoned the neutrality we had so consistently observed" (E. N. van Kleffens, *The Rape of the Netherlands*, p. 110). M. van Kleffens appears somewhat apprehensive of the impression which may be made on his countrymen by this confession; for he proceeds to argue that help could not in any event have reached them in time. This may have been true in the particular case, but hardly affects the moral.

it. Small states lack such power."[1] In modern conditions of warfare a small state cannot defend its independence against a Great Power except by methods which in themselves constitute a surrender of military independence. Interdependence has become an inescapable condition of survival.

The second factor which has destroyed the effective independence of small and weak states is that, in the highly developed conditions of modern warfare, the mere existence of neutral territory in proximity to the belligerents is likely to prove an embarrassment to one side and an asset to the other, so that neutrality, however passive, is rarely neutral in effect.[2] The intensification of economic warfare has probably contributed more than anything else to this result. Prior to 1914 a belligerent might well hesitate, even if some military advantage were involved, to attack a neighboring country which, so long as it remained neutral, would constitute a source and channel of supplies. When in the early years of the present century, the German General Staff elaborated its plan for invading France through Belgium, Holland was excluded from the plan because a neutral port at Rotterdam was essential if Germany was to receive adequate supplies from overseas. The creation during the war of 1914-18 of a wholly new kind of blockade which prevented Germany from drawing the expected economic advantages from the neutrality of Holland revolutionised the position. When the German General Staff drew up its plans for the invasion of 1940, it may safely be assumed that there was no inclination to exclude Holland. It was now clear that the countries of the Western European seaboard could no longer serve in time of war as channels for overseas supplies to Germany. On the contrary, owing to British command of the sea, they were sources of supply to Great Britain; and what was more important still, they helped to shield the coasts of Britain

---

[1] *Izvestia* (leading article), April 11, 1940.
[2] Switzerland is perhaps, thanks to her geographical situation, one of the rare exceptions.

from German attack. A neutral Rotterdam could not serve as an *entrepôt* for German war trade. Rotterdam in German hands might serve as a valuable base against Great Britain. Dutch, Belgian, Norwegian and Danish neutrality was, quite apart from anything these countries might think or do, an asset to Great Britain. The German General Staff drew the necessary conclusion.

The present war has revealed the empty character of the formal independence enjoyed by small states. The only choice now open to them is a policy of peace at any price, which is the negation of a policy; and the humiliations entailed by it, even where it succeeds in sparing them the physical horror of war, have been amply illustrated by such countries as Sweden and Turkey. Small states can no longer balance themselves in dignified security on the tight-rope of neutrality. Still less can they rely on an indeterminate system of collective security which leaves open the identity of the future enemy and the future ally. The small country can survive only by seeking permanent association with a Great Power. The mutual obligation which such association will involve cannot be limited to the contingent liability to do certain things in certain eventualities—the most that the League Covenant ever sought to achieve. It must be a continuing obligation to pursue a common military and economic policy and to pool military and economic resources under some form of common control. Experience has shown conclusively that nothing less than this can in modern conditions assure a reasonable degree of military security. The right of national self-determination is conditioned by this military necessity.

Self-Determination and Economic Power

The threat of military power to the right of national self-determination and to the independence of small states was at any rate recognised by the peacemakers of 1919, though they had little understanding of the nature of the problem created by modern military technique. But wedded as they were to nineteenth-century conceptions of *laissez-faire* and of the divorce between economics and politics, they failed to detect the more recent and more insidious threat of economic power. It is one of the anomalies of the Covenant that, while practical experience of the war of 1914-18 had made its framers well aware of the potentialities of economic power as a weapon of defence, it never occurred to them to consider it as a potential weapon of attack. When some years later Soviet Russia proposed to remedy this omission by a pact of economic non-aggression, the suggestion was ill received. It is indeed true that the definition of economic aggression would meet with still more insuperable difficulties than the definition of military aggression. But the theoretical justification of the proposal was undeniable. The system of the Covenant was defective not merely because it failed to cope adequately with the problem of military power, but because it ignored the problem of economic power. A similar lacuna may be discerned in the minorities treaties concluded in 1919-20. "In their view of what was essential", remarks Mr. Macartney of the framers of these treaties, "they were naturally guided by their own experience. Now the minorities struggle in the West had for a long century past been essentially political. . . . Liberal thought had naturally come to attach the greatest importance to the problems of which it had the chief experience." [1] States bound themselves to accord to minorities the cherished political rights of nineteenth-century democracy. But these did not include the right to work or the right not to starve. Petitions against racial discrimination in such matters as evictions and land settlement were received and discussed at Geneva. But there were a hundred ways in which a well-organised state, which punctually discharged its treaty obligations, could still reduce a minority to penury and despair

[1] C. A. Macartney, *National States and National Minorities*, pp. 281-2.

by such simple devices as refusal to allocate contracts, or to grant financial credits, to firms managed by, or employing, members of the minority. The minorities treaties, like the Covenant, afforded no protection against the oppressive use of economic power; and during the years from 1919 to 1939 it was economic power which counted most.

This fatal neglect of the economic factor by the peacemakers of 1919 was the main theme of Mr. Keynes' famous book on *The Economic Consequences of the Peace:*

> To what a different future Europe might have looked forward if either Mr. Lloyd George or Mr. Wilson had apprehended that the most serious of the problems which claimed their attention were not political or territorial, but financial and economic, and that the perils of the future lay not in frontiers and in sovereignties, but in food, coal and transport.

And again:

> The fundamental economic problem of a Europe starving and disintegrating before their eyes was the one question in which it was impossible to arouse the interest of the Four.[1]

In retrospect it is not difficult to see that the prudent course would have been—and the same would be equally true to-day— to attend first, as an immediate practical measure, to the urgent needs of economic recovery, and then to evolve, in the light of the experience gained, the necessary compromise between the claims of national independence and the imperative exigencies of economic interdependence. What was in fact done was to give unconditional priority to the claims of national self-determination, so far as they could be satisfied at the expense of the defeated Powers, and leave the economic consequences to look after themselves. The growing importance of economic power, and its revolutionary consequences for unqualified political in-

[1] J. M. Keynes, *The Economic Consequences of the Peace*, pp. 134, 211.

dependence and for the right of national self-determination, were ignored.

The causes of this blindness can be easily diagnosed. The peacemakers of 1919 were living in a past world, whose transient conditions they assumed as a postulate of the future settlement. In the nineteenth century, economic interdependence was in some measure a reality. Great Britain, whose commercial and financial predominance made the free flow of goods and credit a paramount British interest, was powerful enough to secure the general acceptance of certain standards of international economic behaviour. There were certain conventional limits beyond which states did not use economic weapons against one another. There was a tacit understanding that certain kinds of economic unity would be maintained. Civilised countries accepted the gold standard, did not depreciate their currencies and did not disown their debts. Moderate protective tariffs were in use almost everywhere. But they were commonly mitigated by acceptance of the most-favoured-nation clause; and the ingenious dodges by which this clause can be rendered virtually meaningless had not been discovered. Quotas and subsidies were in their infancy. The potentialities of national economic power as a weapon of outstanding importance in international politics were undeveloped and almost unthought of. In these relatively idyllic conditions, British predominance assured a certain minimum of real economic interdependence, and even a weak independent state had nothing to fear from economic discrimination. The peacemakers of Versailles assumed that these conditions were perpetual, and that no economic factor militated against the unqualified recognition of the right to national independence.

The settlement of 1919 was thus valid only for economic, as well as for military, conditions which no longer existed. The history of the twenty years between the two wars showed the Great Powers using the new economic weapon against one another and against the small Powers, and the small Powers using the same weapon against one another. There was no profit in the endless controversies on the issue who began first. The question was not a moral one. Modern industrial conditions had enormously developed economic power and the importance of the economic factor, both in national and international politics. In the midst of political disintegration and the multiplication of political units, economic power had undergone a rapid process of concentration. As an American writer puts it, "the contemporary evolution of nationalism has reached an impasse between a popular determination to have smaller cultural units and a will to effect larger economic aggregations".[1] It soon became clear that the satisfaction given in the name of self-determination to national aspirations had aggravated economic problems; and the economic crisis of 1930 revealed the hollowness of the structure long before the iron hand of Hitler supervened to dash it brutally in pieces. The wielding of unlimited economic power by a multiplicity of small national units had become incompatible with the survival of civilisation.

The economic repercussions of the unrestricted right of national self-determination are perhaps in the long run more significant than the military repercussions; for they impinge directly on the daily life of the ordinary man. The world has been changing its shape. A recent Irish writer quotes the observation of a young Irishman that the world is not "the same size as it was in 1916". The demand for prosperity has spread and deepened. "With the change this small country grew a shade smaller; it could no longer provide more than a fraction of its children with the standard they had been taught to expect." The young generation had begun to be dissatisfied with a "walled-in Gaelic state".[2] Political rights have failed to provide a key to the millennium. Just as the right to vote seems of little value if it does not carry with it the right to work for a living

---

[1] C. J. H. Hayes in *International Conciliation*, No. 369 (April 1941), p. 238.
[2] Sean O'Faolain, *An Irish Adventure*, pp. 304-5.

wage, so the right of national self-determination loses much of its appeal if it turns out to be a limiting factor on economic opportunity. The rights of nations, like the rights of man, will become hollow if they fail to pave the way to economic well-being, or even to bare subsistence, and offer no solution of the problems which most affect the man in the street and the man in the field. Just as political democracy must, if it is to survive, be reinterpreted in economic terms, so the political right of national self-determination must be reconciled with the exigencies of economic interdependence.

The Future of Self-Determination

Recognition of the nature of the disease may give us a clue to that re-definition of national self-determination which, like a re-definition of democracy, is so badly needed. If we remember that the principle at stake is the principle of self-determination, and avoid confusing it with the principle of nationality, we shall be clear that this principle is not necessarily one of disintegration. Men may "determine" themselves into larger as readily as into smaller units; and the reaction which we have already noted against the principle as applied in 1919 is the symptom of a movement in that direction. It is true that the individual wants to see the group of which he is a member free and independent. But it is also true that he wants to belong to a group large and powerful enough to play a significant rôle in a wider community and thus lend a sense of reality to the service which he renders to it. If the activities of his group seem trivial and ineffective, his membership of it will become meaningless to him, and he will be open to transfer his loyalties to a larger unit. Where the individual himself is incapable of making this adjustment, it may occur readily enough in the next generation. Once the crabbing and confining effects of small national markets, small national political systems and even small national cultures come to be felt as restrictions on a larger freedom, the days of the small independent national state, the embodiment of the ideals of 1919, are numbered.

These trends have been intensified since the outbreak of war, both in those countries which have been direct victims of military attack and in those which have maintained a precarious neutrality, by a consciousness of the military helplessness and the economic confinement of the small national unit. In December 1940, the acting Norwegian Minister for Foreign Affairs, in a remarkable broadcast from London, spoke of the war-time cooperation between Norwegian and other "freedom-loving forces in the world" as "a work which is at the same time forming the basis for a state which must and shall endure after the war—a political cooperation which will secure our national freedom and protect us from attacking tyrants, and which economically establishes social security and prevents financial crises from destroying economic life and stopping social developments". [1] There is everywhere increasing recognition that self-determination is not quite the simple issue—not the clear-cut choice between mutually exclusive alternatives proclaimed by a cross on a ballot paper—which it seemed in 1919. If it is true that the multiplication of independent states was in fact what the peoples concerned then desired, it is by no means certain that this would be their desire to-day. It is a matter of vital interest to consider here and now what conditions for an effective future organisation of the world are dictated by military and economic exigencies, and how to reconcile these conditions with the strong tendency of human beings to form independent, and potentially hostile, groups for the preservation and cultivation of a common language and tradition, common customs and ways of life, and common interests.

Certain tentative conclusions emerge quite clearly. In the first place, we must discard the nineteenth-century assumption that nation and state should normally coincide. In a clumsy but

[1] *The Times*, December 16, 1940.

convenient terminology which originated in Central Europe, we must distinguish between "cultural nation" and "state nation". The existence of a more or less homogeneous racial or linguistic group bound together by a common tradition and the cultivation of a common culture must cease to provide a *prima facie* case for the setting up or the maintenance of an independent political unit. Secondly, we must lay far less stress than was done in 1919 on the absolute character of the right of self-determination and far more on its necessary limitations. The conception of obligations must be invoked to counteract the undue nineteenth-century emphasis on rights. The right of self-determination must carry with it a recognised responsibility to subordinate military and economic policy and resources to the needs of a wider community, not as a hypothetical engagement to meet some future contingency, but as a matter of the everyday conduct of affairs. Both these conclusions require further elaboration.

The divorce between nation and state, or between "cultural nation" and "state nation", would mean, expressed in simpler language, that people should be allowed and encouraged to exercise self-determination for some purposes but not for others, or alternatively that they should "determine" themselves into different groups for different purposes. There is nothing in such a division incompatible with human nature or with normal human aspirations. Almost all civilised men and women are members of different groups formed to satisfy different needs, and find no difficulty in reconciling the claims of a church, a sports club, a horticultural society and a trade union. Indeed, it can be plausibly argued that healthy social life can exist only where there is some such intertwined network of loyalties and interests, and where no one institution—whether state, church or trade union—makes an all-embracing demand on the allegiance of its members in every field of their activities. Moreover it is clear that such a compromise really can be effected even when one of the loyalties concerned is loyalty to the state. There

is every reason to suppose that considerable numbers of Welshmen, Catalans and Uzbeks have quite satisfactorily solved the
problem of regarding themselves as good Welshmen, Catalans
and Uzbeks for some purposes and good British, Spanish and
Soviet citizens for others.

An extension of this system of divided but not incompatible
loyalties is the only tolerable solution of the problem of self-
determination; for it is the only one which will satisfy at one
and the same time the needs of modern military and economic
organisation and the urge of human beings to form groups based
on common tradition, language and usage. The difficulty of
such an extension is doubtless very great at a period when the
power and authority of the state are everywhere increasing and
are covering, more and more effectively, more and more departments of life, and when economic organisation, education and
the direction of opinion on matters vital to security have become
recognized functions of government. It would be rash to look
for a reversal of this trend. But the very process of concentration and centralisation which this development entails inevitably
ends by setting up a compensating process of devolution; for
the more far-reaching and more ubiquitous the activities of government, the more necessary does it become to decentralise control in the interests of efficient administration. It is in this interplay between centralisation and devolution, in this recognition
that some human affairs require to be handled by larger, and
others by smaller, groups than at present, that we must seek a
solution to the baffling problem of self-determination. "The
troubles of our day", writes Mr. Macartney, "arise out of the
modern conception of the national state: out of the identification of the political ideals of all the inhabitants of the state with
the national-cultural ideals of the majority in it. If once this
confusion between two things which are fundamentally different can be abandoned, there is no reason why the members of
a score of different nationalities should not live together in per-

fect harmony in the same state." [1] Once the broader military and economic framework is securely established, there is no limit to the number or to the functions of the smaller national units of self-government which may be built up within it. In this context the natural and ineradicable desire of the human group for self-determination in the conduct of its affairs can be given the fullest scope and expression.

The other conclusion which requires emphasis is that national self-determination, like democracy, must be re-defined in terms which match the assertion of rights with the equally valid assertion of correlative obligations. In 1919 it was assumed that, once a "nation" was recognised as such, the right of self-determination conferred on it an absolute claim to national independence, and that the concession of this claim must have priority over any serious discussion of mutual obligations between nations. This neglect of the correlation of rights and obligations, based on acceptance, tacit or avowed, of the doctrine of the harmony of interests, was characteristic of the thought and policy of Woodrow Wilson, who assumed, with an unquestioning readiness which seems incomprehensible to-day, that the universal recognition of the right of national self-determination would bring universal peace. Rights were absolute; to recognise a right and make it effective was a good in itself; the assumption of a countervailing obligation was voluntary, and the recognition of the right could not be made dependent on it.

It would be foolish to underestimate the extent of the revolution in men's ways of thinking which will be required to restore the issue of national self-determination to its true perspective as a right exercised within a framework of obligation. For the small nation, it involves the abandonment of the exceptionally favoured position enjoyed by small countries in the nineteenth century, when neutrality was the only price asked of them for military security, and when their territories and their interests

[1] C. A. Macartney, *National States and National Minorities*, p. 450.

(including, sometimes, wealthy overseas possessions) were protected by an overwhelmingly powerful navy for which they
were not responsible and to which they made no contribution,
For the Great Power, it involves the assumption of a direct and
permanent share of responsibility both military and economic
—such as Great Powers have rarely been prepared to undertake
—for the welfare of other nations. For Great Britain—to take
the concrete case—it means making the defence of, at any rate,
some European countries a common unit with the defence of
Britain, and accepting the principle of a common economic
policy which will take into account the interest of, say, French,
Belgian and German industry or of Danish and Dutch agriculture as well as of British industry or agriculture. The military
security and economic well-being of Great Powers, not less
than those of smaller countries, is bound up with the acceptance
of a new conception of international obligation.

The same principles will also apply to the difficult problem
of the right of national self-determination for colonial peoples.
It has often been said that the Allied Governments behaved
inconsistently in 1919 when they asserted the right of self-determination in Europe and rejected it in Africa and Asia.
Logically, this charge is irrefutable. Yet apart from the still
undeveloped capacity of many of these peoples for self-government and from such special problems as that created in India
by the diversity of races and religious, it is clear that to break
up existing military and economic units in the name of national
self-determination would in fact have been a reactionary measure. In Europe the present need is to build up larger military
and economic units while retaining existing or smaller units for
other purposes. In Africa and Asia it is to retain large inter-con-
tinental military and economic units (not necessarily the existing ones in every case), but to establish within these units a far
greater measure of devolution and an immense variety of local
administration rooted in local tradition, law and custom. The
heedless and unwitting extermination of native ways of life and

the imposition of a mechanically uniform system of administration has perhaps been as great a factor in the decay and depopulation of many colonial areas as direct and deliberate exploitation by economic interests. The conception of Africa as a series of vast and more or less uniform areas divided from one another by arbitrary geometrical frontiers must give place to an administrative patchwork based on the self-determination of the tribal unit. In this sense, the "balkanisation" of the tropics is a consummation devoutly to be wished.

It would seem therefore that the international relations of the future must, if the alternatives of complete chaos or brutal domination are to be avoided, develop along two lines: recognition of the need for a larger unit than the present nation for military and economic purposes, and within this unit for the largest measure of devolution for other purposes, and recognition that the right of national self-determination can be valid only within a new framework of mutual military and economic obligation. The crisis of self-determination, like the crisis of democracy, turns ultimately on a moral issue. But it expresses itself in military, and above all, like the crisis of democracy, in economic, terms. There can be no solution of it unless we can solve the economic crisis which is the most conspicuous and most far-reaching symptom of the troubles of our time.

CHAPTER 4

THE ECONOMIC CRISIS

THE economic crisis which underlies the political crisis exhibits
with peculiar vividness the failure of the satisfied countries to
adjust outworn forms of thought to a new and revolutionary
age. The principles of the so-called classical economists, like
most other principles, were never perfectly applied in practice.
Derogations from them were admitted, and here and there bold
thinkers challenged them. But down to 1914 they were generally accepted as the canon of economic orthodoxy; and even
to-day, especially in Great Britain and the United States, some
kind of absolute validity is attributed in many quarters to these
principles. This is natural, not only because theories die hard
and frequently outlive the conditions out of which they arose,
but also because the period in which these principles held sway
was, for both these countries, a period of unparalleled advance
in economic prosperity and in political power and prestige. It
is therefore particularly important for Englishmen and Americans to remind themselves of the variable character of the assumptions made by thinkers on economic subjects in the past.
In the heyday of the nineteenth century, Bagehot recognised
that there had once been "a sort of pre-economic age when the
very assumptions of political economy did not exist, when its
precepts would have been ruinous and when the very contrary
precepts were requisite and wise".[1] But even when classical
economists were candid enough to perceive that their hy-

[1] W. Bagehot, *Physics and Politics* (2nd ed.), pp. 11-12.

potheses had not always been valid in the past, it rarely occurred to them to reflect that these hypotheses might cease to be valid in the future. To-day a more eclectic approach is required. "When we wish to study economics," as a recent writer has said, "we must not restrict our tools of understanding to the concepts of one single 'ism'." [1] It will be found that the new period which has gradually begun to take shape since 1918 has gone back in some respects to the assumptions of the mercantilists, and in others—further still—to those of the schoolmen.

The contemporary world is engaged in revising the system of the classical economists in three essential points. In the first place, it has abandoned the hypothesis of the pursuit of individual interests as the motive force of the economic system. Like the schoolmen, it regards the welfare of individuals as a problem of society as a whole, though like the mercantilists it still tends to identify society with a territorial group. Secondly, it is in process of discarding the quantitative conception of "wealth" as the end of economic activity in favour of the qualitative conception of "welfare", thereby reverting to a point of view familiar to the schoolmen, though on a fundamentally different social basis. Thirdly, and as a result of the abandonment of maximum wealth as the test of what is economically desirable, contemporary thought is feeling its way towards a new conception of the relationship between production and consumption. Modern economic problems revolve round these issues of Individualism and Collectivism, Wealth and Welfare, and Production and Consumption.

Individualism and Collectivism

The classical economists presupposed a society of independent, fully enlightened and completely mobile individuals, each

---

[1] E. Rosenstock-Huessy, *Out of Revolution*, p. 731. A British economist has observed that "Dr. Schacht's true greatness resides in his realisation of the fact that in economics few doctrines are right at all times" (G. Crowther, *Ways and Means of War*, p. 34).

acting for himself, possessed of equal bargaining power, and equally interested in the economic system as producers and consumers. This hypothesis was never even approximately realised. Every European country inherited from the Middle Ages a more or less rigid class structure which had undergone important modifications, but had nowhere been wholly broken down. It is significant that economic individualism achieved its longest lived success in the one important country whose social structure was relatively classless and approximated most nearly to the conditions of equality and mobility: the United States of America.

But if the legacy of the past falsified from the first the individualist hypothesis, this was nothing to the obstacles which were soon to be raised by technological developments. In the age which saw the birth of "classical economics", the industrial system was based on a society of small *entrepreneurs*, independent craftsmen and individual merchants.[1] Individualism bore some relation to economic facts. The smallness of the capital investment required in industry and commerce made this society highly mobile and adaptable. The quick and frictionless adjustment to change required by *laissez-faire* theory was still possible. These conditions were destroyed, as the nineteenth century advanced, by the development of specialised mammoth industries requiring enormous capital investment and a mass army of labour, both of them incapable of rapid and frictionless transference to meet changing demand. The unit was no longer the individual, but the joint-stock company, the trust, the banking corporation, the trade union.[2] The hypothesis of a vast society of equal, independent and mobile individuals was falsi-

---

[1] This was of course not true of agriculture, at any rate in Great Britain; the early classical economists vigorously denounced the vested interests of land-owners, and their triumph coincided with the declining importance of agriculture.

[2] The "closed shop" is the trade-union form of monopoly. The nineteenth-century apostles of *laissez-faire* quite consistently objected to trade unions, which were, in Cobden's words, "founded upon principles of brutal tyranny and monopoly" (Morley, *Life of Cobden*, i, p. 299).

fied to an ever-increasing extent. The individual counted less and less. The forces which dominated production and distribution and exercised a preponderant influence in the economic "society" were a few highly organised interest-groups, growing ever larger and more powerful. What is commonly referred to as "individual enterprise" has been destroyed not, as its advocates sometimes pretend, by "socialism" or by the interference of grandmotherly governments but by the innate trend of competitive capitalism towards monopoly.[1]

Already before 1914 the premiss of classical economics had ceased to be valid, and the issue which is still commonly referred to as Individualism v. Collectivism had become something quite different. As a witty American writer has put it, "the creeds accepted by respectable people described social organisations in the language of personally owned private property, when as a matter of fact the things which were described were neither private, nor property, nor personally owned".[2] The convenient legal fiction which treated limited liability companies as persons became more and more remote from anything real. The issue was no longer whether economic enterprise should be conducted by individuals or by some collective organ (which is what the terms "individualism" and "collectivism" ought to imply), but whether it should be conducted by a congeries of non-official collective organs or by some public authority. In the United States, the individualist tradition was kept alive rather longer than elsewhere, in part by the fashionable American habit of personification, in part by the advertisement given to great personal fortunes gained in industry. Even there, however, Mr. Henry Ford is now the last and unique representative of the tradition. The issue miscalled Individualism v. Collectivism is not really the question whether economic enterprise

---

[1] The innate character of this trend is ignored by those economists who argue that the modern economic crisis is the product not of "individual enterprise", but of monopoly. The trouble is that the individual obstinately refuses to remain an individual.

[2] T. W. Arnold, *The Folklore of Capitalism*, p. 118.

should be controlled by the Federal Government or by men like Mr. Ford, but whether it should be controlled by a corporation responsible to the Federal Government or by some other equally collective, but not responsible, organisation such as General Motors, Bethlehem Steel or Southern Utilities. "The choice . . . is not between competition and monopoly, but between a monopoly which is irresponsible and private and a monopoly which is responsible and public."[1]

Once the issue had taken this form and came to be recognised as such, the result was no longer doubtful. The *laissez-faire* state could remain passive, or intervene only to restrain certain defined malpractices, so long as the units of the economic system were individuals who were not, in isolation, powerful enough to engender frictions dangerous to the social structure. This passivity could not be maintained in face of the growth of mammoth industrial and financial concerns or highly organised combinations of labour. Nor indeed was passivity what big industry really wanted. As President Roosevelt once said, "the same man who does not want to see the government interfere in business . . . is the first to go to Washington to ask the government for a prohibitory tariff".[2] In the days of railway construction (the first industrial enterprise involving the sinking and immobilisation of capital on a really large scale), the state had to intervene for the first time to secure the companies against individual caprice and to secure the individual against oppressive charges. Every modern state has intervened, first, to protect employers against trade unions and, later, to protect the rights of the unions. If we wish to get a correct picture of the social and economic structure of the modern world, we must think not of a number of individuals cooperating and competing within the framework of a state, but of a number of large and powerful groups, sometimes competing, sometimes cooperating, in the pursuit of their group interests, and of a state constantly im-

[1] R. H. Tawney, *The Acquisitive Society*, p. 225.
[2] F. D. Roosevelt, *Looking Forward*, p. 25.

pelled to increase the strength and scope of its authority in order to maintain the necessary minimum of cohesion in the social fabric. We can no longer base our thinking, like the classical economists, on the isolated independent individual. The subject of modern economics is man in society, man as a member of a number of collective groups struggling for power, of which the most powerful, the most highly organised and the most broadly based is at the present time the state. The issue no longer lies between individualism and collectivism. The issue is whether to allow social action to depend on the haphazard outcome of a struggle between interest groups or to control and coordinate the activities of these groups in the interest of the community.

Wealth and Welfare

In an age when even pleasure and pain were regarded as quantitatively measurable, it was not surprising that the classical economists believed themselves to have created a quantitative science of wealth. The price mechanism expressed the preferences of the consumer; profitability determined the preferences of the producer; and the interplay of these factors, both precisely measurable in terms of money, assured the automatic working of the economic system in a manner calculated to produce the maximum of measurable wealth. "Political economy" could thus be conceived as a science comparable with the physical and mechanical sciences. Certain causes produced, in the absence of external interference, certain consequences; and the whole economic system was a perfect self-adjusting mechanism which worked for the benefit of all if everyone pursued his own interest and no political authority meddled with this scientifically determinable process. It was assumed as an axiom which required no proof that the maximum production of wealth conduced to maximum welfare. The profit motive, operating through the individual, worked for the good of the community conceived in terms of maximum wealth. For the first time in history, individual profit was accepted as the test of what was socially useful.[1]

From about the middle of the nineteenth century onwards, the rigours of this doctrine were constantly mitigated in practice by state intervention. The social conscience became increasingly recalcitrant to the view that the principal end of economic activity is to produce as cheaply as possible the maximum quantity of goods which can be sold as dearly as possible. Public authorities undertook the provision of many services and many amenities which, though commonly recognised as socially useful, could not be justified by standards of the price and profit mechanism. The long controversy about municipal trading, which at first turned mainly on the relative efficiency of private and public enterprise, switched over to the issue how far municipalities were entitled to engage in enterprises which did not "pay". The criterion of "welfare" came almost imperceptibly to be distinguished from, and to take precedence over, the criterion of "wealth". Unlike wealth, welfare could not be measured in quantitative terms. Price and profit could no longer be accepted as the sole factors determining the objects towards which the productive resources of the community should be directed. The needs of modern warfare, for which the whole resources of the community must be mobilised, have driven home this lesson. In the war of 1914-18, the controller of the nation's supplies quickly perceived that "it could no longer be assumed that real importance could be measured with sufficient precision by purchasing power".[2] This is in fact an understatement. Purchasing power ceased altogether to be the standard of measurement. "Through application of the principle of pri-

---

[1] "The capitalist creed was the first and only social creed which valued the profit motive positively as the means by which the ideal free and equal society would be automatically realised. All previous creeds had regarded the private profit motive as socially destructive, or at least neutral" (P. Drucker, *The End of Economic Man*, p. 35). We are only just beginning to realise the paradoxical character of the capitalist faith.

[2] A. Salter, *Security: Can We Retrieve It?* p. 58.

orities, the processes of manufacture and trade were made to move in response to a national purpose rather than in response to the wills of those who had money to buy." [1] The war made, or hastened, an economic revolution by proving conclusively that the most effective mobilisation of the national resources for a given purpose is incompatible with reliance on the profit motive.

Unhappily the lesson then learnt was supposed to have a special and exceptional validity limited to the duration of war and without application to the conditions of peace. Mr. Churchill has graphically described the situation which presented itself on November 11, 1918:

> The organisation and machinery of which we disposed was powerful and flexible in an extraordinary degree. The able business men among us, each the head of a large group of departments, had now been working for a year and a half in a kind of industrial cabinet. They were accustomed to unexpected changes enforced by the shifting fortunes of war. . . . There was very little in the productive sphere they could not at this time actually do. A requisition, for instance, for half a million houses would not have seemed more difficult to comply with than those we were already in process of executing for a hundred thousand aeroplanes, or twenty thousand guns, or the medium artillery of the American army or two million tons of projectiles. But a new set of conditions began to rule from eleven o'clock onwards. The money-cost, which had never been considered by us to be a factor capable of limiting the supply of the armies, asserted a claim to priority from the moment the fighting stopped. [2]

The attempt to stem the revolution and to return to an economic system in which "money-cost" was the criterion proved a disastrous failure; and the failure was due to moral, as well to

[1] B. Baruch, *Taking the Profits Out of War*, p. 29.
[2] Winston Churchill, *The World Crisis: The Aftermath*, pp. 32-3.

technical, reasons. In the post-war period it seemed, at any rate
to the younger generation, wholly impossible to identify what
is socially desirable with what "pays" best in terms of cash results. "Market price and comparative cost could no longer be
regarded as the generally accepted regulator of the world's
economic energies. . . . Ordinary men were protesting that
they would no longer submit to having their lives regulated by
the impersonal price signals of international commerce." [1] The
economic crisis of the nineteen-thirties breached the defences
of the last citadel of *laissez-faire*. "The rulers of the exchange of
mankind's goods", said President Roosevelt in his Inaugural
Address on March 4, 1933, "have failed through their own stub-
bornness and their own incompetence, have admitted their
failure and have abdicated. . . . The measure of the restoration
lies in the extent to which we apply social values more noble
than mere monetary profit."

Economic theory has proved far less adaptable than economic
practice to the new spirit of the age. So long as the end of economic activity was merely to create an abundance of goods and
services measurable in terms of money, economics could still
hold its place as a quantitative science and lay claim to an accuracy and an objectivity comparable with those of the physical
sciences. To substitute "welfare" for "wealth" as the criterion
meant frankly to abandon this claim and to transform economics
into a qualitative science, doubtfully entitled to the name of
science at all. Worse still, this transformation would blur the
boundary-line—one of those unreal boundaries dear to the
academic mind—between economics and the other social
sciences. This respect for the supposed purity of economic
science no doubt helps to explain why its adepts have clung
with such blind tenacity to the tattered shreds of orthodoxy.
Even to-day, in Great Britain and the United States the price
and profit mechanism is still commonly defended as the normal

[1] W. K. Hancock, *Survey of British Commonwealth Affairs,* ii, Part 1, pp.
269-70.

test of economic policy, and any departure from it treated as a regrettable necessity imposed by exceptional circumstances. Hence the chronic divorce in recent years between economic theory, and economic practice. Statesmen, driven by social needs, have found themselves compelled to defy all the textbook maxims. Economic theory has failed to give any lead at a time of universal economic distress, and has limped, bewildered and protesting, in the train of economic practice. Such were the penalties of an attempt to defend the principles of the profit system in an age which long ago made up its mind on the necessity of adopting other criteria of what is socially desirable.

The supersession of the profit motive as the mainspring of economic activity has seemed to some to present insuperable difficulties. The profit motive has been so long placed by economists in the centre of their system that people have come to regard it as a central and immutable fact of human nature. But is not this merely an example of the way in which, as Professor Dewey has said, "current social tendencies are read back into the structure of human nature, and are then used to explain the very things from which they are deduced"? [1] The assumption still habitually made that man is actuated in his economic life mainly by the profit motive is coming to be less and less justified by the facts. A large majority of people nowadays work not for profit, but for fixed salaries or wages. Among many salaried workers and higher paid wage-earners to-day, the conditions and nature of the work, and the sense of service rendered or of capacities usefully employed, probably count for more than actual rate of remuneration in determining choice of occupation. Even among those for whom personal remuneration is the paramount factor, only an insignificant proportion can be directly interested in the profits of the enterprise. In some industrial enterprises, bonuses are awarded on a profit basis. But the proportion of these to total pay is generally trifling. If em-

[1] John Dewey, *Freedom and Culture*, p. 108.

ployees as a whole were interested in the profit-earning character of the enterprise in which they were employed, we should
find a marked disinclination to work for government departments which make no profit or for public utility concerns whose
profits are limited, and a corresponding preference for more
speculative types of industry. These symptoms are rarely found
in any grade of worker.

Nor can it be pretended that the modern British investor has
proved particularly susceptible to the attraction of high and
speculative rates of profit. Among other than fixed interest
securities, the greatest popularity in the past twenty years has
been enjoyed by the shares of those large companies whose
profits have remained unusually stable, and whose resources
are so arranged as to equalise dividend payments over a series
of years, so that what is nominally profit approximates as nearly
as possible to the character of interest. The conversion of the
whole of British industry into a series of public corporations on
a non-profit-earning basis would not in all probability have any
marked effect on the attitude either of the worker or of the investor. So drastic a step is perhaps unlikely, if only because of
the burden of control which would be thrown on the state. But
that a progressively smaller rôle will be assigned after the war to
the profit motive in determining what goods shall be produced
and where, what wages shall be paid to those producing them
and what price shall be paid by those consuming them, and
finally in what forms of production the national savings shall
be invested, is one of the most certain lessons of the economic
revolution through which we are passing.

The disappearance of price and profit as the dominant factors
in the economic system involves a profound modification of the
conception of property. Here again current practice has
marched far ahead of the theories of economists. For a long
time past two trends have been increasingly apparent. In the
first place, the social conscience has placed restrictions on the

possession and on the use of great personal wealth. Taxation which, fifty years ago, would have been regarded as confiscatory, has been imposed on it almost everywhere. In many countries large landed estates have been forcibly redistributed. In Great Britain and the United States, the tradition that wealthy men contribute a proportion of their wealth to social and philanthropic objects has grown stronger and is more generally observed. Secondly, the ownership of what Marx called the "means of production" has been divided up and divorced from control. To say that some hundreds of thousands of anonymous shareholders "own" the great industrial enterprises of Great Britain and the United States is almost as meaningless as to call the proletariat the owner of the means of production in Soviet Russia.[1] Public companies are now assumed, and indeed themselves profess, to have "responsibilities" and "obligations to the public", *i.e.* to the consumer. The payment of dividends is restricted in some cases by law, in others by social convention. Everywhere it has come to be accepted that production must serve ends judged useful to the community rather than aim at maximum profit.

The same tendency towards the elimination of the criterion of price and profit, and the substitution for it of a social standard of value, is exhibited in the fixing of wages. The doctrine of the minimum wage, calculated on the professed basis of a reasonable subsistence level, is a direct attack on the classical theory of the free labour market. It is a corollary of this doctrine that the rate of wages has in recent times almost ceased to fluctuate with the prosperity of industry (as classical theory requires), whereas it is commonly assumed (as in the current phrase "the vicious

[1] A railway director, who recently confessed in Parliament that he "still believed in private ownership", went on to speak of "transforming the shareholders into some form of public utility with a larger amount of public control and with the assistance of organised labour" (*Parliamentary Debates: House of Commons*, November 13, 1940, vol. 365, No. 125, cols. 1752, 1758). Even the fiction that ownership implies control is thus abandoned.

spiral") that any substantial rise in the cost of living must automatically involve a rise in wages. Just as profits cannot decently
be allowed to rise above a certain level, so wages cannot
decently be allowed to fall below a certain level. Similarly
unemployment, now universally recognised as a major social
scourge, can no longer be tolerated merely on the ground that
no profits can be earned by employing more people. Yet this
state of affairs was in fact tolerated as lately as 1935. When in
that year the British Government declared it "a misconception
to suppose that a vast quantity of hitherto undiscovered work
capable of giving employment to large numbers of people lies
waiting to be put in hand",[1] it did not mean that it was impossible to discover a vast quantity of useful work which might be
done, but that it was impossible to discover any work on the
doing of which profits could be earned. This regulation of employment by the dictates of profit and loss will have to disappear.
It may be safely predicted that the unrestricted right of industry
to "hire and fire" labour, already abolished or curtailed by war-
time regulations in essential branches of production, will not be
restored after the war. The "welfare" of the workers as a whole
will take precedence over the "wealth" of the producer as an
end of policy. It is clear that the regulating force of the economic system under which we live must more and more be
sought in the realm of ethics rather than in the operations of a
price mechanism; and nearly everyone agrees that the trend in
this direction should be encouraged and intensified.

In this and in other respects, it is becoming apparent that, in
emerging from the world of automatically regulated supply and
demand, we have found our way back to a point of view familiar
in much earlier times. We are reversing what has been called the
"de-moralisation of economics" implicit in the classical system.[2]

---

[1] *A Better Way to Better Times* (Reprint of Statement issued by His
Majesty's Government on Mr. Lloyd George's Proposals), p. 16. The title of
this pamphlet reads a little ironically.

[2] L. Mumford, *Faith for Living*, p. 110.

We are once more thinking, like the schoolmen, in terms of "just price", not of price determined by the "economic", amoral laws of the market. We are working towards the substitution for money values of social values of a different kind. And this by itself means a profound revolution in practice and in thought. Just as the period beginning in the sixteenth century witnessed the "individualisation of society through the progress of money economy",[1] so the retreat from money economy implies a re-integration of society, a move towards collectivisation. The liberal society of isolated independent individuals automatically working in the pursuit of their own profit for the good of all is dead; and it was only in that society that the "laws" of the classical economists were valid.[2] That society and those laws were called into being and justified by a period in which to stimulate an expansion of production was the primary condition of progress. From that period—the period of "scarcity economics"—we have now emerged. Rightly or wrongly, it is now commonly believed that civilised man has mastered the problem of scarcity, and can produce without undue strain on his capacity all that he needs or wants to consume. Not poverty, but unemployment is the scourge of our social system. Our most urgent economic problem is no longer to expand production, but to secure a more equitable distribution of consumption and a more regular and orderly utilisation of our productive capacity. Inequality and unemployment—unemployment both of man-power and of material resources—are the crying scandals of our age. To find the remedy, we must overhaul the whole relationship between production and consumption developed during the past hundred years under the aegis of classical economic orthodoxy.

[1] M. Beer, *Early British Economists*, p. 74.
[2] "The exact laws of the market have no deductive self-evidence at all, but the mere probability which marks every empirical law. The degree of probability of their realisation depends upon how probable it is that the basic social conditions will themselves materialise, that is to say, on the historical fact whether and to what extent liberal society exists" (A. Löwe, *Economics and Sociology*, p. 73).

Production and Consumption

The classical economic system was first and foremost a system of production. It claimed to have discovered the principle of maximum production at minimum cost. Once this principle was applied, everything else would take care of itself. The division of labour was the key to the satisfaction of man's economic requirements. The consumer would always be in a position, through the weapon of purchasing-power, to determine what should and what should not be produced. According to the old maxim, "the buyer settles the price". The interests of individual producer and individual consumer were fairly balanced. The last word would always rest with the consumer.

The practical, though unforeseen, result of this system was to place immense power in the hands of the producer. The founders of the classical school had, consistently enough, denounced all combinations of producers, whether of employers or of employed. But the trend towards collective action was far too strong to be resisted. The growth of large-scale industry controlling immense masses of material and labour made the producer the most influential and dominant force in the late nineteenth- and early twentieth-century state. In the United States, "big business" acquired almost undisputed control of the machinery of government. In Europe, it ousted the landed aristocracy from the monopoly of political office and social prestige. The consumer, who was still the isolated individual of classical theory and was scarcely conscious of his community of interest with other consumers, failed altogether to assert himself. The producer, not the consumer, was able to harness the power of the state to his interests. Even in Great Britain, it was mainly the influence of the export and shipping trades, not that of the consumer, which enabled a long rear-guard action to be fought in defence of free trade. Elsewhere the battle of the tariffs was a walkover for the producer. Nor was the consumer worsted only in the struggle for the support of the state. Not content with this easy victory, and pressing home the opportunities which it provided, the producer through the medium of trusts, cartels and monopolies placed himself more and more securely, and more and more defiantly, in a position to dictate to the consumer. If the ring of soap-producers was firmly and completely closed, the consumer had, in default of any alternative, to take the kinds of soap which the ring chose to put on the market.

Nor would it be right, when speaking of the producer, to think solely of the capitalist, of the *entrepreneur* and of the salaried manager or executive. The organised power of capital was soon matched by the organised power of labour. In the great industrial countries, as has already been pointed out, capital and labour formed a common front against the consumer and shared the same interest in maintaining both the level and the profitability of production. It was true that the worker, though a producer, had a relatively greater interest than the capitalist or the salaried executive in his status as a consumer. But for the comparatively well-to-do worker in regular employment—and it was this type of worker who in the main determined trade-union policy—producer interest, expressed in wages, predominated over consumer interest, expressed in cost of living; and even if this had not been generally true, it was difficult for a cotton operative or a railway worker to foresee how far an increase of his wages would be reflected in increased living costs. In good times, capital and labour might be at loggerheads over the division of the proceeds. But in time of depression, they were half-unconsciously drawn together by the imperative need of making sure that something was left to divide. "Anything that benefits the capitalist system as a whole", an acute critic has remarked, "benefits by necessity this trade-unionist socialist movement as it increases the total national income available for distribution between the classes. Socialism as an opposition from within is salutary and inevitable, but accepts necessarily the fundamentals of the capitalist social system." [1]

[1] P. Drucker, *The End of Economic Man*, p. 29.

The weakening of capitalism in the past twenty years has been accompanied by a weakening of trade-unionism. The war of 1914 shattered the Second International as effectively as it shattered the capitalist system. Soviet Russia, which began by suppressing capitalists, ended by harnessing the independent trade unions to the state. Nazi Germany, which began by suppressing trade unions, ended by treating capitalists in exactly the same way. In recent years it has become clear that capitalism and trade-unionism stand and fall together. Both share in the profits of production, and represent the producer interest against the consumer and the taxpayer.

It would be easy to show how the economic policy of Great Britain, since the last war and especially since 1931, has been dominated by the interest of the producer. Both industry and agriculture have made substantial concessions to labour. But they have more than recouped themselves by subsidies and measures of protection accorded to them by the state at the expense of the consumer and the taxpayer. Commercial policy has been decided in almost every case by a compromise between industry and agriculture, the broad rule being that, where one or the other could show a major interest, that interest was allowed to prevail, the interest of the consumer or of the community being rarely taken into account. The present war has revealed—if it was not clear before—the stranglehold which the producer has obtained on the state machine. When it became imperative for the state to control output for war purposes, the only method by which it could do so was to appoint leading industrialists as "controllers" of the commodities which they were engaged in producing, and to place the control of agriculture in the hands of "war agricultural committees" composed mainly or exclusively of farmers. In the conditions which had been reached before war broke out, perhaps no alternative method would have achieved so rapid an expansion of output. But this method was bound to achieve it with a maximum of advantage to the producer, who was confirmed in his commanding position.

After the outbreak of war a railway agreement was concluded in which the interests of the shareholders and the interests of labour were carefully weighed and balanced, but in which, as a Labour M.P. said in Parliament, "there is nothing to suggest that the public, who are, after all, a very big factor in this matter, have any interest in the arrangements at all".[1]

This predominant influence of the producer interest has been a vital factor in recent economic history, which can only be understood in the light of it. The war of 1914 stimulated the output of a large range of commodities and manufactures, both in belligerent and in neutral countries. After the war, there was a struggle between producers everywhere, supported by their respective governments, to retain as much as possible of the new industries thus developed; and this delayed the elimination even of that part of war-time production which was most obviously redundant. But as the mists of confused thinking slowly cleared, it was revealed that the phenomenon of over-production was not solely attributable to the war or its consequences. The post-war crisis came and went and came again. Depression in agriculture and large-scale unemployment in industry became endemic in nearly every country. The world found itself apparently confronted with a phenomenon which had been inconceivable to the classical economists: chronic over-production. The effects were, of course, cumulative. Over-production of wheat meant that the wheat-grower could not afford to drink coffee or buy new clothes, so that there was over-production of coffee and clothing; and so on throughout the whole system.

The Crisis of "Over-production"

Where then was the flaw in the orthodox assumption that increased facilities of production, by making additional resources available, merely led to new forms of production, and therefore

---

[1] *Parliamentary Debates: House of Commons,* November 13, 1940, vol. 365, No. 125, col. 1745.

to still further increased prosperity, and that over-production was inconceivable except as a transient phenomenon which would right itself by the automatic working of supply and demand? The trouble was that the classical economists presupposed an infinitely mobile society of small producers, in which both capital and labour could be conceived as homogeneous masses of infinitely adaptable material. This presupposition became increasingly invalid in the century after the publication of *The Wealth of Nations*. It was invalidated in three ways. In the first place, industry came to require enormous capital investment which, once made, could not be transferred. Capital sunk in a railway or an ironworks was virtually lost if the railway or the works became redundant, so that the capitalist naturally invoked every kind of expedient to maintain what had become, on classical principles, an "uneconomic" enterprise. Secondly, the increasing specialisation of machinery and labour made impossible those rapid transfers which the classical hypothesis required. Neither men nor machines engaged in producing steel rails or cotton clothing could be switched over at short notice to the production of gramophones or silk stockings. Thirdly, the classical hypothesis underestimated human conservatism. Financiers, employers and workers were equally slow to believe that an enterprise which had flourished and yielded profits for many years could become permanently redundant. Any falling-off in trade was attributed to a passing depression, to "unfair" competition, or to some other incidental circumstance which would soon be eliminated; and every effort was made not, as the classical economists anticipated, to transfer capital and labour to new openings, but to regain the lost positions. This conservatism was especially characteristic of countries like Great Britain, or industries like the textile trade, which had a long record of prosperity behind them. It has been quite as strongly marked on the side of labour as on that of capital. Reluctance to change one's occupation and perhaps also one's home is natural enough; and in addition to this psychological difficulty, the consistent policy of the trade unions has been to place as many obstacles as possible in the way of the transfer of labour from one branch of production to another. The increasing standardisation of wages has contributed to the same result.[1]

While therefore the productive machine, in growing more efficient, has also grown more rigid, so that its tendency has been to go on producing more and more of the same things, what has been happening to the consumer? His demands, in the process of continually increasing, have grown more and more varied. "The fact of real importance which is now emerging from the stress and welter of the immediate past", wrote a British economist in 1930, "is that a radical change has taken place in the world demand for different types of goods and services. There has been a shift in relative demand from the prime necessaries of life, food and clothing and house-room, towards goods and services satisfying secondary needs." [2] This is a perfectly natural process. As production expands and the standard of living rises, consumption goods fall into two categories: "necessaries" and "luxuries" (the terms being, of course, differently applied in different countries and at different periods). The total consumption of necessaries varies mainly with the number of the population, of luxuries with the extent of their purchasing power. Once an article is firmly established in the category of necessaries, further rises in the standard of living do little to increase the volume of consumption. The rise in the standard of living in Great Britain and the United States actually led, in the thirty years before 1939, to a decreased consumption of bread. The time may be near in both countries when no further rise in the standard of living would appreciably increase the consumption of, say, sugar or cotton underwear. The charac-

[1] "The free-moving, self-adjusting, perfectly sensitive competitive capitalism of the theoretical textbooks has disappeared for ever as long as one essential omnipresent market in it—the market for labour—is jammed and rigid" (E. F. M. Durbin, *The Politics of Democratic Socialism*, p. 91, where this point is discussed and illustrated).

[2] A. Loveday, *Britain and World Trade*, p. 86.

teristic of luxuries on the other hand is that the demand for them is infinitely elastic. There is no limit in sight (other than lack of purchasing-power) to the potential demand for motor-cars, tinned foods, fancy articles of clothing, books, *objets d'art*, cosmetics or popular entertainment. It is therefore not surprising that, in the recent period of a rapid rise in the standard of living, "staple" industries have suffered (agriculture has been the most depressed industry of all) and luxury trades have prospered. But the significant point for our present argument is that, while the demand for necessaries is relatively rigid, the demand for luxuries is variable and capricious. "The greater wealth per head, the changes in age and in wealth distribution, the increase in leisure and advance in culture, tend to the same result—instability of demand. Food we must have and clothing and a minimum of house-room, but once these needs are satisfied demand becomes optional." [1] In normal times you can predict with some degree of accuracy next year's consumption of bread, sugar or over-coats. But you cannot guess, even approximately, whether a particular fashion in hats will catch on or not, whether sherry will replace port, whether there will be a rage for silk lamp-shades or steel furniture, whether more or less money will be spent than last year on gramophone records or on greyhound racing.

The acuteness of the economic disequilibrium of the past twenty years has been partly due to failure to solve this funda-mental problem of incompatibility between an increasingly rigid system of production and the increasingly variable de-mands of consumers. There has been a concealed but ruthless battle between producer and consumer in which the producer has had all the weapons in his hands. "The leaders of business have endeavoured to secure themselves to some extent against the dangers of greater fluidity and uncertainty of demand and the rapid changes in the technique of production brought about

[1] A. Loveday, *Britain and World Trade*, p. 92.

by the advance of science, not simply by the rationalisation of individual plants, but by the centralised control of whole industries. To optional demand they have opposed monopoly of supply." [1] By vigorous advertising, the producer has sought to control and dictate demand and to compel the consumer to buy more and more of fewer and fewer things.[2] The slogans "Buy advertised goods", "Buy branded goods", are a subtle device of the advertising agent for lining his own pockets and helping the producer to regiment the taste of the consumer. When all else fails, the consumer must be bribed to buy what the producer wants to sell. If only the consumer will go on long enough buying the same toilet paper or the same boot polish, he will qualify for the free gift of a penknife or a fur coat. For larger objects, systems of hire purchase and payment by instalments perform the same function of subduing the consumer to the producer's will. The reluctance of the consumer to buy what he does not want is branded by the opprobrious name of "sales resistance", which has to be "broken down" by skilful advertising. Twenty years ago, Professor Tawney noted with surprise that people "talk as though man existed for industry instead of industry existing for man".[3] The whole of recent economic history amply illustrates this observation.

In the international sphere this topsy-turvy attitude towards production and consumption was carried to amazing lengths. Imports eagerly wanted by the consumer were reluctantly accepted as a necessary but regrettable condition of the maintenance of exports. Politicians timidly justified British imports of Danish bacon or Japanese bicycles, not on the common-sense

[1] *Ibid.* p. 97.

[2] "Advertising in the past . . . assumed that the public knew what it wanted, and wished for the best of its kind and price. . . . Modern advertising is based on the opposite assumption—that consumers do not know exactly what they want. . . . Not only is the public led to want what the manufacturer is in a position to supply, but he is persuaded to buy more of the commodity than he otherwise would" (T. N. Whitehead, *Leadership in a Free Society*, pp. 184, 187).

[3] R. H. Tawney, *The Acquisitive Society*, p. 49.

ground that they enabled more British people to eat bacon and ride bicycles, but because they enabled Great Britain to get rid of more of her coal and steel. Nearly all international commercial negotiations between the years 1930 and 1939 were conducted on the underlying assumption, not that the producer worked for the benefit of the consumer, but that the consumer was conferring a benefit on the producer by consuming his goods.[1] This assumption could be openly avowed on the most solemn occasions without anyone perceiving its paradoxical nature. At the Assembly of the League of Nations, Mr. Eden claimed that Great Britain had "accepted a steadily increasing percentage of the world's imports" and that this was "no small contribution to the maintenance of international trade".[2] The fact that Great Britain was graciously willing, as a contribution to Danish or Argentine welfare, to eat Danish butter or Argentine meat made Danes and Argentinians graciously willing to warm themselves with British coal. The implication was the same which had already worked so disastrously in domestic markets, *i.e.* that the way to promote trade was to make the consumer consume what the producer wanted to produce, not to make the producer produce what the consumer wanted to consume.

It was not long before some governments learned, and began to apply, the lesson which individual consumers, owing to lack of organisation, had failed to learn, namely that the immense eagerness of producers to sell put it within the power of the consumer to turn the tables on them. Germany applied the lesson with the greatest thoroughness. The main question was, as Dr. Schacht remarked, "whether the rest of the world was willing or in a position to forgo a market comprising . . . 80,000,000

---

[1] The mercantilists held that "it is always better to sell goods to others than to buy goods from others" (Hecksher, *Mercantilism*, p. 116). But this was a logical corollary of their belief that bullion was the best form of wealth to hold. They did not commit the modern absurdity of wanting production in order to give employment.

[2] *League of Nations, Eighteenth Assembly*, p. 64.

people, or whether it wished to keep this market".[1] Those who were least able to forgo it were the countries of Central Europe and the Balkans; and the only way in which they could induce Germany to consume their products was to consume in return the products of German industry whether these were what they really wanted or not. In many countries, producers were selling abroad below cost price in order to induce foreign consumers to buy and recouping themselves at the expense of domestic consumers on whom they could exercise less costly methods of persuasion. In the home market, the effects of over-production were mitigated by the ability of the producer to force his goods on the consumer. In the foreign market, it led to the expedients just referred to (and to many more), and in the end almost completely dislocated international trading. Everyone who attempted to think at all was aware that there must be some fallacy in the reasoning which led to these extraordinary results. But the problem remained unsolved; and attempts at a solution appeared to aggravate the disease.

Expedients and Remedies

The first errors were errors of diagnosis. Mesmerised by the classical view that over-production could not in the nature of things be more than transient, economists for a long time failed to make any serious enquiry into the underlying causes of the trouble. In the first place, little attempt was made to investigate the nature of the alleged "over-production". It may be that at a given moment more rubber, more whale oil or more cotton yarn is being produced than can be absorbed by any known use of these products. It is conceivable that more wheat or more cotton might be grown than the population of the world wanted to

[1] Address to the Economic Council of the German Academy, November 24, 1939. Similarly the international debtor, who could discharge his debt only in goods produced by himself, was in a stronger bargaining position than the international creditor, who could only get paid by consuming goods produced by his debtor.

consume. In such cases, it would be fair to speak of absolute over-production. But the commoner form of over-production is merely over-production relative to the purchasing-power of the consumer. In this sense there may be over-production of lard in Chicago while the share-cropper in the southern states, or the peasant in Eastern Europe, starves for lack of fats. There are no doubt marginal cases in which it is impossible to determine whether over-production is relative or absolute. But the problems are distinct and require different treatment; and it is the problem of relative over-production which has been the grave problem of the past two decades. The second and more serious error of diagnosis, also due to excessive preoccupation with classical theory, was the failure to recognise that relative over-production had become a chronic evil attributable to that disequilibrium between the power of the producer and the power of the consumer which we have just traced.

In these circumstances, the fatal mistake was made of attempting to tackle the problem from the angle of the producer. The producing interests had so complete a stranglehold on the state machine everywhere that there appeared to be general agreement that the right way to meet the crisis was to assist the producer by governmental action; and the first expedients adopted to assist the economic machine to "right itself" were conceived in this spirit. The two most popular methods were to stimulate production by subsidies (including the provision of cheap credit), and to restrict production in order to raise prices. The first method was advocated by many economists, who sometimes appeared to encourage the view that it did not much matter what was produced so long as employment was created by producing more and more, since the profits and wages of the producers would create the necessary purchasing power to purchase goods. Practical men, wisely suspecting some catch in this argument, leaned rather to the method of restriction. Apart from private arrangements carried through by industrial cartels and combines there were official international agreements to re-

strict production of tin, tea, rubber and copper, and to restrict
export (which came in most cases to the same thing) of wheat
and sugar. Both subsidies and restriction proved to be merely
different ways of aggravating the evil of over-production in relation to the capacity of the consumer. Both failed, as they were
bound to fail; and before long the crowning absurdity was
reached of governments subsidising producers to produce goods
which they then paid them to destroy. During the past ten years,
in some of the most civilised countries of the world, wheat and
cotton have been ploughed in, coffee burnt, livestock slaugh-
tered and milk poured away. The expedient of "price stabilisa-
tion" (which always meant keeping prices up and never keeping
prices down) enjoyed unfailing popularity throughout the interval between the two wars; and its universal acceptance was a
disconcerting symptom of the predominant influence of the
producing interests.[1] It was no more successful than any other
of these expedients in solving the problem of disequilibrium.

In the meanwhile attempts had been made to approach the
problem from the angle of the consumer. If the multifarious
commercial devices of advertisement and of the instalment and
hire-purchase systems had not induced the consumer to buy
enough to keep the producer profitably occupied, perhaps the
consumer required some other stimulus. Perhaps the explanation
of his spending too little was that he was saving too much. Thrift
was hastily deposed from the list of major virtues. In Great
Britain, the hoardings were plastered at government expense
with slogans "Spend for Employment" and "Spend for Prosperity"; and economists invented the new theory of "under-

[1] As recently as 1937 a congress of the Farmers' Unions of the British Empire meeting in Sydney demanded the regulation of agricultural production
and export by "commodity councils, producer controlled and financed". It
may be noted that restriction is, on the same short view, as beneficial to labour
as to capital. One of the earliest proposals for international restriction of production was a resolution of the International Miners' Congress at Berlin in
1894 demanding measures to prevent the "over-production of coal" (E.
Halévy, *A History of the English People in 1895-1905*, i, p. 253).

consumption" to explain "over-production". If only the consumer could be induced to overcome his niggardly proclivity to hoard and invest, the problem of over-production would disappear.

It is significant that of all the campaigns promoted in the past twenty years for the purpose of solving the economic problem the campaign for more spending is the only one which has excited any popular interest. The suggestion was soon made that the failure of the consumer to spend might be due not to any desire to save, but to lack of spending power, and that, if this were true, the right way to solve the economic problem was clearly to put more money into the consumer's pocket. In other words, the right policy was not to subsidise production but to subsidise consumption. This conception was the basis of movements like the Douglas Social Credit Scheme and the Townsend Plan which obtained an extensive following. It also inspired in many countries a new kind of prejudice against capitalists, who were denounced no longer as the enemies of the worker, but as the enemies of the "little man", regarded as the typical consumer and harassed *père de famille*. Such movements were a crude, half-articulate protest against the control of the economic system by, and in the interest of, the producer. They rested on the solid ground of principle that the producer exists for the sake of the consumer, not *vice versa*, and that, in the existing state of disequilibrium between production and consumption, equilibrium could be restored only by adapting production to the needs of consumption, not by adapting consumption to the needs of production. In this respect, Social Credit and the Townsend Plan had infinitely more sense in them than the official policies of subsidising or restricting production and of keeping up prices. Nevertheless, in the form in which they were propounded, they were certainly unsound; and economists who had rallied to the fashionable theory of "under-consumption" hastened to make it clear that they did not believe in the efficacy of stimulating consumption by the indefinite creation of consumers' credit.[1]

Meanwhile the attempts of Soviet Russia and Nazi Germany to tackle the economic problem, and claims that they had succeeded in solving it, attracted increasing attention. In democratic countries, the methods by which these results had been achieved excited great hostility; and this hostility hindered an impartial examination of the economic lessons of the policy pursued. The Soviet régime introduced at an early date a system of planned production which in some quarters encouraged the belief that planned production might by itself provide a cure for our economic ills. In attempting to apply the precedent to Western Europe, it was, however, commonly forgotten that Russia was in a primitive stage of economic development, having a vast territory not yet fully exploited, a still rapidly expanding population, a low standard of living, no important exports other than raw materials, and a home market capable, even in staple commodities, of almost indefinite expansion—a combination of circumstances in which the possibility of over-production scarcely existed. The German precedent was more instructive. Here planning was applied from 1933 onwards to a highly developed and industrialised economy which had in the preceding decade been subjected to the stimulus of intensive capital investment from abroad, and which had shown the symptoms of over-production to a marked degree. The method adopted was a programme of planned consumption. In Soviet Russia, there had been little need to plan consumption, for demand automatically outstripped supply in virtually every field. In Nazi Germany, planned consumption, taking the form partly of civilian public works, but mainly of rearmament, was the key to the solution. An immense programme of consumption was

---

[1] Many economists, while rejecting the sweet simplicity of Social Credit, still cling to the belief that depressions can be cured or prevented by some form of credit manipulation. There is no evidence that such devices have ever worked in the absence of planned and managed consumption.

set on foot capable of absorbing all and more than all the productive forces of the nation, and hitherto unemployed labour was rapidly absorbed into the production necessitated by this programme. Both in Soviet Russia and in Nazi Germany, prices were cut adrift from costs of production. The fixing of prices, and the fixing of wages in relation to them, became a social problem, whose solution depended in part on the proportion of the productive forces of the country allocated to the supply of civilian consumption. In Great Britain it was also rearmament —the simplest form of planned consumption—which made the first radical contribution to the cure of the unemployment problem. A more complete solution has now been effected by war conditions, which have allowed the adoption of the same procedure already applied several years earlier in Russia and in Germany.

Planned Consumption

The character of the solution has been obscured in the public mind by the common assumption that a recovery based on rearmament is necessarily transient and is tinged with the immorality of armaments. This argument is a tissue of confused thinking. Armaments are made to be consumed and create no fresh values. They are "unproductive" and "superfluous" in exactly the same way as most of the amenities of civilisation. The economic consequences of the production of armaments are no different from the economic consequences of the production of a pair of silk stockings, a film or a Beethoven symphony. In each case productive resources are applied to create something which the community, rightly or wrongly, wants to consume. It is true that the desire of the community for armaments is extremely variable. But the capriciousness of consumers' demand is one of the problems of the modern social and economic system, and appears here only in a somewhat exaggerated form. The special features of the demand for armaments which have enabled it to be used for a solution of the unemployment problem are two. In the first place, the demand, being unlimited in extent, imposes a system, not merely of planned production, but of planned consumption. Secondly, the plan of consumption is not determined by considerations of price and profit, though these considerations may play their part in determining the most advantageous method of carrying it out.

There is, however, nothing in these conditions which makes them exclusively applicable to the production of armaments. The system of planned consumption followed by the Ministry of Supply does not differ in substance from the system of the Ministry of Food, which has to tackle the same essential problem in terms of foodstuffs; and precisely the same planning of priorities from the point of view not of price or profit, but of the needs of the consumer is undertaken in another sphere by the Ministry of Shipping. If therefore we wish to proceed to a reconstruction of our economic system which will both meet peace-time needs and prevent a recurrence of large-scale unemployment when the demand for armaments has passed away, the first essential is to draw up an infinitely expansible plan of consumption, with graded priorities, which will assure that our productive forces are occupied to their fullest capacity for its fulfilment. What we need, in the words of one of the apostles of Social Credit, is "organisation of consumption first and planning for production only secondly and consequentially".[1]

The extent to which our plan of consumption can be made sufficiently flexible to reflect the capriciousness of consumers' choice will emerge in the course of experience. In the early stages, some restriction of consumers' choice is probably inevitable; and this must be achieved, as a recent writer has put it, through "the directed advance of society towards self-discipline and the habit of discrimination".[2] In any case, few will deny that such a restriction is a lesser evil than the maintenance, for a part

[1] A. R. Orage, *Political and Economic Writings*, p. 251.
[2] G. Chapman, *Culture and Survival*, p. 239.

of the community, of unrestricted choice between a large range of "luxuries", combined with the denial to another part of the community of access to any "luxuries" at all. The first essential of economic reconstruction is that planned consumption must precede and condition planned production. Our economic system must reverse the whole trend of the last century and a half, and once more subordinate the producer to the consumer. As long ago as 1917 Max Weber pointed out that "man's needs are not determined according to his place in the mechanism of production", and that if ever the then popular idea of an "economic parliament" were realised it should be "a parliament elected not by categories of occupation in production, but on the principle of the representation of mass needs".[1] In 1933 President Roosevelt believed "that we are at the threshold of a fundamental change in our economic thought . . . that in the future we are going to think less about the producer and more about the consumer".[2] This fundamental change is the first and most vital condition of economic reconstruction after the war.

Precisely the same conditions apply to the revival of international trade. It should by now be self-evident that the international economic crisis will never be surmounted so long as every country makes it the primary aim of its economic policy to sell more and buy less. The way to a revival of international trade is not to decide what you want to sell aboard and then ascertain what you are compelled to buy from the foreigner in order to induce him to take it, but to decide what you want to buy from abroad and then ascertain what you must produce in order to pay for it. The German-Hungarian commercial agreement of February 21, 1934, was probably the first of recent times in which one party undertook to stimulate the production of commodities desired by the other. This is at any rate the right method of approach. We shall never revive international trade until we succeed in making it pivot on things we want to buy,

---

[1] Max Weber, *Gesammelte Politische Schriften*, p. 299.
[2] F. D. Roosevelt, *Looking Forward*, p. 49.

not on things we want to sell, until we treat exports as a way of paying for imports, not imports as a way of inducing other countries to take our exports. This is precisely what happens when we embark on an armaments programme which is dependent on foreign supplies, and explains why rearmament is good for international trade as well as for trade at home. To bring about the same result in time of peace, we must have the same concentration on the needs of the consumer, and make production, internationally as well as nationally, serve the purposes of consumption.

The second essential of economic reconstruction is the substitution of welfare for wealth as our governing purpose, and the consequent abandonment of considerations of price and profit as the determining factor of production. For the automatic non-ethical process by which consumers' choices were supposed to assert themselves through the mechanism of price we must substitute a system of planned consumption and of prices deliberately fixed to serve ends deemed good by the community. This view of the purposes of price control had already won acceptance before the war when it was agreed that the rents of houses and the price of milk should be so fixed as to place them within the reach of those who most needed them; and since the war the control of food prices for this social purpose has been widely extended. It would be chimerical to suppose that we can return after the war to a world of "free" prices. Once the new view of the function of price has been accepted, many problems of detail remain to be worked out, in theory by the economists, in practice by those who will control post-war policy. It is possible that, in non-essential commodities, price may still provide a useful mechanism for determining the choice of the consumer. The conception of profitability may be useful in choosing between methods of production where the end to be achieved has already been determined on other grounds. In many respects, the price and profit mechanism may prove a good servant once it has ceased to be the master.

There is, however, a further point which brings us to the heart of the problem. If prosperity could be restored, a better life assured to all, and the full utilisation of resources and man-power achieved, by the simple process of expanding consumption and controlling prices, then we should already be on the road to the millennium. If this were true, there would be no answer to schemes like Social Credit or the Townsend Plan—or indeed to the man who explained that he was breaking all the windows in the street in order to improve trade. The flaw in this argument is that it ignores—and here the economists of the "under-consumption" school have rendered a signal disservice—the perfectly sound classical doctrine that increased production can be financed, and increased employment created, only out of savings accumulated by voluntary or compulsory restriction of consumption. As soon as a practical issue arose, the truth of this proposition was immediately recognised by those responsible for British financial policy. When the need for a large-scale rearmament programme became apparent, slogans about spending for prosperity and spending for employment disappeared. The Victorian virtue of thrift and of saving to invest was once more held in honour. But the reaction against seductive "under-consumption" theories was neither swift nor thorough enough. One of the many ways in which the British Government found itself unprepared for war was that it had taken no steps to restrict civilian consumption and thus to make available a large volume of savings to finance war expenditure. These steps had to be hastily improvised after the outbreak of war and proved in most respects inadequate. Nobody now disputes the necessity of such steps. Yet it is still not clearly recognised that what is true of an armaments programme is also true of a programme of social reconstruction. Such a programme can be financed only out of savings. Planned consumption implies not only drawing up a plan of those things which we wish to consume and establishing an order of priority between them, but also restricting the consumption of other less essential or less desirable things and diverting the savings thus effected to finance our necessary programme of production. In other words, we must meet the requirements of peace in exactly the same serious and methodical way in which we meet the requirements of war.

This then is the crux of the economic problem. War stands to-day in a category by itself. Every great civilisation of the past has had its "non-productive" enterprises which have absorbed a substantial part of the resources and labour of the community without regard to profit. Of the three classes of mediaeval society, "those who work" supported "those who pray" as well as "those who fight". Only our modern civilisation has placed war in a category by itself as the sole non-profit-earning enterprise which is universally recognised as having a first and unlimited call on the capacity and on the self-sacrifice of the whole community. War is still the only state enterprise which is not subject to the criticism that it is too expensive. Everyone realises that war imposes economic sacrifices on the whole community (except perhaps on those formerly unemployed or living at the lowest subsistence level), whether these sacrifices take the form of reduced consumption or of longer hours of work. These sacrifices are accepted because the end in view, *i.e.* the winning of the war, is thought worth while. The end involves a programme of achievement which people will in fact make sacrifices to maintain. The execution of this programme brings with it, among other things, full employment; and the vicious circle which we have come to know as the economic crisis is triumphantly broken.

As has already been noted, the production of armaments for purposes of war does not differ in its economic consequences from the production of any other kind of non-productive goods. It is, for instance, clear that the same economic results—the full utilisation of available labour and resources—could be achieved in peace-time by producing armaments and dumping them in the sea, or by building castles and pyramids or, as Mr. Keynes has suggested, by burying bank-notes in disused coal-mines and digging them out again.[1] Such schemes would answer perfectly well to the description of planned consumption not dictated by the operation of the price and profit mechanism. The fallacy underlying them is not economic, but moral. The end in view is not worth while, and people will not be prepared to make sacrifices to attain it. During the economic crisis in the United States, Governor La Follette pointedly observed that those who had "squandered 40,000,000,000 dollars of American money in the most wasteful and futile war of modern history" were not prepared to vote money for public works to relieve distress.[2] The unemployment problem can be solved in time of war because war provides an aim deemed worthy of self-sacrifice. It cannot be solved in time of peace only because modern civilisation recognises no peace-time aim for which people are prepared to sacrifice themselves in the same way.[3] Individual profit, which in the eighteenth and nineteenth centuries provided the motive force of the economic system, has failed us, and we have not yet discovered any moral substitute for it other than war. Nothing but war seems sufficiently worth while. The economic crisis is in essence a moral crisis.

[1] J. M. Keynes, *The General Theory of Employment, Interest and Money*, p. 129. As Mr. Keynes adds, "pyramid-building, earthquakes, even wars may serve to increase wealth, if the education of our statesmen on the principles of classical economics stands in the way of anything better".

[2] D. W. Brogan, *The American Political System*, p. 332.

[3] In this respect the comparison between the Weimar Republic and the Nazi régime is instructive. In the 1920's unemployment was averted in Germany by extensive public works financed by foreign credits. When these credits dried up, the work stopped; for Brüning dared not impose compulsory savings and restriction of consumption in order to maintain them. Hitler financed rearmament without foreign credits on compulsory savings and restriction of consumption. But he too did not dare—or did not attempt—to impose them on any large scale for other than rearmament purposes.

CHAPTER 5

THE MORAL CRISIS

THE moral crisis of the contemporary world is the breakdown of the system of ethics which lay at the root of liberal democracy, of national self-determination, and of *laissez-faire* economics. This system was based on the reconciliation of reason and morality through the doctrine of the harmony of interests. The utilitarian identification of virtue with enlightened self-interest meant that one's highest duty was rightly to understand and steadily to pursue one's own interest. "Personal interest", in the words of Tocqueville, ". . . asserts itself as a social theory." [1] Liberal democracy assumed that individual citizens would recognise the existence of a fundamental harmony of interest between them and would adjust apparent differences of interest on particular points by a process of give-and-take to their mutual advantage. Democracy was the best form of government because it enabled everyone to express his own interest through the medium of the ballot-box. National self-determination was the sure basis of an international community because each nation, in pursuing its own highest interest, was pursuing the interest of the world as a whole, so that nationalism was the natural stepping-stone to internationalism. *Laissez-faire* economics assumed that by promoting their own interest individuals were doing all they could to promote that of the community. If any course of action required of the individual or the nation appeared to involve a sacrifice of interest, there could

[1] Quoted in J. P. Mayer, *Prophet of the Mass Age*, p. 30.

be only one of two explanations: either the sacrifice was illusory not real, or the course of action was wrong. Private interest and public, nationalism and internationalism could never be in conflict with one another.

A significant feature of this system, since it denied the necessity of conscious and deliberate planning for the welfare of the community, whether national or international, was that it dispensed with the need for a moral purpose to direct such planning. It was "a political theory which replaced the conception of purpose by that of mechanism".[1] It had its source in the rationalism of the eighteenth century which, drawing inspiration from the triumphs of science in the material world, explained human behaviour and human affairs in terms of an orderly advance controlled by scientific mechanisms. The nineteenth-century philosophies of Hegel and Marx were typical in their emphasis on the process rather than on the end. Belief in infinite progress, rather than any clear conception of an ultimate end, supplied the sense of a higher purpose. Faith in progress assumed the dimensions of a religion, which did not lack moral grandeur as well as a high degree of practical effectiveness. Man was encouraged to go about his own business and to pursue his own interests in the firm belief that he was thereby contributing to the movement of creation towards some "far-off divine event" which could be hinted at by poets or theologians, but which required no precise definition.

How then was it possible for some two centuries—effectively throughout the English-speaking world and rather less effectively elsewhere—to maintain the colossal paradox of a belief in the harmony of interests, of treating the pursuit of profit as a moral purpose and of making it the motive force of the social and economic system? There are two main answers to this puzzling question.

[1] R. H. Tawney, *The Acquisitive Society,* p. *11.*

The first answer, curious as it may seem, is that, notwithstanding the philosophical premises of liberal democracy and *laissez-faire*, self-sacrifice for a moral purpose, though eliminated in theory, continued to be practised, and even preached, as a private and social virtue. The English-speaking world, where alone the ideas of liberal democracy and *laissez-faire* really became dominant and effective over a long period, developed an immense network of philanthropy and voluntary service; and this development not only provided an outlet for the instinct of self-sacrifice whose utility was denied by the current economic orthodoxy, but performed many of the functions which were subsequently—and in most other countries from the first—taken over by public social services. In the early days, these activities were frequently attacked as incompatible with pure economic and utilitarian principles. The charge was logically irrefutable; for it would have been fantastic to pretend that this host of philanthropists and unpaid public servants, great and small, was pursuing a hidden self-interest. Yet there is no doubt that these theoretically indefensible acts of self-sacrifice were one of the pillars of the system. It might indeed be argued that the ingrained and irrational habits of personal abstinence and public service associated with the puritan tradition played a more important part in building up the liberal and *laissez-faire* society of the nineteenth century than the rational morality of the harmony of interests.[1]

Moreover, a similarly significant anomaly often creeps undetected into theoretical expositions of *laissez-faire* doctrine. Insistence on the purely scientific character of classical economics has not deterred classical economists from professing

---

[1] The same point has been put in a more cynical way: "The strongest basis for individualism is not the intelligence of individuals and their irrevocable devotion to the pursuit of their own self-interest but rather their stupidity and their susceptibility to moral suggestion" (J. M. Clark, *The Trend of Economics*, p. 97).

their faith in free trade with all the fervour of a moral creed.[1]
Professor Robbins, perhaps the most distinguished surviving
English representative of the school, who specifically teaches
that "the economist is not concerned with ends as such", has
nevertheless argued that, under a planned economy, "there will
be still more of the wrong industries in the wrong places",[2]
where the word "wrong" clearly implies a postulated end, and
contradicts Professor Robbins' own thesis of the indifference of
the economist to "ends as such". The fact is that the classical
economists did, as an essential part of their system, unconsciously pass a judgment of value—the judgment that the "right"
end of economic activity is maximum wealth and that any
measure incompatible with maximum production of wealth is
"wrong". The *laissez-faire* system did not, in fact, eliminate
moral purpose. The maximum production of wealth and its
tried instrument, the profit motive, were elevated to the rank
of a moral imperative.

The second explanation of the prolonged and widespread
belief in the harmony of interests and in the profit motive as
a moral purpose is that this paradox did, in this wholly exceptional period of history, and especially in the English-speaking
world which dominated the thought and action of the period,
reflect certain aspects of reality. Expanding markets, developed
by profitable investments, called forth ever-increasing production, the profits of which, seeping down through every stratum
of society, created both a higher standard of consumption and
savings for further profitable investment. Technical invention
kept pace with growing demand. So long as the wheel went on
revolving, the harmony of interests could be plausibly maintained. There seemed no reason why it should ever stop; for it

---

[1] Similarly Marx, who was steeped in the classical economists and took a still
more rigid view of the automatic nature of the economic process, clearly regarded capitalists as morally reprehensible and supporters of the proletariat as
morally praiseworthy.

[2] L. Robbins, *The Nature and Significance of Economic Science*, p. 24;
Economic Planning and International Order, p. 59.

was firmly believed that mankind had discovered that secret
of perpetual motion which was called progress. Unfortunately
this belief was untrue. The wheel had been set in motion by a
driving force which had started in the sixteenth century and
which was bound sooner or later to run down: the impulse of
constantly expanding frontiers and expanding population. Perpetual expansion was the hypothesis on which liberal democracy
and *laissez-faire* economics were based. There were physical
limits to this expansion; and by the end of the nineteenth century they had nearly been reached. The frontiers of the civilised
world had ceased to advance. The leading countries of the world
could already foresee the moment when, some fifty years ahead,
their populations would begin to decline. Under the jolt administered by the events of 1914-18, the wheel ceased to revolve.
In 1923 the United States, which for three generations had been
known to the oppressed everywhere as the land of great open
spaces and unlimited opportunities, closed the door to immigration; and this act more than any other was the symbol of a
world grown static and stereotyped.[1] The onset of the great
economic depression completed the process. "By 1930 the moral
cement that heretofore held democratic Western society together had disappeared."[2] Nobody would believe any longer
that maximum welfare could be attained, or that democracy
could achieve social cohesion, through the free interplay of individual interests. The foundations of liberal democracy and
laissez-faire had crumbled away.

Nor was it possible to take refuge in the third great nineteenth-century ideal, and to find in the rights of nations a basis
of social cohesion and a common moral purpose no longer provided by the rights of man. Shorn of its moral foundation in the

[1] As an American writer has said, "the passage of the restrictive immigration
law of 1923 by the American Congress did more than the Treaty of Versailles
to seal the doom of democracy and capitalism in Europe" (L. Dennis, *The
Dynamics of War and Revolution*, p. 74).
[2] L. Mumford, *Faith for Living*, p. 10.

harmony of interests, individualism, as Nietzsche had demonstrated, could lead only to the doctrine of the morally purposeless superman. Shorn of the same foundation, nationalism, as the
history of the last twenty years has shown, could lead only to
the doctrine of the morally purposeless super-nation or *Herrenvolk*. The bankruptcy of the doctrine of the harmony of interests has rendered barren the hope of achieving international
cohesion, or building the international society, through the free
interplay of national interests. The "good" nationalism of the
nineteenth century, the stepping-stone to internationalism, has
been transformed into the "bad" nationalism of the twentieth
century, the fertile breeding-ground of "economic nationalism", racial discrimination and war. The twentieth century has
brought an ever growing recognition that "patriotism is not
enough"— that it does not provide an intelligible moral purpose
and cannot create a cohesive international society. The harmony
of interests between nations as a basis of international morality
has become no more credible than the harmony of interests
between individuals as the basis of social morality at home.[1]

The Moral Dilemma

A modern philosopher has aptly described the significance
which attaches to the characteristic ideas of an epoch:

> There are certain doctrines which for a particular period
> seem not doctrines, but inevitable categories of the human
> mind. Men do not look on them merely as correct opinions,
> for they have become so much a part of the mind, and lie so
> far back, that they are never really conscious of them at all.
> They do not see them, but other things *through* them. It is
> these abstract ideas at the centre, the things which they take
> for granted, that characterise a period.[2]

[1] The breakdown of the supposed international harmony of interests is discussed in greater detail in E. H. Carr, *The Twenty Years' Crisis*, pp. 65-80.
[2] T. E. Hulme, *Speculations*, p. 50.

The uprooting of these "abstract ideas at the centre", and their replacement by new ones constitutes a fundamental revolution of thought. As a recent American writer has said, "the process of building up new abstractions to justify filling new needs is always troublesome in any society and may be violent." [1] At the present moment we are in the throes of such a revolution. Our conscious thought has begun to reject the abstract ideas which characterised the past 200 years of history—the belief that progress is infinite, that morality and interest coincide, and that society rests on a natural and universal harmony of interest between men and nations. Yet without consciously believing these things, we still unconsciously take them for granted and see other things through them. Hence our thought is confused, and our speech unclear. We repeat ritual words which no longer have any vital meaning. For twenty years phrases like "disarmament" and "removal of trade barriers" served as solemn incantations, whose familiar and traditional sound stirred the emotions but had no effect on action. In war we fight to defend "democracy", though "we are uncertain what the democracy is for which we stand".[2] We fight to restore the independence of nations, though we know well that this independence is impracticable and disastrous. We continue to reiterate these slogans of the past, in vague terms that betray our lack of belief in them, because we still unconsciously take for granted a set of abstract ideas in which we no longer believe. We take them for granted because we cannot live without some basic assumptions, and we have not yet had the courage or the insight to create or to discover the basic assumptions of the coming age. Hence our definitions of peace aims remain negative and not positive, and are rooted in the assumptions of the past and not of the future. "The forces of the nineteenth century", wrote Mr. Keynes more than twenty years ago, "have run their course and are exhausted. The economic motives and ideals of that

[1] T. W. Arnold, *The Folklore of Capitalism*, p. 378.
[2] See p. 16 for this and other quotations.

generation no longer satsify us: we must find a new way, and must suffer again the *malaise*, and finally the pangs, of a new industrial birth." [1] What was then true of the economic world is now not less certainly true of the whole field of political thought and action.

The unique feature of the period from which we have just emerged is that it devised an ethical system which dispensed with the concept of moral purpose. Interest, individual or national, was in itself a sufficiently compulsive social motive. Progress was the self-adjusting consequence of the pursuit of interest by all concerned. Thirty years ago it was still commonly supposed that science, by improving methods of production, would automatically increase the well-being of the human race, and by improving means of communication would automatically promote international unity and concord. No moral issue seemed to be involved. The position which we have reached to-day is that we no longer believe in amelioration by the automatic process of the pursuit of self-interest, that we recognise that progress can be achieved only by deliberate planning, but that we continue to ignore the problem of the moral purpose. We must plan—but to what end? As we saw in the last chapter, and as the war has amply shown, there is no practical difficulty about the solution of the economic problem: what we lack is a sufficiently compelling moral purpose. "The essential thing", wrote Professor Tawney twenty years ago, ". . . is that men should fix their minds on the idea of purpose and give that idea pre-eminence over all subsidiary issues." [2] If the Government—perhaps quite rightly—decide that that essential motive-power shall no longer be the profit motive", said an M.P. recently, "then they will take upon themselves a very heavy responsibility to replace it with something else." [3] Apart from some doubt whether any

---

[1] J. M. Keynes, *The Economic Consequences of the Peace*, p. 238.
[2] R. H. Tawney, *The Acquisitive Society*, p. 97.
[3] *Parliamentary Debates: House of Commons*, August 7, 1940, vol. 364, col. 273.

government is really qualified to abrogate or create motives, the statement is unexceptionable. The economic machine refuses to run until we discover a new moral purpose to replace the now exhausted and inoperative profit motive as the driving force; and this purpose when it is discovered will also provide democracy with the new source of social cohesion which it needs to replace the discarded doctrine of the harmony of interests.

This urgent and widely felt need for a conscious moral purpose explains one of the most puzzling phenomena of recent years: the popular demand, not for more unrestricted liberty, but for more authoritative leadership. In this as in other respects, the dictatorships are the symptom of a world-wide crisis. The appeal of Soviet Russia to opinion, and especially to the opinion of youth, in Great Britain, like Hitler's appeal to German youth or President Roosevelt's appeal to opinion in the United States, must be explained by the sense, whether justified or not, of a developed and deliberate moral purpose which appeared to be lacking in "inert" British democracy. Much has been said—not on the whole unjustly—of the revival of British energy, faith and initiative after the retreat from Dunkirk and the fall of France. But British leadership has hitherto been found wanting in the capacity to harness this national revival to any purpose less transitory and less negative than the defeat of Hitler. Once this goal is reached, there is a danger that the same lack of a common purpose may once more paralyse national policy and bring upon the victor a process of disintegration, perhaps less rapid, but in the end hardly less disastrous, than that which would result from defeat. The months immediately after the war will be fully as critical and as hazardous for Great Britain and for the world as were the summer months of 1940. The essential nature of the crisis through which we are living is neither military, nor political, nor economic, but moral. A new faith in a new moral purpose is required to reanimate our political and economic system.

The corollary of this neglect of moral purpose in the philosophy of the age which is passing away was a correspondingly exaggerated belief in the supremacy of the intellect.[1] During the last twenty years—the tragic aftermath of that great period —we have continued to believe in the existence of a solution of our troubles, a key to our problems, which would one day be discovered by an intellectual process and revealed to us by "experts". Serious people still imagine that there is a "key" to our economic problem, discoverable by ingenious and studious economists, in the technique of credit manipulation or price control or industrial organisation. Ministers and politicians, both in domestic and international affairs, have displayed an altogether exaggerated eagerness to turn to experts in search of a policy. Subconsciously we are still dominated by the Benthamite premiss that, once the right course of action is determined by well-informed and impartial investigation, men will naturally and inevitably pursue this course. It has become bad form in modern political controversy to question the excellence of an opponent's intentions. If he is wrong, it is because he is misinformed, misguided or muddle-headed: error is assumed to be intellectual error. All this is a dangerous illusion, which obscures the real nature of our plight. "Civilisations before us", writes a clever critic, "have died in the midst of their ignorance; but our civilisation, if it is doomed to perish, will have the evil distinction of dying not only with the cure at hand, but on the eve of such a life as has never been known since the days of Eden." [2] It is not knowledge that has failed us, but will, not experts, but leaders. Our civilisation is in danger of perishing for lack of something with which we have dispensed for 200 years, but with which we can dispense no

---

[1] Some typical expressions of this belief are quoted from Comte, Buckle and Sir N. Angell, in E. H. Carr, *The Twenty Years' Crisis*, p. 35.

[2] A. R. Orage, *Political and Economic Writings*, p. 61. It is not certain that other civilisations, any more than our own, have perished through ignorance. Tradition ascribes the loss of Eden not to lack, but to excess, of knowledge.

longer: a deliberate and avowed moral purpose, involving the call for common sacrifice for a recognised common good.

The dilemma of the writer who ventures on the diagnosis of a crisis of this magnitude has been well put by an American critic:

> No one writing on social organisation can escape the demand that he formulate a social philosophy. Not only does the demand come from others, but the writer himself is so much a part of the culture of his own time that he feels uncomfortable if he fails to produce a platform of principles on which he can stand in order to repel attacks.
>
> And yet if we look backward over history, we can see how impossible it is to stand in one age and predict the social philosophy of the next. On what basis could anyone in the Roman Empire predict the peculiar philosophy of feudalism? How could the wisest man in the twilight of the Middle Ages have predicted the philosophy which glorified the trader and made human greed the foundation of justice and morals? How would it have been possible to have foretold the development of the great modern corporation out of a philosophy of rugged individualism? [1]

This scepticism is well grounded. "Reality", as Georges Sorel said, "is protected by an obscurity which philosophy must respect if she does not wish to fall into charlatanism, falsehood or fiction." [2] Yet it is not true that the new social philosophy, the collection of "abstract ideas at the centre", whose acceptance heralds the birth of a new epoch, is the product of idle chance or of the unique imagination of a lonely prophet. The first breath of the coming age can already be felt in the sultry climate of the old. The new ideas are necessarily bound up with social, economic and military conditions as well as with moral trends of thought. There has probably never been a time when so

---

[1] T. W. Arnold, *The Folklore of Capitalism*, p. 332.
[2] G. Sorel, *Les Illusions du Progrès* (4th ed.), p. 2.

many people in so many parts of the world were not only looking for guidance, but were themselves so eager to make their
own contribution to the building of a new order. The eventual
formulation of the new faith, of the new moral purpose which
will revive and reanimate our civilisation, may be reserved for
a great prophet or leader. But the way will be paved by that
gradual and almost imperceptible transformation of the climate
of thought and action of which signs can be already discerned;
and the extent to which this can be effected by common consent
will probably determine the presence or absence of the element
of open violence in the coming revolution. Any one who can
by deed or word promote and hasten that transformation, even
though he may himself have no claim to the rôle of prophet and
no clear vision of the social philosophy and moral purpose of
the future age, is rendering service.

The Moral Function of War

War is the most powerful instrument in effecting this transformation; and it may serve as an introduction to our enquiry
to consider the precise nature of the moral function which war
to-day performs in our society. The issue has been obscured,
especially in the English-speaking countries, by well-meaning
people who, steeped in the nineteenth-century tradition, persist
in regarding war as senseless and devoid of purpose. The wars
of the period 1815-1914, other than imperialist wars necessary
to open up further fields of enterprise to the civilised Powers,
were in fact purposeless. It was silly for European countries to
fight against one another when they could still keep the wheel
of progressive prosperity revolving and maintain social cohesion
by continuous expansion in Asia and Africa. Since the first decade of the present century, however, this has no longer been
possible. To-day it is legitimate to denounce war as cruel and
brutal. But it is thoroughly misleading to describe it as senseless
or purposeless. War is at the present time the most purposeful

of our social institutions; and we shall make no progress towards its elimination until we recognise, and provide for, the essential social function which it performs. If we are to find a substitute for war, we must be clear about the function of war in our time.

The twentieth-century function of war is quite different from its nineteenth-century function. In the nineteenth century the greatest enemy of which civilised mankind was conscious was scarcity. The object of war was therefore to assist the great moral purpose of the accumulation of wealth; and imperialist wars against primitive peoples were the only wars which really served this purpose. Since 1900 the situation has radically changed; and some people, observing that "the great wars of the twentieth century are not between the poor and starving countries of the world, but between the richest", have drawn the conclusion that "there is no longer an economic imperative driving nations to fight".[1] But this is hardly the point. In the twentieth century civilised mankind is no longer predominantly conscious of the evil of scarcity.[2] It is now widely believed that, at any rate in the most advanced countries, there is plenty for all and that the principal evil is not the insufficiency but the maldistribution of wealth: the two great enemies are unemployment and inequality. Against these evils, which liberal democracy and *laissez-faire* capitalism cannot cure, large-scale war provides an effective, if short-term, antidote. In these circumstances, as a British economist has remarked, "it seems dangerous to say that there are no redeeming features in the economics of war".[3] The familiar argument that war "never

[1] *International Conciliation*, No. 363 (October 1940), p. 349.

[2] It is worth noting that the three Great Powers whose people still enjoy a relatively low standard of living and are conscious of scarcity as a primary problem—Japan, Italy and Soviet Russia—have all shown readiness in the past twenty years to embark on "colonial" wars of the nineteenth-century type, combined with a marked reluctance to become involved in large-scale war of the twentieth-century type.

[3] G. Crowther, *Ways and Means of War*, p. 11.

pays" fails to impress an age which no longer believes that what "pays" is always and necessarily right.

Of the effect of war in creating employment enough has already been said. While the intellectuals and the well-to-do classes everywhere continued to regard the war of 1914-18 as an unmitigated disaster, large masses of people learned during the next twenty years to look back on it as a time of secure and profitable employment. In the present war ample employment has been accompanied by the profound and widespread fear—such as hardly existed last time—of a return to unemployment after the war. The association between full employment and war is now fully understood; and the psychological reactions of this understanding are wholly incalculable. Moreover, the war of 1914-18, in almost every country in Europe, did more than any other event of the past hundred years to mitigate the more glaring forms of economic and social inequality. The experience is likely to be repeated—is already being repeated—in the present war. It is useless to-day to condemn the economic consequences of large-scale war because it is destructive of accumulated wealth. This is not the main consideration, so long as it mitigates the evils of unemployment and inequality. Any substitute for war must perform these functions not less effectively.

Nor can we regard the function of war as solely or predominantly economic. It strikes much deeper into the roots and recesses of human nature. An incontrovertibly accurate observation, rarely made because it seems almost indecent to our conventional judgments, appeared in a recent leading article in *The Times:*

> Save when immediate tragedy comes their way, an enormous number of ordinary peaceable citizens are personally, at this time of horror and trial, extraordinarily happy. There is work to be done, now in this island, by them.[1]

[1] *The Times*, October 7, 1940.

It is absurd to treat Hitler's confession that, in August 1914, he fell on his knees and thanked heaven for "granting him the happiness of living at this time" [1] as a symptom of peculiar moral depravity. The sentiment has long been a commonplace, and was uttered almost at the same moment by Rupert Brooke in a poem which appears in the anthologies. Apart from the emotional excitement associated with war, it provides a sense of meaning and purpose widely felt to be lacking in modern life. Hence war has become the most powerful known instrument of social solidarity. In the advanced countries of the world, war or preparation for war is to-day the only moral purpose with the recognised capacity of inspiring the degree of self-sacrifice in all classes of the community necessary to keep the political and economic machine in motion. Before 1939 this was not yet wholly true of those favoured countries which could still draw on the rapidly diminishing returns of nineteenth-century prosperity and security, though it was already becoming true even of them. Now there is no escape. We cannot return to the old peace: it is dead. We cannot escape from war until we have found some other moral purpose powerful enough to generate self-sacrifice on the scale requisite to enable civilisation to survive.

There are two movements to-day purporting to offer to the world a universal principle or purpose which supersedes war: Christianity and communism. [2] Christianity suffers from the defects of all movements which are obliged to embody their ideals in creeds and institutions. But while the formal articles of the Christian faith no longer command the assent of the masses, except in a few not very important countries, and while Christian churches have been in the past—and perhaps still are—

[1] Hitler, *Mein Kampf*, p. 177. A young German engineer is quoted as saying in 1931: "If war came, someone would need my strength and my intelligence. Now no one needs me" (S. King-Hall, *Total Victory*, p. 155).

[2] The vital force of religions other than Christianity is often underestimated. But none of these religions has at the present time any serious claim to universality or any considerable influence on Western civilisation.

as frequently associated with the cause of reaction as with the cause of progress, it would be a mistake to minimise the rôle played even to-day in Western civilisation by what are vaguely called "Christian ideals" or "the Christian ethic". There is here a source of common feeling which, however obscure and inarticulate, helps to keep in being an underlying sense of common values and of unity between peoples.[1] It is not inconceivable that the new leadership for which the world craves may arise from within the Christian church. But this hypothesis appears to presuppose a transformation of Christianity, or a revival of its primitive spirit, which would in itself amount to a revolution. Those who believe that a "return to Christianity" is the clue to our problems must face the task of re-creating Christianity before they can use it as a foundation on which to rebuild the world. "If the Christian spirit is to exert a controlling influence on these modern developments", a wise Christian thinker has said, "it can only be by means of 'new thoughts which have not yet been thought', by fresh insights and conceptions that are still waiting to be born." [2]

Communism, like Christianity, has suffered from the shortcomings of those who practise it. Its creed has the major defect that, true to the nineteenth-century tradition of Marxism, it expresses itself in terms of a material process rather than of a moral end. But it has in fact generated among its followers a strong sense of moral purpose; and like Christianity it propounds values common to all peoples. Communism has been an important factor in the revolution through which we are passing and has a direct relevance to our immediate problems

[1] Discussion of the place of religion in the revival of moral purpose is rendered difficult by an apparently calculated vagueness in the current use of the word. "The most essentially religious thing in us", says a contemporary writer on education, "is that by virtue of which we cohere as a society" (F. Clarke, *Education and Social Change*, p. 70). If we interpret "religion" in this sense, our conclusions about it may obviously be quite different from those which we should reach about "religion" as interpreted by, say, the Pope or the Archbishop of Canterbury.

[2] J. H. Oldham, *Christianity and the Race Problem*, p. 215.

and needs. It still has a number of enthusiastic and
disciples in many countries; and if Soviet Russia pla
tinguished and successful part in the war against Nazi G
its prestige will be enhanced. The cooperation betw
Western peoples and Soviet Russia in the war should пеip to
resolve the antithesis, incidental rather than fundamental, between the secular ideals of Christianity and those of communism. Even if the "abstract ideas" of the future society derive
directly neither from Christianity nor from communism, they
will probably owe something to both.

The Search for a Moral Purpose

Any attempt at the present time to forecast the moral foundations and assumptions of the coming order may well seem
both ineffectual and presumptuous, especially to the multitude of those who, through preoccupation with current tasks,
through indifference, or—most frequent of all—through a sense
of helplessness, are content to turn a blind eye on the future.
But anyone who has an active faith or hope in the future of our
civilisation will find it hard to abstain from such speculation,
however conscious he may be of its hazards and uncertainties.
In this spirit, it is proposed here to attempt in outline some
estimate of the conditions which must be fulfilled by any movement or creed likely to make a widespread appeal to the contemporary world and to provide the sense of a common purpose
essential to the survival of civilisation:

(1) The new faith must speak in positive rather than in negative terms, striving for the achievement of good rather than for
the avoidance or suppression of evil. It was a sinister fact, significant of the frustration of the epoch, that the great aims of
the past twenty years expressed themselves in terms either of
a return to the past or of mere avoidance: to prevent war, to
reduce armaments, to remove trade barriers, to cure unemployment. Even to-day those who perceive the inadequacy of the

negative war aim of destroying Hitler tend to define their purpose in the almost equally negative word "security", social and
international. President Roosevelt's promulgation of the "four
freedoms" contained sound doctrine. But it would have been
better if it had demanded not the liberation of mankind from
evils, but the pursuit of positive goods. To prevent war we must
create a new order; to reduce armaments we must build a common pool of armaments for a common purpose; to remove trade
barriers we must plan international trade; to cure unemployment we must organise men for the fulfilment of urgent and
necessary tasks. We shall fail if we merely entrench ourselves
to protect what we possess, or what we possessed in the past. A
positive and constructive programme is the first condition of
any effective moral purpose.

(2) Champions of one class have often appeared from the
ranks of another; and it would be foolish to hazard any guess
as to the social stratum from which the new leadership will be
drawn. But whoever may be its prophets, the new faith will
make its appeal predominantly to the "little man"—to the unorganised consumer rather than to the organised producer, to
the individual of small possessions and no importance who feels
himself helpless in the midst of great impersonal organisations
dominating the life of the community. It will therefore proclaim
its independence of these organisations—of big business, of trade
unions and of the great political parties—and aim at the emancipation of society from the vested interests which they have
come to represent. The ascendancy of big organisations is a
prominent and unhealthy feature of modern life. Even where
they purport to be representative, they have acquired a life and
interests of their own, and the individual no longer feels himself
represented by them. The need for organisation may well be
greater than ever. But the world is in a reckless mood, and will
respond eagerly to an appeal to tear down existing organisations, to do away with their abuses and to start again. The new
faith must restore to the individual, to the "little man", his sense

of being the constituent member of the community, and thus make democracy once more a reality.

(3) The new faith must address itself first of all to the solution of the economic problem; for the running sores of our present social order—unemployment and inequality—are predominantly economic. This does not necessarily mean that the new faith will express itself in economic terms. Indeed it has been shown that the economic problem cannot be solved except through the common recognition of a new moral purpose. But this fact cannot be used to support the argument that the economic problem is merely incidental and subsidiary. Man does not live by bread alone. But without it he does not live at all; and there is a real sense in which bread is the first essential element of his moral as well as of his physical welfare. The immediate impulses which lead to war and other social disorders may, as has often been said, be psychological and moral: envy, fear, injured pride, thwarted ambition. But there is ample evidence to show that these impulses flourish in a soil of economic maladjustment. There is nothing paradoxical or one-sided in the view that the building of a new economic order is the most urgent task which confronts us after the war.

(4) The new faith will approach the unemployment problem, not by way of prevention, but by way of the creation of needs vast enough to make a full call on our resources and morally imperative enough to command the necessary measure of sacrifice to supply them. All frontal attacks on the problem of unemployment have failed, and are bound to fail, because the essence of that problem is not to create work for its own sake—a process economically easy but morally impracticable —but to create work destined to fulfil a purpose felt by the community to be worthy of self-sacrifice. Once this purpose is recognised—as happens in the case of war—the problem of unemployment is automatically solved, or is reduced to the proportions of a technical problem of the mobility of labour. The new faith must solve the unemployment problem by providing

a moral purpose as potent as was religion in the Middle Ages or as is war to-day.

(5) The new faith will have to revive and renew the ideal of equality which, however imperfectly realised, lies at the root both of Christianity and of communism, and which was deliberately rejected by the capitalist system.[1] Of the vitality of the modern demand for equality there is no doubt whatever. It has appeared in the form of the demand for equality between individuals, between classes, between nations. It has been at the root of every recent revolution and of most recent wars. Nor is it a demand which could be satisfied by the formal political or legal equality of the nineteenth century. It is specifically a demand for economic equality—for equality of economic resources or equality of economic opportunity. This problem too requires, in the first instance, a positive and constructive rather than a purely negative and destructive programme. Our deliberate purpose should be to build up equality rather than to break down inequality. Assuming that the process of equalisation can be achieved by gradual rather than by violent methods, the first step is to secure the distribution to all of what may, on a generous interpretation, be called the necessaries of life; and since, in the area with which we are most likely to be concerned, this should not be difficult of attainment, the distribution of the necessaries of life may be supplemented by the distribution of many of the amenities and luxuries. It would, however, be idle to suppose that the whole process can be confined to the positive and constructive. Disproportionately great wealth has become in itself an offence to the public conscience; and on this ground, as well as on grounds of practical necessity, there will inevitably be a levelling down as well as a levelling up. The degree of sacrifice and the numbers from whom it will be required depend on too many circumstances to be measured

---

[1] "The principle of accumulation based on inequality was a vital part of the pre-war order of society" (J. M. Keynes, *The Economic Consequences of the Peace*, p. 19).

in advance. But they must, at any rate at the outset, be substantial, and it would be unwise to belittle them. Some may find most irksome not the material sacrifice, but the sacrifice of freedom involved in the probably inevitable rationing and standardisation of staple products. The luxury of the exclusive enjoyment by a limited class of things not accessible to the many has played a considerable part in our civilisation. Since no approach to equality will ever be carried far enough to bring about a complete equalisation of the rewards of labour, this luxury will doubtless persist, though the individuals enjoying it may change. But it will have to be enjoyed in the sphere of non-essentials rather than of essentials.

(6) The new faith, reversing the nineteenth-century trend, will lay more stress on obligations than on rights, on services to be rendered to the community rather than on benefits to be drawn from it. The former emphasis on the rights of man was proper to an age when the social structure suffered from excessive rigidity, and it was necessary to break down artificial barriers standing in the way of development and expansion. This condition is no longer present. The most serious danger confronting society at this time is that individualism, masquerading in the guise of the rights of man, may be carried to a point fatal to social cohesion. The catchword that "the state was made for man, not man for the state", legitimate as a protest against the tyranny of totalitarianism, must not be used to cover a denial of social obligation. Among the formerly recognised rights of man, there is little doubt that the rights of property have become in recent times a disintegrating factor. Some democrats have taken the same view of the right of free speech when invoked on behalf of the enemies of democracy. Many observers have attributed the growing danger of disintegration to the industrial system. "An industrial world cannot maintain itself against internal disruptive forces without a great deal more organisation than we have at present." [1] "Modern indus-

[1] B. Russell, *Icarus, or The Future of Science*, p. 29.

trial society suffers from a dangerous lack of social integration, and certain characteristics of industrial activity are likely to increase this condition unless steps be taken to prevent it." [1] It may be suggested that the most fundamental factor jeopardising social cohesion is the cessation of the apparently automatic and almost effortless expansion which was characteristic of the nineteenth century and which made possible the recognition of the profit motive as a moral force. The unquestioned belief in progress provided not only a sense of common purpose, but a certain prospect of increasing advantages to be shared in common. Even in terms of taxation, the benefits of social order were extraordinarily cheap. The nineteenth century became accustomed to think far more of the claims of the individual on society than of the claims of society on the individual. Rights were more important than obligations, benefits more conspicuous than services, in the social balance-sheet. Now that we have fallen on less prosperous days, the perpetuation of this point of view threatens the social order with bankruptcy. If society is not to break up, we shall have for a time to contribute more to maintain it and be content to draw less benefits from it.

(7) Just as the social problem is complicated by the one-sided emphasis of the past on the rights rather than on the obligations of the individual, so the international problem is complicated by an exclusive recognition of the rights of nations. The new faith will have to provide for a readjustment of this attitude. Here too the approach should be positive and constructive. It is less important to dwell on the evils of sovereignty than on the building up of a wider form of international community. The task will be infinitely harder than the task of building up social cohesion within the nation, both because there is as yet hardly any basis of international loyalty or consciousness on which to build, and because governments, the most powerful and closely-knit forms of organisation yet invented, have a

[1] T. N. Whitehead, *Leadership in a Free Society*, p. 231.

vested interest in the old order. It can hardly be achieved except on the basis of the principles already laid down; and it will not be achieved without strong leadership. The war, by overriding national frontiers and national distinctions and introducing new forms of cooperation between those engaged together in it, has laid foundations on which the new faith can build. Whether this faith can achieve sufficient vitality to seize the opportunity remains an open question. On the answer appears to depend the future prospect of any international order worth the name.

(8) Finally, the new faith must reopen the classical debate between liberty and authority and achieve a new synthesis. It will perhaps need to correct the one-sided nineteenth-century emphasis on liberty corresponding to the one-sided nineteenth-century emphasis on rights. This is especially true of the international order, where the collapse of authority—represented in the nineteenth century by British sea-power and by the Concert of Europe—has been complete. But in general the most important task is to reinterpret the concepts of liberty and the authority in the social and economic sphere. The traditional nineteenth-century system provided for the exercise of authority by the controllers of capital. This authority is now passing—after a transitional stage of uneasy compromise between capital and trade-unionism—to the state. The transfer of authority is not unnaturally resented by those who once exercised it as a deprivation of their liberty; and this explains why liberty has readily become in recent times a conservative and even a reactionary slogan. But it is not so resented by the masses, who do not necessarily see in the increased authority of the state a loss of liberty for themselves. It is highly significant of the trend of British opinion since the war that the Government has been criticised far less for its encroachments on individual liberty (which have in fact been enormous) than for its failure to exercise in full the almost unlimited authority conferred on it by the Emergency Powers Act. Popular authority as much as popular liberty will be the keynote of the new faith.

There is all the difference in the world between an examination of the conditions which a new faith and a new moral purpose must fulfil and an assurance that this faith and this purpose will come to birth. They cannot be generated by an intellectual process, which can do no more than demonstrate the need for them if civilisation is to be saved. The war has brought the final proof of the bankruptcy of the political, economic and moral system which did duty in the prosperous days of the nineteenth century. It has also provided—at any rate for the British people and for the whole English-speaking world—a moral purpose which has revived the national will, increased the sense of cohesion and mutual obligation, bred a salutary realisation of the gravity of the crisis, and at the same time created the hope and the opportunity of a new ordering of human affairs. But it is essential to recognise in all humility that this purpose is the product of war, that it is directly inspired by the needs of war, and that it is animated by the potent forces of a common enmity and a common fear. There is no guarantee that out of it will grow a more permanent purpose to create in time of peace a new world based on new principles and new social philosophy. All that can be said with certainty is that the war will not leave us where it found us. It will be the prelude either to the fairly rapid decay—or perhaps the violent overthrow—of the civilisation which has prevailed in Europe for the past 300 years or else to a decisive turning-point and new birth. It is no obstacle that such a new birth may imply a revision of some of our estimates of human nature; for as has been truly said, revolutions "exploit another part of human nature hitherto neglected".[1] Whether the revolution through which we are passing will achieve this result, we cannot yet tell. But there is no excuse for mistaking the character of the issue. The crisis cannot be explained—and much less solved—in constitutional, or even in economic, terms. The fundamental issue is moral.

[1] E. Rosenstock-Huessy, *Out of Revolution*, p. 607.

PART II

SOME OUTLINES OF POLICY

CHAPTER 6

BRITAIN AT HOME

WHEN we pass from the consideration of underlying principles and problems to the examination of practical issues of policy, we move from a field in which some broad degree of certainty is attainable to one in which everything is tentative. The outlines of the crisis which we are traversing are sufficiently clear for us to understand its general character. We know the direction in which the world is moving, and in which we must move with it or perish. But we cannot gauge the rapidity of the movement; we can only guess which countries will take the lead in it and which will fall behind; and there are almost certainly new developments in store of which we have as yet no inkling and which may powerfully modify its course. In particular, the assumption—natural to most British people—that Great Britain is destined to play a predominant rôle in the ordering of the world after the war will not be realised unless the people of Great Britain maintain in time of peace the same sense of common purpose and obligation which has been developed under the impulse of war. If we are now to examine the problems of peace from the specific angle of British policy, we must be perfectly clear about this initial requirement. Halévy believed that, already in the twenty years before 1914, "England felt an increasingly powerful conviction that her vitality was less than that of certain other nations".[1] This is in any case true of the twenty years before 1939—"the years of the locust", as they

[1] E. Halévy, *A History of the English People in 1895-1914*, i, p. x.

have been called.[1] The fact that there is now a widespread consciousness of the decline in British unity, initiative and determination during that period, combined with a marked revival of these qualities since 1940, provides the firmest ground of hope that this revival will not end with the war.

This leads us to the important point that social and international policy have become inseparable. Mr. Winant, at the moment of his appointment as American Ambassador to Great Britain, said in New York that "the democracies had been caught unprepared in their social policy as well as in their armament, and that their failure to solve the problems of unemployment and security had played into the hands of Fascism and National Socialism".[2] There is no reason to dissent from the view expressed about the same time in a German newspaper that "a great national emergency like war will be best surmounted by a people that has found the right answer to the gigantic enigma of its social and political problems".[3] If this is a revolutionary war, concerned as much with social as with national purposes, the revolution must begin at home. It is inconceivable that we can play a leading part in the reconstruction of the world and leave the structure of society in Britain unchanged and unaffected. A successful foreign policy for Great Britain is now possible only on the basis of a substantially altered outlook which will inevitably reflect itself in almost every branch of domestic policy; and what we can achieve in Europe and the world will grow out of, and is in large measure dependent on, what we can achieve at home. There is a further reason for giving precedence to domestic policy. An important start can be made here even while the war is going on. In foreign policy, too much depends on military prospects and on changing alignments to permit of concrete decisions being taken in advance, much less applied. In domestic policy there

[1] A. Cobban, *The Crisis of Civilization*, p. 156.
[2] *The Times*, February 10, 1941.
[3] *Frankfurter Zeitung* quoted in *The Times*, January 3, 1941.

are decisions which can and should be both taken and applied without further delay.

This book being primarily concerned with international problems, no attempt will be made to elaborate in detail a domestic policy. But certain broad outlines may be sketched, bearing mainly on those points where changes in home policy seem most indispensable to a successful foreign policy or involve precedents applicable to it.

Public Works

In the whole sphere of domestic policy the least controversial item, and therefore the easiest to begin with, is the necessity of an extensive building programme. Nearly every great civilisation of the past has been known for its characteristic buildings: Egypt for the pyramids, Greece for her temples, Rome for her baths and aqueducts, the Middle Ages for their castles and cathedrals, the cities of the Renaissance for their town-halls or guildhalls, the monarchies of the seventeenth and eighteenth centuries for their palaces. Few of these great public works of former ages would have passed any modern test either of profitability or of utility. The most famous of them were undertaken for the glory of God, or the glory of the state, or the glory of the monarch. Their economic rôle was that, while creating employment, they were neither profit-earning nor in the ordinary sense of the word "useful"; and they were undertaken because the community, or those who controlled its activities, thought these objects sufficiently important to devote its resources to them.

It has often been asked why nineteenth-century civilisation has left hardly any great buildings which future generations will contemplate with delight. Great buildings are, almost of necessity, public works; and the age of *laissez-faire* and individual enterprise confined public works within the narrow limits of proved utility. In nineteenth-century Britain, traces of the long-standing tradition of non-productive public works survived in the building of churches and museums. Moreover, unquestioned faith in the stability of existing civilisation led to a predilection for durability as something which could be ultimately justified in terms of profit, so that some of the immense private building of the Victorian age is redeemed from contempt by its strength and massivity. But the contemporary British attitude to public works has not yet altered very much from the Victorian view that, if they cannot be justified in terms of profit, they must be confined within the strict limits of proved necessity. Magnificence for the sake of magnificence still seems incompatible with the democratic spirit. Even religious people would be shocked by an expenditure on cathedrals, religious monuments and bishops' palaces comparable—in relation to the total resources of the community—with that eagerly undertaken 500 years ago. The grandiose building schemes of the dictators are treated with mockery or denounced as an attempt to exploit the masses for personal glory. Some Indians are said to resent on the same grounds "the incredible pomp of Lutyens' government buildings at New Delhi".[1] In recent times the development of motor traffic has compelled large expenditure on roads; and these could not, like the railways of the nineteenth century, be left to private enterprise. But public works in general have been limited by strict devotion to "economy". The school buildings of Great Britain constructed at the public expense are mean and paltry in comparison with those of other leading European countries. A project to build a new bridge at Charing Cross was rejected a few years ago on the ground of expense which, placed in the perspective of 1941, would have been that of twenty-four hours of war.

In 1920 the British Government was forced for the first time to contemplate public works as a means to provide employment. For the next twelve years an Unemployment Grants Com-

[1] Negley Farson, *Behind God's Back*, p. 445.

mittee was intermittently occupied in making grants to local authorities for schemes of sewerage, water and electricity supply, road-making and so forth. But its operations were always restricted by the assumption that it was undesirable to divert any appreciable volume of capital investment from "normal trade channels".[1] Where we have made most remarkable progress in the present century is in the recognition of housing as a proper charge on public funds. Housing has been perhaps the most extensive social reform undertaken by the British Government since 1920, and probably the most effective palliative of unemployment. If the building of splendid monuments is incompatible with democracy, the building of decent houses for the mass of the population clearly is not. The use of public funds to provide large numbers of people with cheap houses was applauded by many who would still at that time have thought it improper to provide the same people with cheap bread, milk, meat or clothing at the public expense. In these confused minds, something may have survived of the old tradition that building is a form of activity in which the state can properly engage without strict consideration of profit. On the other hand, a serious concession was made to old-fashioned views of "private enterprise" by giving preference to a system of subsidised building by private contractors. The unhappy results of this system, and the superiority in every respect of the housing undertaken directly by local authorities, are a clear pointer to the policy to be adopted after the war, when the time comes to complete the process of slum clearance throughout the country and to replace the houses destroyed by bombing from the air.

The present outlook for public works in Great Britain is brightened by several favouring factors. There is a now almost universal recognition of the need for radical replanning of the whole country carried out under the direction of a national planning authority with power to control site values and build-

---

[1] *International Labour Office: Studies and Reports Series*, C, No. 15 (*Unemployment and Public Works*), p. 30.

ing operations everywhere. The principal aims in view will be
the better distribution of industry over the country, the wider
dispersal of population, and a reduction in the size of our great
urban units. A century ago there were natural reasons for the
huddling together of the principal industries and of business
life in a few crowded areas. With the electrification of industry
and the development of communications, these reasons exist no
longer. Strategic arguments have come to reinforce arguments
drawn from considerations of health and practical convenience.
It seems plainly undesirable—to take only the most glaring case
—that a quarter of the population of Great Britain should live
within a radius of some twenty miles from Charing Cross, that
a considerable proportion of the population of London should
have no normal access to the countryside, and that large numbers of the working population should daily spend a period of
from one to two hours—and sometimes more—in travel.

The replanning of industry, a new public works and transport policy and a new housing programme are thus closely
interconnected and are urgently required. The Government
must not only take the initiative in setting these measures on
foot, but must itself set an example. The experience of the war
has shown that there is no essential need to concentrate all the
organs of central government in the same spot; and the present
dispersal of government departments seems likely to become
permanent. A case could be made out for more drastic reform.
There is much to be said for dealing with the unwieldy agglomeration of London by removing the capital to a new and more
central site, perhaps somewhere in the Midlands. London would
thus remain the commercial centre, but not the seat of government; and such a change would by itself stimulate the much
needed overhaul of our whole system of administration. In any
event the formulation of a replanning policy is vitally necessary
if confusion is to be avoided. Pressure to begin work immediately on the conclusion of hostilities will be irresistible; for

the need to build will be urgent, and building will be one of the most effective means of providing employment in the critical period of demobilisation. Unless plans are laid in advance, chaos will be the inevitable result.

The Social Minimum

Both housing and public works, though they provide immediate employment, bring only deferred benefits to the mass of the public; and it would be rash to suppose that they will by themselves exhaust the demand for reconstruction in the field of domestic policy. A far more fundamental reorganisation of our national economic system and equalisation of our standards of living will be necessary. We must begin by firmly setting the consumer, not the producer, in the centre of our economic system, and by making planned consumption, not planned production, the starting-point of our policy. This means the introduction of a minimum standard for all in the essentials of life. No new principle is involved in any of the methods by which this aim may be achieved. For many years free medical services and free education have been provided for all who could not afford to pay for them, and free sanitary services for nearly all. Domestic consumers have long paid for water, not by the gallon, but by a fee roughly proportionate to their standard of living. Free or cheap milk was supplied before the war to certain categories of people, and free meals to school children. During the war, staple foodstuffs are being sold at prices kept deliberately low by subsidy. The community accepts the obligation of seeing that a certain standard of physical well-being is brought within the reach of all its members.

The conception of a minimum standard of nutrition as an aim of public policy has made great strides in the past few years. The impulse has come from two quarters. The feature of the breakdown of the economic system which most keenly touched the popular imagination and scandalised the public conscience was the widespread deliberate restriction of production, or the direct destruction, of essential foodstuffs at a time when a considerable proportion of the human race was notoriously undernourished. The question was unavoidable why, instead of encouraging and subsidising restriction or destruction, governments should not have distributed the produce to those who needed it most; and the straightforward answer that nobody was prepared to foot the bill failed to satisfy an age already disillusioned with the fruits of capitalism. The other impulse came from the producers, who perceived that such a plan would be an effective way of enlarging their markets and threw their weight behind the campaign for increased consumption of foodstuffs. Scientific research was undertaken, nationally in Great Britain, and internationally, at Geneva, into standards of nutrition; and minimum standards of nutrition necessary to maintain health and well-being have been worked out. Thanks largely to the publicity enjoyed by this work, the opinion has gradually spread among responsible people in this country that the provision of cheap food, like the provision of cheap housing, to those who could not otherwise afford it is a proper charge on public funds.

The shortcomings of existing diets are due in part to ignorance as well as to poverty. Since the war, propaganda and popular instruction on diet have been undertaken at the instance of the Ministry of Food. They have been directed primarily to recommend and encourage the use of the best substitutes for foodstuffs in short supply. But they have also helped to inculcate some of the principles of a more healthy diet—an interesting example of a valuable initiative neglected in time of peace and rendered possible by the stimulus of war. There will be general agreement that this educational activity should not come to an end with the conditions which have evoked it. The methods of remedying the more serious shortcoming of diet due to poverty are more difficult and more controversial. The fixing of minimum prices for essential commodities, combined with government subsidies sufficient to ensure a plentiful supply, may be practically the most convenient, though theoretically the least perfect, method. The system of differential prices introduced in the case of milk has obvious drawbacks, but may be the best solution for some foodstuffs. Free distribution to those in need may conceivably be necessary for others.[1] In one case only, payments in cash seem unavoidable. The problem of the varying number of children per wage-earner's family can be fairly met only by a state system of family allowances. This is a large and intricate problem, which should be explored before the energies and the goodwill generated by the war have been allowed to evaporate.

Many who welcome such a programme in principle are still perturbed by the question "Can we afford it?" or "How much can we afford?" It is fallacious to seek an answer to this question in a study of budget figures or in any other purely financial calculation. The housing subsidies of the past brought prosperity to the building trade; it has often been held that they were the largest single factor in relieving unemployment after 1931. The distribution of cheap or free milk assures the milk producer of a regular market. In short, to subsidise consumption is almost always the soundest way of subsidising production. The same is true even if the goods concerned are not produced in this country. To stimulate the consumption of Dominions wheat, Danish bacon or Mediterranean citrus fruit means to buy from customers who will purchase in return the products of British industry, and so stimulate industrial production. In setting up our minimum requirements and in seeing that they are met, we help to create the prosperity which will enable us to pay for them. The only limit of what we can "af-

[1] In 1939 a "food stamp plan" was introduced in certain American cities, under which stamps to the value of 50 cents a week were issued to persons in receipt of relief, entitling them to purchase foodstuffs listed as being in surplus supply.

ford" is the extent of our resources in materials and man-power; and so long as any substantial part of our population is unemployed, it is absurd to pretend that this limit has been reached. But in order to reach that limit—and here is the crux of the problem—some national authority must be in a position to determine, as it does in war, the priority of requirements and to secure the allocation of materials and man-power to meet them. And in establishing this priority, the criterion—as in time of war—must be what is socially desirable in the interests of the consumer, not what brings most profit to the producer. The establishment of the social minimum and the cure of the unemployment problem are different facets of the same process.

Once this principle is accepted and applied, two extensions of it may be considered. The first call is naturally for the primary necessities of life—food, housing, clothing and fuel. Provided we are prepared to accept the necessary discipline, there is no doubt that all these can be supplied in ample quantities without undue strain on our resources. But there is no reason in principle to limit ourselves to the bare minimum. It it is not unreasonable to contemplate the eventual inclusion in our scheme of free electric cookers, subsidised radio sets or cheap motor-cars, of national theatres and concerts, of free holiday trips and so forth. In the age of potential plenty which we have now attained, it may be short-sighted to turn an unemployed musician into an inferior builder or agricultural labourer when we might subsidise him to supply good music to those who would not otherwise hear it. Local transport at a nominal and uniform price would help to ease the housing problem. Once it is clearly established that the purpose of our economic system is to produce things wanted, directly or indirectly, for consumption, not things which it is profitable to produce, the limits of what is practicable in the way of achievement can in all probability be set fairly high.

The other desirable extension of the conception of the social minimum is from the national to the international sphere. Standards of nutrition existing in Great Britain before the war, defective as they were, were far in advance of those of most European countries or of our own dependent Empire. The raising of standards in these countries, as well as in Great Britain, even at the cost of some immediate sacrifice to ourselves, should be one of our war aims and an essential part of our post-war policy. The problem of nutrition is preeminently one which calls for solution on something like a world-wide basis. The planning of different types of production appropriate to different areas, of the distribution of foodstuffs and of their exchange against other commodities is a vast international problem which leads us into the heart of difficult and contentious issues of industrial and agricultural policy. An immediate line of approach to this problem should be through a study of the nutritional needs of different areas, of the sources from which these needs can be most effectively met, and of the methods by which necessary supplies can be made available. What is done in the relatively non-contentious field of nutrition may then perhaps serve as a precedent for that wider extension of a more equal prosperity which is essential if peace is to be maintained in the future.

Industry

There has never been a time, at any rate since the inauguration of the postal services, when Great Britain has totally rejected the practice of state trading. But the *laissez-faire* tradition has been responsible for a strong prejudice against the direct sale of goods or services by the state. As the organised life of society has grown more complex and more and more needs have appeared which could not be met by unfettered private enterprise, a number of compromise arrangements have been effected, ranging from public utility companies with special privileges and obligations created by Act of Parliament to municipal trading enterprises and, more recently, to quasi-public boards and corporations operating with direct responsibility to government departments. Simultaneously with the creation of new institutions, existing institutions, once independent in fact as well as in name, have been brought under *de facto* public control. The Bank of England has become virtually an agency of the Treasury, controlling on its behalf the operation of the other banks; and the status of the railways would be little altered for any practical purpose if they were placed under the direct authority of the Ministry of Transport. The controversial issue of state trading has thus been conveniently shelved. The once popular demand for the "nationalisation" of various enterprises has become in most cases superfluous and meaningless.

The enterprises which became most rapidly and most naturally subject to *de facto* public control were those in which monopoly was either necessary in order to secure the requisite capital investment (public utilities, transport) or convenient for some other reason (banking, broadcasting). The further extension of public control over industry at large is being accelerated by the fact that practically all essential branches of production have now taken on monopolistic forms. Producers everywhere have combined to protect themselves against competition and to promote their own interests. The present war, like the last, has been instrumental both in hastening the process of combination and in bringing industry under state control. Every important branch of production in Great Britain has its controller who is an official of the Ministry of Supply or of the Ministry of Food, and whose function is to see that production is determined by the needs of the community as a whole and not solely by the interests of the producer. Such control will need to be perpetuated after the war; and this can perhaps be best achieved by organising each branch of production as a semi-public board or corporation, autonomous in the day-to-day conduct of its business but responsible to the state on broad issues of policy.[1]

There are two main purposes which the future state control of industry must be designed to serve. The first is the defence of the interests of the community as a whole, and of its weaker members in particular. The state in Britain has never long maintained an attitude of complete indifference and impartiality towards industrial problems. Prior to the nineteenth century, its interventions were mainly directed to one of two ends—to protect industry against foreign competition and to secure an abundant supply of cheap labour. In the early years of the industrial revolution, it assisted employers by prohibiting combinations of workers. Then, from about 1840 onwards, there was a swing in the opposite sense, and the state found it increasingly necessary to protect the worker against the employer. In 1940 the situation has changed once more. The great industrial organisations have grown so powerful that the intervention of the state is necessary, if for no other reason, in order to protect other sections of the community.[2] Both employers and workers are now highly organised for the defence of their interests, and are apt to bridge their differences by a compromise which weighs adversely both on the unorganised body of consumers and on the growing and equally unorganised mass of unem-

[1] Though the growth of monopoly is one of the factors which has accelerated the development of state control, it does not follow that that control should necessarily be established on a monopolistic basis. There seems no reason why two, three or several autonomous corporations, subject to the same measure of control, should not be organised to cover the same field of production: such an arrangement would preserve some at least of the unquestioned advantages of competition and comparison.

[2] In the United States the Sherman Act, the first piece of anti-trust legislation, goes back to 1890, but until 1933, when President Roosevelt initiated a new "anti-trust" drive, it had remained largely ineffective. In Great Britain a strong committee appointed by the Ministry of Reconstruction reported in 1919 in favour of the establishment of governmental machinery to supervise industrial and retail trade combinations. But no action was taken on the report. The apparent inability of government to uphold the interests of the community against those of "big business" is a disquieting feature of modern democracy.

ployed. The two great social functions of production are the primary one of producing goods for the consumer and the incidental one of providing jobs for the worker. State intervention must in future be directed above all to the protection of these two interests.

The second purpose which state control must serve is to coordinate the series of problems—or aspects of the same problem—which revolve round the fixing of prices, wages and return on capital. The *laissez-faire* system, under which the relation between these three factors was settled by the self-adjusting mechanism of the market, broke down irretrievably when the growth of monopoly enabled both prices and wages to be fixed by processes of collective bargaining and pressure, and when the establishment of state control over currency, credit policy and the capital market destroyed the automatic operation of the third factor. There is now no authority other than that of the state which can treat these three interdependent factors —as they must be treated—as a single whole. During the war the state does, in effect, exercise control over prices, wages and return on capital. But the machinery is wholly defective, and the control is exercised in watertight compartments without any apparent overriding conception of a single policy. The dangers of inflation and the "vicious spiral", of which much has been written, result from this lack of policy. It is no doubt necessary and desirable that the right methods of industrial control should be hammered out by process of trial and error. But it is important to remember that this is no mere rough-and-ready war-time device which can serve its purposes and be discarded at the end of hostilities. Ever since the breakdown of *laissez-faire*, we have lived in an economic interregnum. Prices, wages and return on capital, released from the automatic discipline of the survival of the fittest which was the essence of a free market, have responded to different and uncoordinated stimuli; and our whole economic structure has lapsed into chaos and disaster. The establishment of a single coordinated and planned control over these three factors is a permanent need of modern industrial civilisation.

The nature of the machinery of control will also require consideration. The form which obviously suggests itself as appropriate is tripartite, representing workers, employer and state.[1] But two important reservations must here be made. First, the representatives of the state cannot be confined to mediatory functions, but must be regarded as the custodians of the public interest and must in that capacity have in the last resort an overriding voice. Experience has shown that employers and workers in any given enterprise or branch of production may have a common interest in raising or maintaining prices, or in restricting production and employment, which may be contrary to the interests of the rest of the community. Secondly, the dichotomy of "worker" and "employer"—the legacy of *laissez-faire* capitalism—is obsolete and has ceased to be a suitable basis for the organisation of industry. The term "employer" is still used to denote two distinct categories of person which formerly coincided, but in practice rarely now coincide—the director or manager who "runs" the business, and the financier whose capital is staked in it. The future control of industry must be based on the conception that the whole staff of workers, clerks and managers enjoy a common status as servants of the public in whose interest the enterprise is conducted; and the much canvassed idea of giving the "workers" a "share in the management" must be realised on this basis. The "employer-financier" is even more obsolete than the "employer-manager". Most of the capital of

[1] When President Roosevelt set up an "Office for Production Management", whose personnel represented employers, workers and state spending departments, he explained that "in every process of production there were three elements—management, labour and the buyer-user" (*New York Times*, December 21, 1940). Similarly the "National Defence Mediation Board" established in March 1941 to mediate in industrial disputes which threaten to interfere with war production was composed of three representatives of "the public" (of whom one was chairman), four of employers and four of employees. Nazi German control of industry is based on the same tripartite principle.

contemporary British industry is "owned" by a large anonymous body of investors, or by large corporations which are themselves "owned" by a similar body of investors. The notion that the "employer" is the proper person to represent the interest of the capital invested in the enterprise which he controls is in many cases pure fiction—and sometimes a dishonest fiction at that. State control of industry is to-day almost as necessary in the interest of the "little man" whose savings are directly or indirectly invested in it as in that of the consumer for whom production ultimately takes place.

The problem of the future financing of industry is closely concerned with the question how far state control shall be extended over the field of production. The necessity of control over those great industries whose magnitude makes them tantamount to national institutions and whose well-being is essential to that of the community is no longer seriously contested. In these cases control clearly implies limitation of profits. But enforced limitation clearly carries with it the corollary of guaranteed profits at an approved rate; and in its war-time dealings with industry, including the railway companies, the Government seems to have been guided by the general principle that enterprises should be enabled to earn a "reasonable" rate of profit, generally identified with the average rate of the last few pre-war years. Government control of industry leads inevitably to a system under which the capital invested in industry becomes a fixed interest-bearing, guaranteed security, abandoning the hope of high interest in return for gilt-edged status. This should have no adverse effect on those great staple industries which already conduct their affairs on "safety first" lines and whose ordinary shares have long been recommended by stockbrokers as suitable investments for fathers of families. But it may fairly be asked whether the speculative element involved in the hope of high profits is not a necessary stimulant to the development of new lines of production and perhaps to the opening up of new markets. An affirmative answer cannot be given without some hesitation. Every important industrial enterprise—including those whose affairs are conducted on the most conservative and least speculative principles—now spends large sums both on technical and on market research. It would be absurd to suggest that either those engaged on the research or the directors responsible for the policy are actuated primarily by the thought of pecuniary advantages which may accrue to them from its results. On the other hand there have been inventions covered by patents and deliberately left unused because their use would threaten some existing source of profit. Human nature is many-sided, and we can afford to neglect no opportunity of stimulating the development of fresh ideas and new inventions. The balance between gilt-edged and speculative investment, each of which has its rôle to play, must be preserved.[1] It is perfectly arguable that, while industries which, owing to their essential character and monopolistic organisation, have attained gilt-edged status are rightly and necessarily subjected to limitation of profits and brought under government control, the field of speculative investment and unlimited profits should still remain open to fresh and untried lines of production. In this field, there may still be room for the old-fashioned *entrepreneur*—the man who "undertakes" new ventures—who has vanished from the more stable industries. The fact that such new lines may, if they enjoy success, stabilise themselves in the course of ten or twenty years as essential industries and develop in the direction of monopoly and state control, will not deter the enterprising kind of capital which looks for quick profits.

It thus seems possible to conceive for the future a mixed economy in which essential industries and essential services will

---

[1] It has been impressively argued that in recent years this balance has not been maintained, even in the conditions of a free market, owing to the growing popularity of fixed-interest-bearing securities and dislike of speculative investment (A. G. B. Fisher, *The Clash of Progress and Security*, pp. 161-3). Mr. Keynes, writing in 1936, expected "to see the state . . . taking an ever greater responsibility for directly organising investment" (J. M. Keynes, *The General Theory of Employment, Interest and Money*, p. 164).

be conducted in the form of autonomous units under government control, paying interest rather than profits on the capital invested in them, while luxury industries and services or new lines of production will continue to operate in the conditions of a more or less free market. In the category of essentials, the consumer will be protected against exploitation in the form of inflated prices but will have to submit in return to some measure of standardisation—which is, in fact, already imposed on him by monopoly conditions. In the category of "luxuries", the consumer can be left to protect himself by the weapon of refusal to buy and can continue to enjoy a large freedom of choice. This division has in fact been growing up for some time. The necessities of the war, and of the coming peace, will serve not so much to introduce a new principle as to enforce a far wider definition than has hitherto obtained of "essential" industries and services, so that the type of organisation which has hitherto applied in the main to public utilities and other similar enterprises will be extended to most or all of the "key" industries. Problems have arisen, and will no doubt continue to arise, from the coexistence of these different forms of enterprise. But there is no reason to suppose that they will prove insoluble.

Agriculture

Agricultural policy is one of the most difficult problems confronting Great Britain after the war. Great Britain occupies an altogether exceptional position in that only 7 per cent of her population draw their livelihood from agriculture (a far lower proportion than in any other important country) and that the period of her greatest supremacy and greatest relative prosperity in the world was the period in which her agricultural production was most neglected. Both the economic system and the foreign policy of Great Britain have hitherto been based on the assumption of a large volume of imported foodstuffs. The future of British agriculture cannot be considered intelligently except in the framework both of general economic policy at home and of foreign policy.

Two general considerations have to be borne in mind in framing agricultural policy:

In the first place, the market for agricultural products is less elastic than the market for industrial products and for services. The more primitive the community, the greater the proportion of agricultural products in its total consumption. In a progressive society, the proportion of available purchasing power expended on agricultural products tends to diminish. In a period of rising standards of living (especially if there is no corresponding increase in numbers of population), the relative importance of agriculture is bound to decline. This has been happening throughout the civilised world in the last thirty years. The rapid fall in agricultural prices throughout that period in relation to the general price has been due to a misguided attempt to expand world agricultural production at the same rate as other forms of production.

Secondly, output per head of population engaged in agriculture is everywhere lower in terms of value (in Europe lower by 60 to 100 per cent) than output per head of population engaged in other forms of production. The discrepancy is greatest for grain crops raised by small-scale peasant production, as in South-Eastern Europe; least for grain crops raised under prairie conditions with a minimum of human labour, and for specialties like milk, butter and bacon produced intensively for a highly concentrated and relatively wealthy market. Notwithstanding technical improvements in agriculture, there is no prospect in any predictable future that the man employed in agriculture will be equally "efficient"—in the sense of producing output of equal value—with the man engaged in other forms of production. Broadly speaking, a shift of man-power from agriculture to industry results in increased national production and a higher standard of living, while a shift of man-power from industry to agriculture produces the opposite results. The countries which enjoyed the lion's share of the great nineteenth-century wave of prosperity achieved this result by an enormous increase of the proportion of their man-power engaged in industry. As Mr. Churchill once said of Great Britain, "our population could never have attained its present vast numbers, nor our country have achieved its position in the world, without any altogether unusual reliance upon manufactures as opposed to simple agriculture".[1] The more recent eagerness of many countries to industrialise themselves, though sometimes denounced as perverse and mistaken, has been inspired by the same ambition. Hitler knows perfectly well what he is doing when he seeks to concentrate industrial production in Germany and preaches a "back to the land" policy for France and other subject countries.

We have long ago departed from the standpoint that maximum production is the sole aim of economic policy. These fundamental elements of the agricultural situation are not necessarily decisive. But as underlying realities they cannot be ignored. Deliberately to prefer forms of production which are less "efficient"—in the sense of yielding a lower output per man employed—is exactly on the same footing as to promote the production of "substitute" materials at high cost in preference to importing "natural" materials paid for by other and more efficient forms of production. This course is justified in some cases by special considerations. But we must be clear what the considerations are which dictate the agricultural policy of Great Britain. The arguments which must determine the level of agricultural production in Great Britain fall into two categories— those relating to foreign policy and military security, and those relating to social policy at home.

The argument for an expansion of the domestic production of foodstuffs on strategic grounds has been frequently and effectively used since 1914, and is naturally potent to-day. But it re-

[1] Winston Churchill, *Liberalism and the Social Problem*, p. 195.

quires careful scrutiny. War-time needs may prove a fallacious basis for permanent policy. All modern experience shows that the most indisputable material condition of capacity to wage war, and therefore of the status of a Great Power, is a large industrial production and a large population of skilled industrial workers. Great Britain could never have become a Great Power, and still less can remain a Great Power to-day, on the strength of industrial production for the home market. She achieved her position, and—given her size—can only retain it, as a great exporting country; and she can only retain extensive foreign markets so long as she remains an extensive importer of foodstuffs. These are two sides of an equation. You cannot subtract from the one without subtracting from the other. The importance of arresting the decline in the British mercantile marine—an unavoidable symptom of declining trade—needs no emphasis. A small and densely populated island like Great Britain, once she becomes involved in war, will need to import to the limit of her capacity; and if her capacity to import is interrupted she is doomed to defeat. To be dependent on imported foodstuffs is no greater an evil than to be dependent on imported munitions. While therefore the increased production of foodstuffs in Great Britain is highly desirable on strategic as on other grounds, it would be disastrous, on strategic grounds as well as on general grounds of foreign policy, if this result were achieved by any serious curtailment of peace-time imports of foodstuffs. This is so important that it must be an overriding consideration in any sane agricultural policy for Great Britain. The aim must be to keep the land in a condition in which it is potentially capable of maximum production in an emergency rather than to aim in normal times at a maximum which can be achieved only at the expense of other forms of production.

Nor can we afford to ignore the relation of British agricultural policy and the British market to schemes of international reconstruction after the war. If Great Britain is to play a predominant rôle in Europe and in the world, her cooperation cannot be limited to military and political commitments. Any international system will prove ineffective which does not involve a harmonious dove-tailing between the economic interests and systems of different countries. Everyone remembers the embarrassments of the period when British politicians and British diplomats at international conferences denounced the wickedness of the industrial quotas established by other countries to exclude British manufactures while simultaneously protesting the innocence of British agricultural quotas designed to exclude foreign foodstuffs. Quotas will in one form or another remain. But we must not repeat the naïvety of supposing that we can retain our position as a great industrial and commercial Power if we are not prepared to take practical account of the interests of the countries whose prosperity depends primarily on their agriculture. To take only three of the most obvious of our post-war international problems, our relations with the Dominions, our relations with the United States and our relations with post-war Europe, all involve considerations closely affecting agricultural policy. Decisions must not be taken in one field which prejudge issues vital to our interests in another.

The social arguments bearing on the future place of agriculture in the British economy are more intangible and therefore more difficult to assess. The member of Parliament who recently spoke of putting the land to "the most productive of all human uses, namely, growing wheat",[1] presumably used the word "productive" in a mystical sense which would be proof against any rational refutation. The sentimental view of agriculture as a "natural" occupation as opposed to the "artificial" conditions of industrial life has little relation to modern mechanised farming. It is clear that British agriculture, maintaining the tradition of the pre-industrial age, has avoided some of the evils of nineteenth-century industrialism—notably the rejection of any responsibility for the physical and moral well-being of the

[1]*Parliamentary Debates: House of Commons*, March 19, 1941, vol. 370, No. 39, col. 1941.

worker. But the paternalism of British agriculture, now rapidly passing away, developed abuses of its own. In the replanning of the economic system, the dispersal of urban agglomerations, the maintenance of high standards of health and social amenity for all categories of workers, and the establishment of a proper balance between town and country are factors of primary importance. In this sense a unique opportunity presents itself of ruralising industry and of industrialising agriculture. Industry and agriculture need to be organised as interrelated parts of national production. But no satisfactory result can be achieved by treating them as rivals and seeking to aggrandise one at the expense of the other. Here again much harm has been done in the past twenty years by approaching the future of British agriculture as an isolated problem. It can be properly considered only in the framework of a general social and economic policy.

There is one factor which differentiates agriculture from any other branch of production except mining, and which calls for specialised treatment, *i.e.* its dependence on an infinite variety of natural conditions. A uniform national policy—in the sense of a policy which applies the same regulations and offers the same inducements throughout the country—fails to take account of this variety of conditions and is a costly anomaly. Suppose it to be an established fact that the cultivation of wheat or sugar beet is essential to the maintenance of soil fertility and a prosperous agriculture in East Anglia. This may be a cogent argument for subsidising wheat or sugar beet grown by East Anglian farmers, but it is no argument at all for paying the same subsidy on wheat or sugar beet grown in the West Midlands, where different conditions may render the cultivation of these crops superfluous, or where they can be profitably cultivated without subsidy or with a subsidy at a lower rate. There is no solution of this problem except a regional system of control adjusted to local conditions. Agriculture throughout the country must be fitted into a centrally conceived, but regionally administered, scheme of production.

All these factors require to be taken into account and balanced against one another in considering British agricultural policy. It is clearly important that, whatever man-power and resources are employed in agriculture, the maximum output obtainable from them should be obtained. It is also important that every necessary step should be taken to maintain the fertility and potential capacity of the land. All measures and all forms of research designed to increase the efficiency of British agriculture should therefore be encouraged. But agricultural policy must be framed with regard to other interests besides that of agriculture, which cannot in Great Britain be the sole, or even the paramount, consideration. In the light of these principles, the directing lines of policy should run somewhat as follows:

(1) There should be no attempt to increase the number of men employed in agriculture (though the increased employment of women may be desirable). But every effort should be made by improved equipment, by research and agricultural education, and by the direct penalisation of inefficient farming to raise the value of output per man employed.

(2) Increased production of foodstuffs must be absorbed by increased consumption (through subsidies and cheap or free distribution where necessary) and not balanced by decreased imports.

(3) The aim should be to increase production of foodstuffs for which there is a rapidly expanding market provided prices are fixed to correspond with purchasing power (dairy produce and vegetables) rather than of foodstuffs for which the market has in normal times nearly reached saturation point (cereals and sugar).

(4) The aim should be to direct production from foodstuffs which can be easily transported and stored, and of which large stocks can and should always be held in the country (cereals and sugar) to foodstuffs which can be less easily

transported and stored (dairy produce, vegetables, fruit).

(5) Every effort should be made to keep the best land under cultivation and to hand over land which cannot be made productive except at high cost for afforestation or urban and industrial development. This requires collaboration between the authorities responsible for agriculture, for town planning and for the location of industry.

(6) The formal ownership of land, like the ownership of industrial enterprises, has become a matter of no great importance. But a standard of professional efficiency should be required of farmers, and no unqualified person should be allowed to control or farm agricultural land.

(7) The execution of this policy calls for the establishment of a National Land Commission, having regional commissions working under it, on which the interest of the farmer, the agricultural worker and the consumer should be equally represented.

Forms of Government

Political forms grow out of the conditions which they are required to meet and can rarely be devised in advance to meet emergencies whose character is still unknown. It has already been shown that the survival of democracy depends on its ability to establish control over those economic forces which have hitherto defied its authority or themselves controlled it, and to restore a sense of common obligation as a necessary corollary of the common enjoyment of rights. These changes represent a change of spirit and a shifting of forces rather than a change of political forms. Nevertheless some changes of form are not excluded, and present trends suggest the directions which they may take.

The most important constitutional development of recent years in almost every country has been the growth in the power of the executive at the expense of the legislative assembly, extending in countries where democracy has been abandoned to the total or virtual disappearance of the latter. This development has been intensified by the emergence of the head of the executive as a unique figure, no longer *primus inter pares*, but set well above his colleagues. The phenomenon of the growing importance of personal leadership is by no means confined to the dictatorships. Fifty years ago Bryce gave to a chapter in *The American Commonwealth* the title "Why Great Men Are Not Chosen Presidents". The implied generalisation was perhaps even then unduly sweeping. But it could be made by an acute observer of American institutions. Nobody would make it in the age of Theodore Roosevelt, Woodrow Wilson and Franklin Roosevelt—all outstanding men of their generation. In 1916, and again in 1940, British democracy turned in the hour of crisis to personal leadership. France found a great leader in 1917. Her failure to find one in 1940 was a cause—or perhaps a symptom of the cause—of her defeat. In Great Britain probably the keenest political debates of recent times have turned, at any rate in the minds of most people, on the question who should or should not be Prime Minister; and the experience of the second year of the war showed how difficult it was to bring controversy to a head in the House of Commons so long as the personal issue of the premiership was not in question. Forward-looking people in Great Britain at the present time are perhaps more preoccupied to know what individual leaders will direct British policy after the war than what will be the party complexion of the House of Commons. It is difficult to imagine any effective choice which could be presented in the near future to the electorate of Great Britain—or indeed of the United States—except in the form of a choice between rival leaders. Policies tend more and more to be symbolised by leaders rather than by parties.

There are several reasons for this growing prominence of the executive and its head. Some of these reasons are directly connected with the nature of those economic forces whose effective control is now the most serious task of democracy. To exercise this control is an extremely complex business, for which a representative body like the House of Commons or the Congress of the United States is ill equipped. It has been calculated that in the parliamentary session of 1937–38, out of 487 hours devoted by the House of Commons to legislation, 209 hours were occupied by Bills providing for "economic organisation of industry and agriculture".[1] Such legislation is necessarily highly technical, and does not lend itself to public discussion by an assembly of laymen. To implement it requires the constant issue of regulations and other forms of executive action. The best that Parliament can do is to confine itself to a somewhat vague pronouncement of its intention, and then give wide powers to the executive to carry this intention into effect. This procedure has evoked protests in recent years both from theoretically minded democrats and from interests opposed to the controls which were in fact established by this method. But there is no other way in which democracy can assert its authority over the economic system. When the war made this problem really urgent, the British Parliament by the Emergency Powers Act of May 22, 1940, delegated virtually the whole of its powers to the executive, requiring every subject of the Crown in the United Kingdom to place himself, his services and his property at the absolute disposal of the Government. Mr. Bernard Shaw made the apt comment that Great Britain had achieved, by the passing of an Act of Parliament in two and a half hours, that nationalisation of the means of production which Soviet Russia had failed to bring about in twenty-three years. The comment would have been true as well as apt if the executive had been as resolute in using these powers as Parliament was in conferring them. What was necessary in the crisis of the war will be not less necessary in the crisis after the war. The extremely complex problems of the post-war period can be faced, in Great Britain

[1] Stafford Cripps, *Democracy Up-to-Date*, p. 59.

and elsewhere, only by an increasing delegation to the executive of the powers of the legislative assembly.

Besides the complication of the measures required, there is another and perhaps more important reason why legislative assemblies are ill-fitted to cope with the problem of controlling the economic system. An elected assembly necessarily represents a number of powerful economic interests. In modern times these interests exercise control over Parliament mainly through highly organised party machines dependent on them for financial support. The theory of nineteenth-century liberal democracy was that, since the interests of each and the interests of all ultimately coincided, the interplay of interests in a representative assembly produced the results most conducive to the good of the community as a whole. The growing strength of economic organisations has deprived this hypothesis of any reality it may once have had. Experience has shown that it always pays powerful organised interests to compose their differences at the expense of the weak and unorganised. The well-organised producers will forget their internecine rivalries in their common desire to keep up prices against the unorganised consumer. Representative assemblies can find no cure for unemployment so long as the unemployed have no organisation and contribute to no party funds. It is true that the executive, and the bureaucracy through which it works, is not exempt from economic influence. But this influence is less direct and continuous. In the great democratic countries bureaucracy, though its many defects include a certain professional interest of its own, takes on the whole a relatively detached and impartial attitude towards competing economic interests. A decision on economic policy conducive to the good of the community as a whole is at the present time more likely to emanate from a committee of civil servants than from a representative assembly dominated by economic vested interests.

In this important respect, the head of the executive is in a unique position. Unlike the civil servant, he is in close touch with that interplay of interests which underlies all political activity and which can be ignored only by framers of utopias. But like the civil servant, he is relatively disinterested. Having reached the highest position in political life, he has nothing to hope in the way of future promotion from placating powerful interests within his party. If he is a strong personality and a popular figure, he is probably more necessary to his party than his party is to him, and he can up to a point rule, rather than be ruled by, the party machine. This ideal is not always realised in practice. Few men are wholly proof against flattery or against certain forms of social inducement of which wealthy interests readily dispose. But modern democracy seems likely to depend more and more for its efficient working on a head of the executive strong enough to stand above, and if necessary to dominate, the interplay of economic interests which finds expression in representative assemblies. It is significant that recent great political leaders in democratic countries have often been at variance with the parties and party machines which they were supposed to represent. Theodore Roosevelt, Woodrow Wilson and Mr. Lloyd George split and broke their respective parties. Mr. Winston Churchill has always been a bad party man. President Franklin Roosevelt has established a powerful personal ascendancy over the Democratic party machine; and when the Republican Convention of 1940 was faced with the task of finding a candidate likely to appeal to the mass of voters, it rejected all the nominees of the party managers and chose a complete outsider—a recent recruit to the party. These are signs of the times. A certain defiance of the party system, whose main field of activity is the legislative assembly, seems characteristic of successful leadership in modern democracy.

The shift of power from Parliament to the executive has been facilitated by modern methods of publicity. The process began with the growth of the popular press. On the one side, the executive began to feel that it might be quite as important to gain the support of the press for its policy as to gain the support of the House of Commons. On the other side, the press offered a forum for the airing, as well as for the creation, of public opinion, which could thus exercise an influence on the executive independently of Parliament. The process was intensified by the invention of broadcasting, which has given to the executive—and especially to the head of the executive—an extra-parliamentary means of influencing public opinion immeasurably more potent than the platform speech. To come well over the air is now a more valuable asset for the head of a democratic government than to be an effective parliamentary orator. Moreover, science has provided not only this modern method of creating opinion, but a modern method of ascertaining opinion. The "straw vote" or "public opinion poll" was first introduced in the United States, but is now widely used in Great Britain, by political as well as by business organisations, as a convenient instrument for testing public opinion. A curious debate in the House of Commons ensued in August 1940 on the revelation that this method was being employed by the Ministry of Information. The Minister concerned defended it as "a scientific method of discovering public opinion",[1] and justified it as a war-time measure by the unrepresentative character of a war-time House of Commons. Some more intelligent parliamentarians uneasily perceived that Mr. Duff Cooper had proved too much; for if this were really a "scientific method", it might well be superior even in peace-time to the rough-and-ready method of treating the voice of the House of Commons as an expression of the voice of the people.[2] While such a device could never be adopted as the official test of the popular will, it has undoubtedly placed in the hands of the executive a means of ascertaining

---

[1] *Parliamentary Debates: House of Commons*, August 1, 1940, vol. 363, col. 1548.

[2] *The New Statesman and Nation* of August 10, 1940, recorded "the impression that the press and the House of Commons both felt that they had a vested interest in the interpretation of public opinion and that they must destroy an interloper".

public opinion in many ways more reliable and accurate than that provided by the parliamentary machine.

The modern tendency is therefore for the executive to appeal to the electorate, and for the will of the electorate to be impressed on the executive, direct and, so to speak, over the head of the legislative assembly; and this has accelerated that transfer of power from the legislature to the executive which had already been set in motion by other factors. In the United States the presidency is likely to become more important than Congress. There may be sharp periodical reactions against this trend. But it will be intensified by the growing concern of the United States in world affairs. The experience of the last few years has shown that the constitutional powers of Congress are an obstacle to any effective foreign policy in periods of crisis. Inevitably the American people will sooner or later need and demand a foreign policy. It will probably prove easier for a skilful President, having public opinion behind him, to circumvent Congress than to amend the constitution; and the power and prestige of Congress will insensibly decline. In Great Britain, Parliament is already losing power to the Cabinet and, still more, to the Prime Minister. Fifty years ago, it would have been absurd to find the centre of gravity of the British Constitution anywhere but in the House of Commons.[1] In the latter part of the twentieth century, it may fall to a new Bagehot to record that the most important function of the House of Commons is to serve as an electoral college registering the people's choice of a Prime Minister. The most significant part of the work of the House of Commons at the present time is that which is directly concerned with the administrative functions of the executive. It is never

[1] It may be noted however that the House of Commons is, by origin and tradition, not an organ of government, but the watchdog of the people over the government. According to one recent critic, "many of its present defects probably arise from the recent 'democratic' tendency to convert it into a sovereign parliamentary assembly on the Continental model governing the country through a committee of ministers" (E. Percy, *Government in Transition*, p. 108).

more effective than when it is criticising the actions or the composition of the Government, never less effective than when it is attempting to legislate or to direct policy.

If therefore we look forward to probable lines of constitutional evolution in Great Britain, it may be significant to observe the greater continuity, and therefore the greater potential strength, of the executive assured by the American and Swiss constitutions. In the United States the President and Vice-President (the former appointing the Cabinet), in Switzerland the Federal Council (which is the supreme organ), are elected for four years and are not removable during that term, though they are subject to regular and unrestricted criticism by the representative organs. If we consider the opposite extreme, as exhibited in the Third French Republic, of a legislative assembly in full control of the executive, and exercising the right to dismiss it at any moment, there will be little doubt in which direction British institutions are likely to evolve. The most desirable reform of Parliament itself lies in the direction of an extension of the committee system and a reduction of the time spent in public session. Much of the most useful legislative work of Parliament is already done in small committees. Small standing committees dealing with foreign affairs, defence questions, colonial questions, questions of health and local administration and so forth, would facilitate more intimate relations between the great departments of the executive and groups of M.P.s especially interested in their work, and would help to avoid the grave inconvenience of frequent public debates at critical times on such matters as foreign or defence policy.

This shift of power within the constitution from a popular representative assembly to a popular responsible leader represents, not a diminution of democracy as such, but a change in the form and character of contemporary democracy. It is part of the issue which confronts every democracy of achieving a compromise between two extremes: the appointment of all public servants by election, being the nearest practicable mod-

ern approximation to "direct" democracy, and what has sometimes been called "plebiscitary" democracy, involving the
choice by popular vote of a leader who appoints subordinates
responsible to himself to carry on the business of government.
Certainly neither extreme could be realised in its pure form
without destroying democracy itself. But both elements enter
into any workable system. The constitution of the United States
runs to both extremes. The emergence as the strongest constitutional power of a President whose principal officers of State
are personal nominees responsible only to himself is a victory for
the "plebiscitary" principle.[1] On the other hand, nowhere but
in the United States has there been such a plethora of elective
appointments to public office, though many observers of the
American scene have regarded this system as a weakness, and
there has been some mitigation of it in recent years. In Great
Britain, the judiciary and the civil service, both appointed by
methods other than election, have long been regarded as pillars
of British democracy. Even in the working of our representative institutions, popular faith in frequent resort to the electoral
process has perceptibly weakened within the last twenty-five
years. Before 1914, it was a familiar part of House of Commons
tactics for the Opposition to challenge the Government to "go
to the country". Since 1918, this challenge has been rarely heard
or rarely pressed. In recent times it is easier to think of cases
where democracy has been discredited by inopportune elections
than of cases where it has been damaged by failure to hold an
election at a crucial moment. The German republic died in 1932,
before Hitler battered it to pieces, of a surfeit of elections.

This issue plays an important part in a problem of great importance for the revitalisation of British political life: the reform
of local government. The growing complication and concentration of government has produced an urgent need for devolution

[1] "The presidency has a distinct flavour of the plebiscitary monarchy of the
Bonapartes", wrote Professor Brogan in 1933 (*The American Political System*,
p. 120). The flavour is still more noticeable to-day.

—a need whose more obvious war-time aspects have been met by the creation of twelve Regional Commissioners. But little progress has yet been made towards an answer to the question how to reconcile an increase of delegated authority from Whitehall with the more old-fashioned elective forms of local self-government. This is not, as is sometimes supposed, a question of principle. Democracy does not consist in the multiplication of elections or of elected officers. The experience of the United States demonstrates the dangers of undue devotion to the ballot-box as an instrument of local government. In recent years the municipal administration of several important cities has been handed over, with results which apparently gave widespread satisfaction, to nominated non-responsible "commissions". While no such drastic change need be sought in Great Britain, there has already been a substantial reduction in the number of elected bodies; and this process may well be carried further by future reforms. The test is practical rather than theoretical. Where elections are regarded with apathy by a high proportion of the electorate, and have the effect of placing control over local affairs in the hands of small organised groups representing party, or other less respectable, interests, neither the prestige nor the reality of democracy is enhanced by retaining them. On the other hand, the civil defence and other services organised during the war have revealed in the British people an immense reserve not merely of devoted service, but of initiative and capacity for leadership, which had never been tapped by our peace-time organs of local government. The problem is to utilise this material and evoke this local patriotism in time of peace by giving to such voluntary services and organisations a real function to perform in our local administrative system. Such cooperation of citizens in the business of administration is a truer form of self-government, and may represent more of the essence of democracy, than voting in a multiplicity of local elections; and the issue is not affected by the question whether such activities are under the direction of an official appointed by a

Minister responsible to an elected House of Commons, or of a town clerk appointed by, and responsible to, an elected council. The determining factor in making democracy real and effective is not to multiply the number of direct channels through which popular authority flows, but to create among the maximum number of people a lively sense that they, and people like them, are administrators as well as administered, and that the conduct of government is part of their business and their responsibility.

None of these changes would affect the essence of democracy; most of them are, in fact, suggested by the experience of other democratic countries. The gravest danger to British democracy to-day lies in that conservatism which regards democratic institutions inherited from the nineteenth century as sacrosanct, and fails to recognise that changes in these institutions are essential if democracy is to remain a reality in the twentieth century.

CHAPTER 7

BRITAIN AND THE WORLD

THE difficulty of framing any programme for future action in international affairs may perhaps best be appreciated if we consider the uncertainties which would have faced the critic confronted by a similar task towards the end of the Napoleonic wars. An intelligent observer in 1814 might perhaps have foreseen that, notwithstanding Napoleon's downfall, the tide of democracy and nationalism, which had received its impetus from the French Revolution and from the Napoleonic campaigns, would sweep triumphantly onward and that the attempt to dam its flow by a restoration of the old eighteenth-century order would end in ignominious failure. He might have predicted that the increasing use of machinery would lead to a substantial expansion of industry, though he would almost certainly have underestimated its importance. But he could hardly have guessed that the nineteenth century would witness an increase of population and of material prosperity unparalleled in human history; or that Great Britain would become the predominant Power in every quarter of the globe; or that Germany and Italy would emerge as strong and united nation-states; while if he had understood as clearly as Metternich the incompatibility between the ideas of democracy and nationalism on the one hand and the continued existence of the Hapsburg Empire on the other, he might well have doubted the capacity of that Empire to survive for another hundred years. Some of the main underlying trends might have been correctly traced. The details would have eluded the most percipient critic.

The framing of policy to meet concrete problems requires an understanding both of underlying general trends and of the day-to-day details of the situation. Those who seek to discuss the problems of the post-war world are too often offered the choice between the two extreme positions: the position of those who believe that we should, in the light of a few broad general principles, construct the framework of a future world order into which the pieces can, when the time arrives, be smoothly and conveniently fitted, and the position of those who argue that speculation on future conditions of peace is futile and dangerous, since we cannot foresee the circumstances in which the war will end. It seems both unnecessary and disastrous to accept either position. If the general diagnosis of our fundamental problems presented in the previous chapters is sound, we can draw from it some substantial conclusions as to our future policy. The tentative nature of these conclusions, and the likelihood that many of them will have to be qualified in the light of new developments, should be kept in mind throughout.

Having recognised the paramount importance of planning for the future, we need however to be on our guard against current well-advertised offers of ready-made systems of world organisation. One popular approach is to plunge immediately into the elaboration of some constitutional framework for the whole world or for whole continents—a federation, a revived League of Nations, a "United States of Europe"—to be set up by agreement at the end of the war. There is a kind of naïve arrogance in the assumption that the problem of the government of mankind, which has defied human wit and human experience for centuries, can be solved out of hand by some neat paper construction of a few simple-minded enthusiasts. Except in so far as they keep public opinion alive to the necessity of radical change, the supporters of projects like Federal Union exercise a pernicious influence by grossly over-simplifying the problem and by obscuring the need to study with patience and humility the historical perspective and the economic organisation of the world for which they prescribe. Projects of a revived and re-vised League of Nations have the advantage of building on something which has existed and enjoyed in the past a measure of popular support. But the tradition of the League of Nations is one of frustration and—more fatally still—of association with the interests of a particular group of Powers; and its ideology was also derived from nineteenth-century political traditions which have already proved inadequate to solve our modern problems. It is conceivable that the name of the League of Na-tions, and such goodwill as attaches to it, might be used in the creation of a new order. The so-called technical organisations of the League will certainly survive in one form or another, perhaps being affiliated to the International Labour Organisa-tion. But those who contemplate a revival of the League of Na-tions in substantially its previous form, with a few modifications designed to "strengthen" it, are open to the same condemnation as the proponents of Federal Union. The ideals of the French Revolution and of the American War of Independence are to-day inadequate—in part, even irrelevant—for the solution of modern problems of government.

There is indeed a real danger that—as happened to some extent in 1919 and after—legalistic discussions about sovereignties, leagues and federations may serve as a red herring to divert public opinion from those practical issues of cooperation and interdependence, military and economic, on which the future depends. A constitution, in Burke's famous phrase, is "a vest-ment which accommodates itself to the body".[1] Until the body politic of a new order begins to take shape, it is premature to seek for elaborate constitutional vestments to clothe it. The Statute of Westminster did not lay the foundations of the Brit-ish Commonwealth of Nations. It registered certain relation-ships which had already established themselves and which it was convenient to put on formal record. The new and broader

[1] Burke, *Works* (Bohn ed.), vi, p. 146.

commonwealth of nations can only be built up out of some such network of relationships, flexible in character and inspired by no undue itch for uniformity, to which it may some day be possible and convenient to give a more precise legal shape. At the present stage interdependence is a practical, not a constitutional, problem. It is a dangerous, if popular, illusion that it can be solved by a committee of ingenious constitutional lawyers to everyone's satisfaction and without impinging on anyone's interests. What we are required in fact to surrender is not a mythical attribute called sovereignty, but the habit of framing our military and economic policy without regard for the needs and interests of other countries.

To begin, then, with constitutional structures is to begin at the wrong end. Because we have recognised both the fact and the necessity of increasing interdependence among nations, we should not therefore consider ourselves entitled to envisage a utopia where the lion—or even the eagle—will lie down on equal terms with the lamb. Foreign policy will not cease to exist for those who possess power (for those who do not it was always something of an illusion); and it will be as necessary to take account of the realities of power in the new world as it was in the old. We should take as our starting point the international situation which may be expected to emerge at the end of the war, and in particular—since we are concerned primarily with British policy—the place of Great Britain in that situation.

Miscalculations of the Past

It is extremely important that there should be, at the end of this war, a clear understanding of the changed position of Great Britain since the palmy days of the nineteenth century. Lack of this understanding was responsible for many of the disastrous incidents of the period 1919–39. The confusions of British foreign policy in this period were rather the result than the cause of the decline in British power and prestige in international affairs; and they occurred because the change in the situation was not realised and faced either by British statesmen or by the British public. The uniqueness of the British position in modern history is due to one central fact. Thanks in part to the skill and inventiveness of her people, in part to the comparatively high degree of political development already attained by her before 1800, but most of all to the fortunate disposition of her natural resources, Great Britain had a long start over the rest of the world in that vast process of industrial development which made the nineteenth century one of the most remarkable periods of recorded history. Throughout the middle years of the century, Great Britain was the principal supplier to the world of nearly all staple industrial products, drawing in return from the rest of the world supplies of foodstuffs, raw materials and a few specialised luxuries.[1] She was thus able to lead the way in a remarkable rise in the standard of living, and to acquire an overwhelming preponderance in that form of military power which best suited her needs—the first, and down to the end of the century the only, large-scale mechanised navy. The solid basis of the two-Power naval standard and of all that it implied was the fact that, as lately as the eighteen-seventies, British exports exceeded those of the two next greatest Powers combined. This disparity could not possibly endure. Great Britain possessed no monopoly of natural resources or capacities. Where she had led, other favourably situated countries having larger territories and larger populations could follow. By 1913 Great Britain, Germany and the United States ranked approximately equal as exporting countries. The total production of Germany was as great, that of the United States more than twice as great, as that of Britain.

[1] It is instructive to note that Hitler's New Order is a conscious and deliberate attempt to create for Nazi Germany by military force the same position which Great Britain, in exceptionally favourable natural conditions, gradually built up for herself in the nineteenth century. In twentieth-century conditions this position cannot be attained by Great Britain, by Germany or by any other Power.

These changes were quickly reflected in the international situation. The Boer War gave Britain an unwonted and transient sense of failure, and showed the rest of the world that she was less invincible and less invulnerable than had been supposed. The configuration of European politics was quickly re-shaped. The German threat to British supremacy took more obvious and more aggressive forms. The German naval programme, by compelling Great Britain to accelerate construction and to concentrate her fleet in the North Sea, was a grave embarrassment to Britain as a world Power. Great Britain replied by taking France into her defensive system, thereby revealing her weakness and insensibly modifying the whole basis of her policy. Meanwhile the picturesque career of Theodore Roosevelt hastened the process of drawing the United States closer to Europe. A basis of common tradition with Great Britain, as well as the fact that Germany was the spearhead of an attack on those free and liberal nineteenth-century ways of life which belonged as much to the American as to the British tradition, made it certain that in the new three-cornered distribution of world power, the United States would ultimately throw her weight on the British, not on the German, side.

Though Britain's unique supremacy in industrial power had disappeared before 1914, many of its adjuncts—especially her undisputed pre-eminence in finance and shipping—still remained almost intact. The war undermined these, and thus further weakened her position as a world Power. She was no longer the greatest producing or the greatest exporting country in the world. She was still, in virtue of her vast nineteenth-century investments, the largest creditor country. But she sold large blocks of her investments to the United States in order to finance the war; and the income from the remainder, instead of being reinvested abroad as in prosperous nineteenth-century days, was increasingly required in the period between the two wars to pay for the excess of imports over exports. In shipping she still led the way. But the overwhelming predominance which had once given her, with a few minor countries, a virtual monopoly of the carrying trade of the world belonged to a distant past. This decline in economic power was reflected in a falling-off of military strength. After 1918 a revival of the two-Power naval standard was not to be thought of; and the comparatively small margin of British superiority over the Japanese navy gave Japan an effective preponderance of power over Great Britain in the Far East. In the air, Great Britain did not attempt seriously to compete with other European Powers.

These conditions explain the most distressing and unsatisfactory feature of British foreign policy between the two wars —its failure to establish any proper coordination between ends and means. Public opinion expected, and Ministers too often encouraged it to expect, a policy which, if it were to be effective, implied both capacity and readiness to take immediate military action in almost any part of the world to enforce it. At no time after 1919 did Great Britain possess that comfortable and easy margin of military superiority which alone makes such a policy possible. The root of this discrepancy between policy and resources lay in the traditional character of the British outlook and in the obstinate refusal of the British people—admirable in many respects, yet dangerous—to recognise that Great Britain no longer occupied the same position of effortless supremacy which she had enjoyed almost throughout the nineteenth century. One thing which made it easy to entertain this comforting illusion was that the decline had been relative, not absolute. The standard of living was still rising. The general structure of British economic life was unaltered. In spite of unemployment—and the unemployed, having little political influence, were too often treated as a minor incident—Great Britain seemed to be still moving upward in the scale of prosperity. While Germany, having lost the war, knew that her international position had been compromised and took heroic steps to retrieve it, Great Britain relapsed easily into the comfortable belief that, having won the war, she was stronger and more impregnable than ever, and that no special exertions were called for on her part. It was readily assumed that the international status of Great Britain was unchanged, or had even been enhanced by the victory of 1918; and any qualms were silenced by vague perorations about the League of Nations or Anglo-American cooperation.

The illusion received added encouragement from a corresponding failure on the other side of the Atlantic to realise the fundamental transformation which had come over the international scene. At the end of the war it was assumed in many quarters as a matter of course that the hegemony of the world had passed from London to Washington. Max Weber writing in Germany in November 1918 believed that the world supremacy of America was "as inevitable as that of Rome in the ancient world after the Punic War".[1] But the transfer was not so quickly or easily effected. The United States were as reluctant to assume, as Great Britain was to abandon, the prerogatives of military and economic predominance. Hence there was, throughout the twenty years between the two wars, a constant failure on both sides to make the necessary adjustments to the changed situation. The Washington Conference proceeded on the tacit assumption that Great Britain and the United States were henceforth equal partners in world supremacy. But no political partnership between states is ever equal except in name (which helps to explain why the pretence of equality is always so rigidly kept up); and no provision was made, at Washington or elsewhere, for that effective leadership without which effective action is impossible. Hence Great Britain embarked on policies, at Geneva and elsewhere, which could not have been consistently maintained—and ought not to have been initiated—unless American power had been at the disposal of Great Britain; and the people of the United States, far from casting themselves for the rôle of world leadership, confined their policy for the most part to the defence of American interests, narrowly inter-

[1] Max Weber, *Gesammelte Politische Schriften*, p. 283.

preted. The period between the two wars was an interregnum in international leadership, due to the inability of Great Britain to perform her old function and the unwillingness of the United States to assume it.

Failure to recognise this fact led to misunderstandings, of which the most curious and most revealing arose over the affairs of the Far East. After 1931 Great Britain was patently unable by herself to curb the power of Japan. The United States, lacking the psychology of leadership and taking refuge in the irrelevant point that British financial interests in the Far East were larger than American, were unprepared for any concrete action. In 1932 American diplomacy by half-promises of sympathy and support busily encouraged Great Britain to act, and discredited the British Government for its failure to do so. But in 1937, when British diplomacy more cleverly declared itself ready to participate in any action initiated by the United States, the latter developed the same inertia as Great Britain had displayed five years earlier. From 1936 onwards American opinion severely condemned Great Britain for her failure to intervene effectively in the affairs of Europe. But this condemnation did not imply on the part of the United States any corresponding readiness to act themselves. After the present war broke out, many people in Great Britain found it difficult to understand the passionate desire of Americans to encourage and assist the British war effort, combined with an equally passionate determination not to involve their own country in the war. The psychological basis of the American attitude to international affairs for the past twenty years has been the conviction that Great Britain has a prescriptive and immemorial right and duty to take the lead where a strong lead is required, and that it is the business of good Americans to encourage and support Great Britain in so far as they approve what she is doing. Throughout the whole period, both Great Britain and the United States constantly attempted to pursue political and economic policies based on their respective nineteenth-century traditions and incommensurate with their present power; and confusion and mis-understanding were the inevitable result. The conception of a responsibility for leadership resting on the United States has hardly yet begun to take root.

Britain's Changed Status

Nothing can be more important, in framing Great Britain's post-war international policy, than to form as clear a view as possible of the changes in her status which the war will have brought about. One of the primary needs for readjustment will be psychological. At the close of the war, however favourable its issue, Great Britain will have little temptation to repeat the error of supposing that victory has enhanced her military or economic power. Behind the short-lived exultation of victory her self-confidence will have received a salutary shock. In 1918 it could reasonably be felt that British seapower had been the predominant factor in the defeat of the enemy. French military power had no doubt also been invaluable; but this could equally be counted on in any further struggle against Germany. The assistance of the United States in money, in material and in man-power had substantially eased the later stages of the war and perhaps hastened the victory. But there was no sufficient ground to suppose that victory could not ultimately have been achieved without it. The light-hearted boasting of irresponsible Americans that they had won the war provoked amusement rather than indignation. Now all this is changed. The assumption that French military and naval forces constituted a reliable and permanent adjunct of the British defences—a convenient assumption under which Great Britain concealed from herself the relative decline in her own power—has been shattered. It is clear, and has been frankly admitted, that Great Britain could not defeat Germany in the present war single-handed without American aid in the things which she most needs. The realisation of this fact will have psychological consequences whose character and extent can as yet hardly be estimated. In any event, one result of the change can hardly fail to be a temporary, if not a permanent, weakening of Great Britain and of Western Europe as a whole in relation to the United States and to the non-European world as a whole. Much will depend on the success of British policy at home in recovering a sense of moral purpose, in reorganising the life of the community and in increasing the national capacity for production. Much also will depend on the success of British foreign policy, on lines to be discussed in later chapters, in bringing about a tolerable economic reconstruction of Europe. But it is difficult to imagine any contingency—other than a complete German victory over the United States as well as over Great Britain—in which Europe or any European country would be likely to remain the undisputed centre of the world. The world of the twentieth century may eventually find its centre of gravity across the Atlantic, or it may continue to have many centres. But it will not, like the nineteenth-century world, have a single centre in Europe—or, more specifically, in London. The revolutionary change in Great Britain's status may be expressed by saying that, instead of being the one great world Power, she will become one of two or three, or perhaps more, world Powers.

This change will have economic symptoms and implications. The most important of these is that the world will no longer have a single economic and financial centre. It is still not clearly enough recognised that the nineteenth-century system of relatively free trade and a single international currency standard depended on the fact that a large proportion of the international trade of the world was negotiated and financed in London. Modern talk of "managed" trade and "managed" currencies sometimes carries with it the implication that nineteenth-century trade and nineteenth-century currency required no management, and that management is not only unnecessary but intrinsically undesirable. This is an illusion. The international trade of the nineteenth century was "managed" by the mer-

chants of Great Britain, who offered the readiest and most convenient market for a large proportion of the merchandise of the
world. The international currency was "managed" by the city
of London, which discounted bills, made loans and advances,
adjusted exchange values and arranged the necessary minimum
transfers of gold. London ceased to play this rôle in 1914, has
never regained it, and cannot now regain it. Failure to find some
other orderly method of conducting and financing international
trade, or even to perceive that some other method was required,
has been responsible for the economic and financial anarchy of
the ensuing period. After twenty-five years it is time to understand that international trade and finance must be organised on
a new basis and that nineteenth-century precedents are value-
less and misleading. Counsel has too long been darkened by idle
dreams of a return to free trade or a restoration of the gold
standard.

Another aspect of the change which will present peculiar difficulties to Great Britain—and not only to her—is the impending
radical modification of Great Britain's status as a creditor nation.
In the days of her nineteenth-century prosperity, Great Britain
helped to create markets for herself in almost every part of the
world by loans designed to promote the development of the
borrowing countries. Moreover, she did not normally, before
1914, retain the interest paid on these loans; she re-invested it in
the same or other overseas countries, thereby rendering the
whole process cumulative. This revenue did not therefore really
enter into the balance of payments, and British imports were
fully paid for by British exports and by receipts from British
shipping and other services. As we have already seen, the situation was modified by the war of 1914-18 in two important
ways. In the first place, Great Britain was compelled by the
necessity of financing purchases from abroad, especially from
the United States, to sell a substantial part of her overseas investments; and after 1918 the interest derived by Great Britain from
such investments never attained anything like its pre-1914 di-

mensions. Secondly, the interest received by Great Britain from her remaining overseas investments became for the first time after 1918 an indispensable item in her balance of payments. There was now a considerable gap between British imports on the one side and British exports and shipping and other services on the other. Interest on overseas investments was no longer re-invested abroad, except in small and diminishing amounts, but was used to bridge this gap.

The modification of Great Britain's economic status in the world after the present war will therefore be profound. She will have parted, directly or indirectly, with a large proportion of her most lucrative overseas investments, so that instead of an income from this source of £200,000,000 a year—the estimated figure for 1938—she may be able to count on not more than, say, £50,000,000 a year. Moreover, this revenue may be offset by obligations contracted during the war, so that Great Britain might conceivably end the war on balance as a debtor, not a creditor, nation. Even if this extreme contingency is not realised, there is no doubt that Great Britain after the war, in order to make her balance of payments meet, will have either to import considerably less than she did before the war or to export con-siderably more. Some fall in imports might not prove incom-patible with the maintenance of the 1938 standard of living. But it should be borne in mind that any such reduction in foreign trade would react detrimentally on our shipping and on the revenue derived from it, and thereby aggravate the problem of making both ends meet; and it is difficult to believe that if the reduction were at all considerable, the general level of prosper-ity would not suffer. Great Britan will therefore be faced, if her standard of living is to be maintained, with the difficult task of increasing her exports at a time when a large number of other countries both in Europe and elsewhere are better equipped than ever to produce many of those goods which they formerly im-ported from Great Britain. There are only two ways of escape from this dilemma. Britain can only regain her prosperity if she develops new lines of production, and thus puts herself once more in the forefront of the producing world; and she can only regain her prosperity if the standard of living, and consequently consumption, all over the world, undergoes a substantial increase and thus provides once more that expanding market which was the basis of nineteenth-century well-being. This means in practice two things. Great Britain will have to produce more than before in order to maintain—and a *fortiori* to increase —her present standards of living; and she will have to regard rising standards of living in other countries as a matter of direct interest to herself.

This change in Britain's position will also have its repercussions in every country whose trade with Great Britain has been an important factor in its economic life—that is to say, throughout a large part of the world. Of late years it has sometimes appeared to be taken as a matter of course in commercial negotiations between Great Britain and other countries that the trade balance should be "passive" for Great Britain and "active" for the other country, this condition being the natural reflexion of Great Britain's position as the major creditor nation and purveyor of shipping and financial services. In the decade before the war, some countries had begun to realise that the only way to maintain a market for their own produce in Great Britain was themselves to buy more British goods. But the economic and psychological strain of readjustment to a new situation in which other countries will be unable to sell to British importers substantially more than they buy from British exporters is bound to be considerable.[1] It will be greatest of all in the United States, which will, according to all reasonable expectation, replace Great Britain as the principal creditor country and the most important financial centre in the world. It is difficult to see how

---

[1] It is unnecessary to raise here the issue of bilateral and multilateral trade. Multilateral trading would alter the incidence in particular cases, but would not affect the basic fact that other countries as a whole will in future have to buy from Great Britain almost as much as they sell to her.

disaster can be avoided unless the people of the United States adjust themselves fairly rapidly to the view that this position can only be maintained, as Britain maintained it in the nineteenth century, by offering a large and expanding market to the products of the rest of the world. But it should be recognised that such an adjustment will involve a profound modification of tradition, an abandonment of deep-seated prejudices and, above all, an unusual readiness to over-ride sectional interests, in a country where a high degree of natural economic self-sufficiency has hitherto made foreign trade seem relatively unimportant.

The Rôle of the United States

Of all countries affected by the changed status of Great Britain, the United States will be affected most. The problems of adjustment confronting Great Britain are matched by problems of adjustment equally difficult and delicate confronting the United States. Both sets of problems are inter-connected, being often merely opposite facets of the same situation. There is a dangerous tendency in some quarters to assume that the close cooperation and consciousness of common interests and policy established between the two countries during the war will remain unimpaired in the post-war period; in other quarters an equally dangerous tendency to assume a return to conditions approximately the same as those prevailing before the war. Neither of these prognostications is likely to be fulfilled. The end of the war will bring to light again many of the rivalries and jealousies temporarily suppressed by the sense of common danger and common effort. But the whole picture will have been transformed, both by the tremendous experience through which both countries will have passed and by the changed character, psychological and economic, of the relations between them; and while some old problems will have disappeared, new ones will be found to have arisen. The problems of readjustment to a new status which will confront both countries after the war will present themselves mainly in the concrete form of problems of Anglo-American relations. If the position of Great Britain as a world Power has since 1919 been dependent in large part on the character of her relations with the United States, this will be still more conspicuously true after the present war.

Actually as well as potentially, the United States will almost certainly emerge from the war as the strongest world Power. The head of the Office for Production Management recently declared, perhaps with a conscious echo of the former British two-Power standard, that "the United States can out-produce any other two nations in the world".[1] The claim is probably not exaggerated. Doubt exists not of the capacity of the United States to lead the world, but of their readiness to do so. There has hitherto been a marked reluctance on the part of Americans to admit that the position attained by them entails any responsibilities save, perhaps, those of a humanitarian order. Nor are the difficulties purely psychological. The spoken or unspoken assumption, which underlies many discussions of this subject on both sides of the Atlantic, that the United States are destined to play in the twentieth century the rôle of world leadership played by Great Britain in the nineteenth century is wholly uncritical and requires careful scrutiny.

When Great Britan rose to unchallenged world supremacy a century ago, she had a 300-year-old seafaring tradition, territories under her rule in every continent, an industry in the early stages of an unprecedented expansion, a low degree of self-sufficiency in terms of the requirements of modern civilisation, a politically mature governing class, a rapidly increasing population and a static and weak landed interest. These interconnected factors conditioned British development and the character of British power. Not one of them is present in the United States to-day. Here we have a vast continuous territory

---

[1] *The Times*, August 5, 1941.

favoured by an unusually high degree of self-sufficiency,[1] a strong continental, isolationist and specifically anti-European tradition, a rigid constitution which impedes prompt action, a nearly stationary population, a powerful agricultural interest and an industry which, while still possessing an immense potential capacity for development, is already haunted by the same problems which everywhere confront modern industrialised society. These factors will clearly have an important bearing on the prospects and conditions of American world leadership. Will the desire persist to build up and maintain an overwhelmingly powerful navy, and to use it to police the world? Will there be a regular outflow of Americans ready and eager to play their part in developing and governing the backward regions of the world? Will the American Constitution be so modified, either in the letter or in its practical working, as to make it possible for the United States to have an active foreign policy? Will the United States offer an extensive market for the products of the rest of the world and thereby become a great centre of international commerce? Will American financiers or the American Government be content to become the bankers of the world, lending far and wide on a long- and short-term basis in order to keep the machinery of world finance running smoothly? Few people would confidently answer any of these questions—much less all of them—in the affirmative. Yet if they are not so answered, it becomes rash to speak of a twentieth-century American leadership of the world comparable in character to nineteenth-century British leadership. History is never content merely to change the actors and to repeat the drama. American leadership may develop on some different pattern peculiar to itself.

Two essential issues of foreign policy will confront the Amer-

1 The United States provide the solitary instance of a country combining a high degree of self-sufficiency with a high standard of living. The only important countries which rival the United States in self-sufficiency are low-standard countries: Soviet Russia, India and China.

ican people after the war, one political, the other economic.
Will they undertake permanent political and military obligations outside the Western hemisphere? and will they open their
markets to foreign trade freely enough to make the United
States the commercial and financial centre of the world? The
answer to these questions is difficult, speculative and liable to be
affected by contingencies which may occur before the end of
the war, including direct American participation in military
operations. Nevertheless, the future policy and status of Great
Britain as a world Power is so much dependent on the answer
that some consideration of them must be attempted.

The political question calls for two preliminary caveats. Two
qualities characteristic of British politics appear in a magnified
form in American political life. In the first place, a genuine strain
of idealism is matched by an underlying shrewdness and caution, so that while idealists are listened to, applauded and supported both morally and materially, caution plays a far larger
part in the eventual decision than these demonstrations might
have led the onlooker to expect. It is a source of strength as well
as of weakness that in America, more than in Great Britain, any
crank can obtain a friendly hearing if he presents his case at-
tractively enough. The popularity recently enjoyed by schemes
for the incorporation of Great Britain and the British Dominions in the American Federation or for still wider unions
with foreign states should not mislead the observer into taking
them seriously. Secondly, American public opinion shares in an
enhanced degree British ignorance of political conditions abroad
and more specifically in Europe. There is a constant liability to
be gulled by special pleaders, and a constant inclination to assume that any state of affairs which is regarded by Americans,
living several thousand miles away, as right and fair can be
brought about and maintained through sheer goodwill and
common sense, and without imposing any kind of obligation on
those well-meaning Americans who sponsor it. Hence Ameri-

can foreign policy, like British foreign policy, often appears highly irresponsible. Causes are supported, or solutions advocated, which cannot in the long run be upheld without the application of force on a large scale. Yet this by no means implies that American opinion will be in favour of using American power to uphold them. One of the gravest dangers ahead is that American influence will be employed to frame a peace settlement of a character which could be maintained only by American power, and that American power will not in fact be available to maintain it.

A further danger arising from the remoteness of the United States from Europe is a lack of synchronisation in material conditions and in trends of thought. Woodrow Wilson's influence in 1919 was, taken for all in all, reactionary because the contemporary American political philosophy which he brought with him to Europe had belonged to the Europe of fifty years earlier and no longer fitted the Europe of his own day. The world since then has grown smaller, and continents are drawing nearer to one another. But North America has not yet felt the full blast of the revolution which is sweeping over Europe and is not yet alive to some of its implications. Hence American opinion is still inclined to express itself in the nineteenth-century language of liberal democracy, national self-determination and economic *laissez-faire*. In domestic affairs, political action has been far in advance of political terminology. In international affairs, President Roosevelt's leadership may achieve the same result. But while nearly all Americans ardently desire to see greater unity in Europe and frequently express surprise and indignation at the lack of it, the unguarded and unqualified reiteration by leading Americans of nineteenth-century slogans like national liberation and self-determination sometimes seems calculated to hamper the chances of bringing it about.

The crux of the question is, therefore, not so much what international solutions will be supported by the American Gov-

ernment or by American opinion, but whether any commitments will be assumed to impose and maintain these solutions.
Promises to consult have been too often given, and too often
proved ineffective, to have any substantial value. Nothing but
precise commitments, involving preparatory measures taken in
common, will suffice. There seems a greater chance that these
may be undertaken in the Far East than in Europe; but even so
much is highly problematical. It is true that there has been a
mighty swing away from isolationism, and that the expected
reaction after the war will not wholly nullify its effects. But
these effects are more likely to be seen in a development of
American spheres of interest and activity than in commitments
to other countries, which are doubtfully compatible with the
requirements of the constitution. By far the most hopeful symptom of more active American participation in world affairs is
the acquisition of military bases in foreign, and especially
British, territory. If this process is extended, and if the bases
are retained after the war, willingness to employ American
armed forces to defend them may be assumed; and the "mixing
up" of British and American interests will have assumed some
degree of permanence. This line of advance is more hopeful
than the quest for contingent political commitments which,
if obtained, will be hedged about with uncertainties and qualifications calculated to make them meaningless and ineffective.
The present war, following on that of 1914-18, seems to most
European, and to many American, observers to have demonstrated that the Western hemisphere is henceforth inevitably
involved in any major European upheaval. Increasing recognition of this fact is likely to make the United States more ready
and eager to play the rôle, and to develop the military strength,
of a Great Power. But there may be the same reluctance as there
was in nineteenth-century Britain to interpret this rôle in terms
of formal or permanent commitments on the European continent.

The question whether the markets of the United States will be thrown open to international trade is equally difficult and perhaps still more fundamental; for American policies outside the Western hemisphere will be dictated in some part by the extent of her commercial and financial interests. The dilemma is plain enough. The terms of the "Lease-Lend" Act betray a lively appreciation of the embarrassments of a country seeking export markets but unable to name any imports which it would be disposed to receive in payment. At the end of the war the American tradition of generosity will probably allow the American Government and American philanthropists to finance exports of supplies required in Europe and elsewhere for relief and reconstruction without any serious question of repayment. But this process cannot be prolonged indefinitely, and the dilemma must then be faced. It will crop up in several forms. The simplest form of all will be the question whether the interest of those Americans, including the American Government, to whom debts are owed from abroad will predominate over the interest of those Americans who want protection against an influx of foreign goods in payment of those debts. The dilemma will appear in other forms in the question whether American importers will purchase agricultural products from the great South American states in payment for the manufactured goods which American exporters wish to sell there, and in the question whether American importers will purchase European manufactures in payment for the agricultural products, including cotton and tobacco, which American exporters wish to sell to Europe. The United States are in the uniquely embarrassing position of being equally interested in agricultural and in industrial exports.

Where nearly everything depends on a balance of conflicting interests within the United States, the outsider will hardly care to hazard an opinion on the probable outcome. It may suffice to record a few significant factors which will play a rôle, though not necessarily a decisive one, in the future course of American economic policy:

(1) Though the United States are the greatest exporting country in the world, the proportion of the national wealth derived from foreign trade, and the proportion of the population dependent on it, is far lower than in Great Britain or in many other countries: the influence exercised by interests predominantly concerned in foreign trade is therefore relatively small;

(2) Financial interests, especially those concerned with foreign investments, are under a cloud, and can only exercise influence by indirect means;

(3) The working of the constitution makes a positive economic policy, like every other kind of positive foreign policy, extremely difficult: for example, the agricultural interests in the Senate, where they are heavily over-represented,[1] may be powerful enough to veto agricultural imports from the Argentine, but not powerful enough to force on the industrialists the concessions necessary to increase agricultural exports to Europe;

(4) Apart from constitutional machinery, the American tradition, while supporting a high tariff, regards *laissez-faire* in other respects with superstitious veneration. In domestic affairs, large departures have been made from the hallowed principle. In international affairs, the veneration appears undiminished: for instance, a fanatical and purposeless devotion to the obsolete doctrine of most-favoured-nation treatment has virtually limited the Cordell Hull trade agreements to commodities of which the other party is the sole or main supplier.

[1] Not more than one-third of the population of the United States is dependent on agriculture, and this proportion is probably decreasing. But agricultural interests predominate in some thirty-four out of the forty-eight states of the Union, each of which elects two senators.

These handicaps in the way of a positive economic policy may
be overcome by strong and determined leadership. But the issues confronting American statesmanship in this field are of
grave import for the United States themselves, for Great Britain
and for the rest of the world.

The Rôle of Great Britain

The discussion of Anglo-American relations, while it remains
a capital problem of British post-war policy, cannot be carried
at the present stage to any conclusion; for too much depends on
factors which are largely beyond British control. But the more
the underlying conditions and psychological difficulties of readjustment are understood on both sides of the Atlantic, the
less likelihood there will be of a recrudescence of dangerous
jealousies and frictions. The same is true in the main of British
relations with the other countries of the English-speaking
world; for most of the same forces have been at work, though
in a modified degree. The second world war in a quarter of a
century has for the second time rallied the British Dominions
spontaneously to the support of the mother country, and provided powerful evidence that they too cannot afford to disinterest themselves in the destinies of Europe. On the other
hand, strategic interests will tend in the future to strengthen the
ties of three at least of the Dominions—Canada, Australia and
New Zealand—with the United States. Financial interests may
point in the same direction. Little has been said in public about
war-time financial arrangements between Great Britain and the
Dominions. Canada may well emerge from the war as a creditor
of Great Britain, though she will doubtless remain a debtor of
the United States; and it is not impossible that a common interest
in gold may forge new links between the United States and
South Africa. It is perhaps unlikely that Great Britain will be
in a position to resume lending to the Dominions on anything
like the old scale. But she will be able, if she pursues a wise

policy, to offer the same extensive market as of old to Dominions produce—a market which neither the United States nor any other country can readily provide—though it will have to be recognised in the Dominions that the days of an overwhelmingly "active" trade balance with the mother country are past. Post-war relations between Great Britain and the Dominions present a less difficult problem than relations between Great Britain and the United States, both because the required readjustment will be less radical and because mutual understanding is closer and more deeply rooted in tradition. But the two problems will be similar in kind, arising as they do from shifts in the balance of military and economic power and complicated as they are by many cross-currents of sentiment and tradition. Moreover they will react on each other; for they are in a sense merely two aspects of the same problem—the organisation of the English-speaking world. But it is important to remember that the solution of this problem must be sought in the first instance in the realm not of constitution-making, but of military, economic and psychological readjustment.

Beyond the confines of the English-speaking world the course of British policy can be more confidently charted. In the Far East, it is true, Great Britain's rôle must on the whole remain a subsidiary one. She cannot act effectively there unless the full weight of the United States is thrown into the scale, and she may fairly expect to leave the main initiative to Washington. But elsewhere it would be fatal for her, both politically and economically, to have the air merely of waiting to see what the United States will propose. In large parts of Europe and Africa and in the Middle East, Great Britain—if she sets a wise course and recovers that sense of a mission which alone can preserve her from decay—will continue to exercise a rôle of leadership and pre-eminence. How much she can achieve will no doubt be influenced, here too, by the amount of moral and material support which she receives from the rest of the English-speaking world. But a clear and decided British policy will make the active cooperation of the United States and the Dominions more, not less, certain. The tradition of waiting for a British lead is still firmly ingrained in American minds; and almost everywhere a strong British lead will be welcomed, not resented, by the other English-speaking countries. This is particularly true of Europe—a continent against which Americans retain all their prejudices and where they are particularly reluctant to assume responsibilities except of a humanitarian order. Europe is still the danger zone. The future power and prestige of Great Britain are most intimately involved in her handling of the European problem.

CHAPTER 8

BRITAIN AND EUROPE

THE conclusion recorded at the end of the last chapter that
Great Britain should be prepared to play an active rôle in post-
war Europe will be contested; and the present chapter will be
devoted to an examination of it. It may be taken for granted
that there will be after the war a body of opinion in Great
Britain—how strong cannot be guessed in advance— in favour
of restricting to a minimum the part of the world with which
Britain should actively concern herself. According to this view,
Great Britain would retire from active participation in European affairs, and seek to establish a limited kind of world order
based on cooperation between the British Empire and Commonwealth of Nations and the United States of America, thereby
maintaining her status as a world Power but not as a European
Power. It will be argued that an English-speaking group could
rely on a unity of political tradition and thought which would
give it a far higher degree of real, as opposed to formal, cohesion
than would be enjoyed by any wider combination; and it would
be cemented and defended by a tacit or overt naval alliance between Great Britain and the United States. This conception is
the modern form of the doctrine of splendid isolation. More
emphasis than the Victorians would have thought necessary is
laid nowadays on the importance of close identity of policy
with the United States. But the negative aspect and principal
attraction of the doctrine—the rejection of any direct interest
in the European continent—remains constant.

Splendid Isolation?

It would be rash to minimise the strength of the feelings, and the force of the arguments, which can be mustered in support of this view. The familiar allegation that modern inventions, especially military aviation and long-range artillery, have deprived Britain of her former insular position and made her more essentially part of the continent of Europe than she was before 1914 has been overdone. There was never an idyllic age in which Britain enjoyed complete immunity from risk of invasion from Europe. Fear of invasion was as keenly felt in 1803 and 1859 as in 1914 or 1940-41. The invention of steam was held to portend the end of British insularity in exactly the same way as the invention of the aeroplane nearly a hundred years later.[1] But these fears have hitherto proved unsubstantial. The fact that in the war of 1914-18, for the first time in several centuries, people were killed by enemy action on the soil of Great Britain was observed as a noteworthy fact, but does not appear to have influenced the subsequent British attitude towards Europe. Whether the fact that the same thing has happened on a much larger scale in the present war will exercise a stronger influence and produce any fundamental change of outlook, is a matter of speculation. It would be imprudent to count on such a result. If the war ends without any even partially successful attempt at the invasion of this island, the sense of secure insularity, however illusory, may be reinforced rather than weakened by the experience.

Moreover, one sequel of the war, though not perhaps an immediate one, is almost certain to be a reaction of distaste against Europe as a whole, and a popular inclination to isolate Britain from any superfluous contact with so intractable a reality. This

---

[1] "Steam has infinitely multiplied our intercourse with Europe", wrote the future Lord Salisbury in 1860, "and has provided facilities for an invader which none of us are as yet able accurately to estimate" (Gwendolen Cecil, *Life of Robert Marquis of Salisbury*, i, p. 302).

inclination may well be enhanced by the presence in this country of a large number of refugees from different European countries, all claiming the support of Britain for their respective and often contradictory projects and ambitions. The habit of regarding the British Isles as something separate from, and alien to the traditions of, the European continent is deep-seated and of long standing; and it may be further strengthened after the war by a still more marked reaction of a similar kind in the Dominions and the United States. It will be urged with some plausibility that detachment from Europe is a condition of closer cooperation with the English-speaking world overseas, and that Great Britain is faced by a choice between this world and the continent of Europe as a choice between two incompatibles.

The probable strength of this movement makes imperative a searching re-examination of the whole problem of Britain's relation to Europe. If detachment from Europe is an impracticable policy for Great Britain—far less practicable at the present time than it was in the nineteenth century—then it is of the highest importance to bring home this situation in the clearest possible terms to opinion in Great Britain and in the English-speaking world overseas. There are, in fact, cogent reasons why Britain cannot, without prejudice to her vital interests, wash her hands of the European continent and refuse the leading rôle which it will certainly be open to her to play in its post-war reorganisation. These reasons are both military and economic.

The Balance of Power

The factor which has profoundly modified the military situation of the island of Britain situated on the western confines of Europe is not, as is commonly said, her own increased vulnerability to modern weapons—this point is open to question, and defence may have developed as rapidly as offence—but the changed situation in Europe due to the increasing size of the unit of power. As has been shown in an earlier chapter, both the military factor and the economic factor, on which military power has come more and more to depend, are rendering obsolete the small and even the medium-sized independent unit. The size of the units which count effectively in international politics grows steadily larger. There is no longer room in Europe to-day for those three or four important and strong countries whose more or less equal rivalries enabled Great Britain in the past to secure herself through the policy of the balance of power. Much nonsense has been talked in recent years about the balance of power. But the confusion of thought resulting from the attempt to brand it as a morally reprehensible policy has been less serious than the confusion resulting from the assumption that it is a policy which can be applied at all times and in all circumstances. The principal military reason why Great Britain can no longer, consistently with her own safety, abandon Europe to its own devices and retire into a non-European world order dominated by the English-speaking countries is that the balance of power in Europe has hopelessly broken down.

The recent history of this familiar doctrine is worth some attention. For three centuries, British policy in Europe was, put concisely, to keep Europe at arm's length but at the same time to prevent Europe from coming under the effective control of a single Power. During and after the peace settlement of 1815 she achieved this result, as she had done many times before, through the balance of power. She was concerned to see Austria, Prussia and Russia sufficiently strong to provide a guarantee against any fresh outbreak of aggression by France. She was equally conscious that, if France were rendered totally powerless, these three Powers might themselves become strong enough to destroy the possibility of any balance. She therefore insisted on the comparatively lenient treatment of France, and afterwards opposed the claim of the members of the Holy Alliance to constitute themselves dictators of Europe. By holding the balance between conflicting groups of European Powers Great Britain succeeded throughout the remainder of the nineteenth century in averting any serious threat to herself from the Continent and in preventing the outbreak of any general European war. This was no doubt a self-regarding policy. But the familiar charge that Great Britain for her own advantage kept Europe in a state of permanent disunion would be more convincing if there had been more conspicuous evidence at any time of a desire for unity among the European countries themselves.

This period came to an end with the conclusion of the Anglo-French Entente in 1903. The essence of the balance of power was that there should be in fact, irrespective of the attitude of Britain, a tolerably even balance between rival Continental groups. So long as this existed, Britain could from time to time throw in her weight on one side or the other to prevent the balance from being disturbed, while remaining permanently uncommitted to either side; and the impartiality implied in this permanent detachment from Continental rivalries was an essential part of the policy of the balance. By the end of the nineteenth century the state of affairs which made this policy possible and successful was rapidly disappearing. The condition expressed in the old Latin motto of the balance, *Cui adhaerer praeest*, was no longer fulfilled. Germany, well organised, highly industrialised and with Austria-Hungary as a pliable tool, had become more than a match for the rival group consisting of France and Russia. Britain could no longer readjust the balance by a slight inclination to the weaker side, while retaining her traditional aloofness. She was now compelled by Germany's strength to throw in her whole weight, to enter the arena, and herself to become a member of one of the rival groups. For this reason the Anglo-French Entente was not a guarantee of peace, but a portent of war. It was the end of the policy of the balance of power as practised by nineteenth-century Britain. The policy had broken down because its essential condition, a fairly even balance of forces on the Continent itself, was no longer present.

The years after 1919 witnessed a probably half-unconscious attempt on the part of Britain to revive the defunct policy of the balance. Both France and Britain attempted to give concrete shape to the vague ideal of a League of Nations by fitting it to the needs of their traditional policies. For France, the League of Nations was a group of European countries (with some irrelevant non-European appendages) encircling Germany and holding her firmly in the fetters of Versailles. For Britain, the League was an instrument for resuscitating the balance of power. Germany on the one hand, and France and her satellites on the other, seemed to constitute that approximately equal balance of forces which would permit Britain to resume her nineteenth-century rôle of impartial aloofness and adjustment. The Locarno Treaty was the highwater mark of this conception, and was greeted with an enthusiasm accorded to no other achievement of British foreign policy in the inter-war period. Both France and Britain failed—and for the same reason. The belief that France and her minor satellites constituted an effective counter-weight to Germany—the presupposition on which both French and British policies were based—was pure illusion. France and her allies had not the strength to maintain an effective encirclement of Germany. Britain could no longer successfully pursue her nineteenth-century policy because the even balance of Continental forces was not, as she supposed, attainable. In the years after Locarno, she found herself compelled more and more often to throw in her weight on the French side; and after 1934, she openly reverted to the policy of the Anglo-French Entente. Finally, this too broke in her hand; for France was no longer equal to the rôle of a Great Power.

If Britain is to profit, at the end of this war, by the experience of the past, it is imperative that the past should be clearly understood. At no period of her history has Britain been able to disinterest herself altogether in the affairs of the Continent. The period in which she came nearest to doing so—the so-called period of "splendid isolation"—was the period in which she could successfully practise the policy of the balance of power precisely because the rival Continental Powers were in fact more or less equally balanced. This condition no longer exists and, so far as can be judged, is unlikely to recur. The policy of 1919 was based on the underlying assumption that Germany's power could be balanced by the combined power of an agglomeration of weaker states headed by France. The assumption was false. Its acceptance by Britain was the product of wishful thinking born of a desire to resuscitate the nineteenth-century balance of power. The possibility of restoring the balance did not exist after 1919; and British policy, based on a false premiss, ended in disaster.

Will there be any chance, at the conclusion of the present war, of reviving the defunct balance of power in such a way as to enable Great Britain to resume with safety her detached and effortless nineteenth-century attitude towards Europe? This is the hope of British isolationists; and popular discussions suggest that, as after 1919, a good deal of wishful thinking is still current on the subject. The initial assumption is generally made that Germany will be permanently weakened by dismemberment or forced disarmament. How far this is a desirable or a practicable policy will be considered in the next chapter. For the moment it is merely necessary to note that the permanent weakening of Germany, whether desirable or not, cannot be effected by a single stroke, but would require the permanent application of force on a large scale to maintain it. Such a policy has in fact little resemblance to the old-fashioned doctrine of the balance, which implied the co-existence on the European continent of a number of equally independent and more or less equally matched states. But the fundamental issue which it raises is much the same. Is there likely to be after the war, on the continent of Europe, a Power or combination of Powers possessing the strength and the will either to keep a penalised and partitioned Germany in permanent subjection or to act as a balance to a strong and independent Germany? If the answer is in the affirmative, Great Britain may hope to retire once more into the splendid and comfortable isolation of the nineteenth century. If not, Great Britain must for her own safety face from the outset the responsibility of playing an active part in European affairs.

The prospect of creating this convenient counterweight to the menace of German power on the Continent without the constant and active intervention of Great Britain depends on the realisation of one or more of three hypotheses, which must be examined in turn. These are: (*a*) that France can be restored to the status of a great military Power, (*b*) that a number of small Powers, grouped together by a League of Nations, a series of regional federations or alliances or some other suitable device, can form a combination solid and powerful enough to maintain or reinforce the balance, and (*c*) that the full return of Soviet Russia to the European family of nations will re-establish the balance in the form familiar before 1914.

(*a*) That the reinstatement of France as a Great Power should be a hope entertained by many Englishmen is comprehensible. But before this hope can be treated as an assumption capable of forming a sound basis for policy, it requires to be coolly and critically examined. The fall of France in June 1940, however unexpected it may have been at the moment when it occurred, was not an isolated and inexplicable accident, but the culmination of a process which had been developing for three-quarters of a century. The year 1870 transferred military supremacy on the Continent from Paris to Berlin. In 1917 British and American support saved France from disaster by a hair's-breadth. In 1940 the relative decline of France in face of Germany had gone too far to be arrested any longer. It is unnecessary to consider how far this decline should be attributed to France's relative deficiency in industrial resources, to the failure of her population to expand, or to the persistence of an individualist tradition which did not conduce to the efficient large-scale organisation either of political or of economic life. Whatever importance may be assigned to particular causes, the whole process was clearly too deep-seated and too radical to justify any hopes of a prompt reversal.[1] It would be the height of rashness to assume that France, broken, discredited and divided against herself, can recover within a single generation the strength, the unity and the determination to restrain the power of Germany. Nor is there any reason to suppose that France—even were she much stronger than seems likely—would have the will to serve as a bulwark against renascent German aggressiveness. Recent events have revealed a deep-seated vein of anti-British feeling in France. A British victory will no doubt once more drive it underground—as it remained partially latent throughout the period of the Anglo-French Entente. But to repeat the mistake of ignoring it would be another case of wishful thinking. Nor would it be wise to underestimate the strength of disagreeable feelings left behind in this country by the surrender of June 1940. To build up friendly relations with France after the war will be a slow and necessary task. To rely on a revived alliance with France as a cardinal factor in British policy after the war would be reckless folly. So far as real military power is concerned, it would be prudent to count on something like a vacuum on the continent of Europe between the western frontiers of Germany and the English Channel or the Atlantic seaboard. Should Great Britain decide to disinterest herself in the Continent, this vacuum would eventually be filled by Ger-

[1] A well-known British well-wisher of France wrote recently: "Even were the French people to rally to the standard of Free France and to play their part in ridding their own country and Europe of the Nazi and Fascist curse, the memory of the men of Vichy, as voluptuaries of humiliation and devotees of dishonour, would prevent many minds from accepting French guidance in European reconstruction. France would still have to work out her own salvation, to save her own soul before it could again illumine Europe with the radiance of its light" (Wickham Steed in *Free Europe*, November 15, 1940, p. 11.)

many, whatever temporary measures might have been taken to weaken or destroy her power.

(*b*) The notion that a group or groups of smaller Powers could be used to restrain a weakened Germany and to hold the balance against her entered largely into the conception of the League of Nations and especially into the French view of that institution. Its fundamental fallacy lies in the consideration, developed at length in a previous chapter, that military and economic conditions have destroyed the reality of the independence of small states, and that these states can play no effective rôle except through military and economic cooperation, deliberately organised and permanently practised, with a Great Power. This result cannot be achieved through the cooperation of however large a number of minor countries with one another, since the nucleus of effective power is lacking. Moreover, it is notorious that, reluctant as are most of the smaller countries to accept the leadership of a Great Power, they find it still more difficult to cooperate with one another. The example of the countries of Central and South-Eastern Europe during the past twenty years, and more recently of the Scandinavian countries, is conclusive evidence on this point. No lesson of recent history is more cogent, or more important to bear in mind, than the futility of attempting to use a combination of minor Powers as a counterweight to Germany.

While, however, these conditions are of general application, the position of the highly developed small countries of Western Europe and of the less developed small countries of Eastern Europe differs in some respects. In the small countries of Western Europe, there was widespread loyalty to a somewhat vague conception of the League of Nations as an impartial guarantee of peace. But the more precise conception of the League as a defensive coalition against Germany under French leadership was decisively rejected. It is conceivable that opinion in these countries may have been sufficiently modified by the present war to induce them to enter into a permanent coalition under active British leadership. But it may be taken for granted that, if this leadership were withheld, these countries would contain in themselves no focus of resistance to a revival of German power or to its advance to the western shores of Europe.

In Eastern Europe, the conception of a combination of smaller Powers as a counterweight against Germany is still more chimerical. No part of the peace settlement of 1919 proved more hollow than this. From the critical moment when Germany began to regain her strength, she found no difficulty at all in playing off Poles and Slovaks against Czechs, Hungarians against Roumanians, Bulgarians against Greeks and Croats against Serbs. Only the most hardened of wishful thinkers, or those most ignorant of conditions in Eastern Europe, can be deaf to the lesson of experience—not confined to recent history —that these countries will readily accept the patronage of a strong Power in order to pay off old scores against their neighbours. There is no reason to suppose that this experience would not be repeated. Moreover, Eastern Europe presents a special problem owing to the presence there of another Continental Great Power besides Germany. In 1919 some of the smaller countries were deliberately supported and encouraged to aggrandise themselves in the hope that they would constitute a barrier between Germany and Russia—the notorious policy of the *cordon sanitaire*. This unintelligent policy had the result, which might have been expected, of creating a strong bond of sympathy between Germany and Russia. A return to it would inevitably produce the same result; for it is presumptuous folly to suppose that any external power could in the long run maintain in that area a settlement distasteful to Russia as well as to Germany. If the countries of Eastern Europe are to free themselves from the domination of Germany, it is essential for them to act in close and willing cooperation with Soviet Russia, and to reserve for Russia a determining voice in the eventual organisation of that region. The problem is the same which we shall encounter everywhere of reconciling the rights of national self-determination with the necessary obligations of military and economic interdependence. But to attempt to organise these countries independently of Russia as a bulwark against Germany would be a fatal policy.[1] It would antagonise Russia; it would recreate the Russian-German alliance; and it would break down under the first strain with consequences disastrous to both countries themselves and probably also to the peace of the world.

(c) The third assumption which requires examination is that Soviet Russia can be used as a counterweight to Germany, and the balance of power in Europe thus conveniently restored without the need of permanent intervention by Great Britain. The temptation to indulge in this form of speculation will be particularly strong if, as may well occur, Russia is felt to have played a large and decisive part in the final defeat of Germany. Soviet Russia enjoys considerable prestige if not as the birth-place, at any rate as the first testing-ground, of the modern revolution; and she is a country of almost unlimited natural re-sources. But just as there was a tendency before June 1941 to underestimate her military capacity, so there may be a danger of exaggerating it in the closing stages of the war. Fifty years hence Russia may have become a great industrial Power. But at pres-ent, Russian industrial development judged by Western stand-ards is still limited; Russia is relatively weak in skilled industrial man-power in the Western sense of the term; her capacity for sustained military action beyond the limits of Russian or former Russian territory remains to be proved. If Great Britain were to retire from Europe, it cannot safely be assumed that Soviet Russia, with such support as she might muster on the Continent, would be permanently strong enough to hold Germany in sub-jection or to counter-balance German power.

Nor is there any reason to suppose that Russia herself would be prepared to play such a rôle, however convenient it might

---

[1] Such a policy was widely advocated before Soviet Russia's entry into the war and may be heard of again. Its dangers must be strongly emphasised.

be for Great Britain. Historical precedents must be invoked with caution. But the study of Russo-German relations during the last two centuries reveals some features which may be regarded as constant even in the much changed conditions of to-day. Russia and Germany have some common, and some conflicting, interests which tend to rise alternately to the surface. They are rivals for the exercise of a predominant influence in Eastern Europe. But a common interest unites them against any other Power which attempts to play a leading rôle there. This consideration should deter Great Britain from any ambition to intervene directly in this region. But it should also serve as a warning that Russia, if left without any support in Europe other than that of minor Powers, might well find a basis of accommodation with Germany. Another important element in the situation which is sometimes over-looked is that Russia, like Great Britain, is not a purely European Power and that her policy cannot be determined solely by European factors. If Great Britain is ready to take her share of responsibility for a new order in Western Europe, there is a reasonable prospect of securing the whole-hearted cooperation of Russia in Eastern Europe. But it would be a dangerous miscalculation to assume that, if Great Britain withdrew from Europe altogether, Soviet Russia would continue to act as a watchdog over Germany, so re-establishing the policy of the balance and ushering in a period of durable peace on the Continent.

The three assumptions commonly made in support of the belief in a resuscitation of the European balance of power are thus all devoid of solid foundation; and Great Britain must courageously face the fact that the policy of the balance is irretrievably bankrupt. The situation is no longer that which existed throughout the greater part of the nineteenth century when the Continental Great Powers were effectively balanced against one another. We can no longer entertain the illusion of the nineteen-twenties that France and a group of minor Powers, whether associated by an old-fashioned alliance or by the newfangled device of collective security, can provide an effective balance against Germany. Soviet Russia may be expected to play an active part in the building of a new order in Eastern Europe, but cannot be counted on to bear the whole burden of maintaining the balance against Germany. No other Great Power enters into the picture. Once British influence and power were withdrawn, the essence of Hitler's New Order would reappear in some altered guise, and Europe west of the Russian frontier would coalesce sooner or later into a single military and economic unit of enormous concentrated power. Even if Great Britain could form with the English-speaking peoples overseas a unit as closely integrated as the Continental unit—and this hypothesis is wildly improbable—her exposed position on the verge of the Continent would surely become untenable. Great Britain is, for good or evil, involved by military necessity in the affairs of Europe; and those who desire the maintenance of British power must accept the inevitability of British commitments in Europe. An attempt to escape from her responsibilities there will now for the first time—a thing which has never been possible before—unite the greater part of the Continent against her. For reasons of her own security Great Britain can no longer stand aloof from Europe and take refuge in community of English-speaking peoples; and American interest, being bound up with the survival and security of Great Britain, is identical with British interest in maintaining British power in Europe.

The Economic Factor

If therefore the military factor seems to preclude a policy of isolation from Europe, what can be said of the economic factor? To-day the direction of trade is more predominantly determined by political and military power than in any other period of modern history; and there seems little likelihood of a reversal of this trend. For Britain to isolate herself from Europe to-day would mean, in a sense which would not have been true in the

nineteenth century, to disinterest herself in trade with Europe.
A large and powerful Continental unit from which Britain was
excluded, while it could not attain complete self-sufficiency,
would certainly be in a position to render itself independent of
many products and manufactures habitually exported from
Great Britain to Europe before 1939. The question whether
Britain can afford to abstain from active participation in European affairs turns partly on the question whether Britain can
afford to dispense with a large part of her former European
markets.

This question is not difficult to answer. As has already been
said, any substantial approach toward self-sufficiency can in all
probability be achieved only at the cost of a decline in the standard of living; and Great Britain must maintain her industrial
output if she wishes to remain a Great Power. Her "invisible
exports" have suffered a considerable decline which can hardly
be retrieved. The maintenance of British exports is therefore
vital. In 1913 Europe (including Russia) took 34 per cent, of
British exports. After the last war, the percentage fell below 30,
recovered in 1931 to 34, and had declined again by 1938 to 30.5.
In 1913 Europe took 51 per cent, and in 1938 59 per cent, of
British re-exports—the result of an important *entrepôt* trade
from which Britain could be wholly excluded by a European
unit organised independently of her. In several parts of the
world the recent falling-off of British trade must probably be
accepted as permanent. In 1913 Britain sent 16 per cent of her
exports to the Americas, in 1938 only 12 per cent. In 1913 Asia
(excluding India, other British possessions and Asiatic Russia)
took 8.7 per cent of British exports, in 1938 only 4.4 per cent.
In 1913 India with Burma took 13.3 per cent of British exports,
in 1938 only 7.7 per cent. In the Far East and in Latin America
it is prudent to reckon with a continued reduction of markets
for British trade. There would have been little inclination to
contest the vital importance of making good these losses by an
expansion of British trade with Europe but for the somewhat

exaggerated hopes which have been entertained of an almost unlimited increase in exports to the British Empire (India excluded). In 1913 the Dominions took 17.5 per cent, the colonies and protectorates 6.2 per cent of British exports; in 1938 the corresponding figures were 29.8 and 12.2 per cent respectively.[1] These encouraging statistics have been taken to provide support for the view popular in some quarters that the future of Britain lies in turning her back on Europe and developing her prosperity on the basis of still closer economic relations with her overseas Empire. Since 1919 advocacy of isolation from Europe has almost always been associated with the demand for closer trade relations with the Dominions.

This hypothesis of expanding imperial trade will not, unfortunately, resist a closer examination of the facts. Even the percentages quoted are to some extent misleading; for they conceal the fact that the period was one of declining British exports, and that the absolute increase in British exports to the Empire was altogether less impressive than the percentages might suggest. This is, however, a minor point. The hypothesis of an imperial market sufficiently expansible to compensate Britain for declining trade elsewhere was open on other grounds to grave doubts, even before the Ottawa Conference of 1932 had put it to the test. The British delegates to that Conference were already sceptical of its validity. "The United Kingdom is so highly industrialised", said Mr. Baldwin, "that it is vital to the physical existence of her people to find adequate markets for her products", and he went on to explain that more than half her export trade was in fact taken by foreign countries.[2] Was there any reasonable prospect that the Dominions and colonies taken together could fill this void? A careful study of British trade with

[1] The figures for 1913 are taken from the *Board of Trade Journal*, February 13, 1930, where the necessary adjustments are made for the changed status of Eire.

[2] *Imperial Economic Conference at Ottawa, 1932: Appendices to Summary of Proceedings* (Cmd. 4175), p. 122.

the Dominions showed that they were beginning to follow the path taken by India and by other countries whose trade with Great Britain had so regrettably fallen off. The proportion of consumption goods to total exports to the Dominions (and in the case of the United Kingdom "consumption goods" meant primarily textiles) was declining, and the proportion of capital goods (iron, steel and machinery) was increasing. In other words, the Dominions, like other countries, were beginning predominantly to import from Great Britain the wherewithal to make it unnecessary for them to import in the future the consumption goods which had formed the staple part of their imports in the past. Some day the colonies themselves might strike the same trail.

But if the hypothesis of an indefinitely expanding market in the Dominions had been of dubious validity before 1932, the sequel of the Ottawa Conference wholly destroyed the possibility of continued belief in it. The able historian of British Commonwealth relations gives to his section devoted to the post-Ottawa period the expressive heading "Imperial Self-Insufficiency, 1932-38"; [1] and he traces the rapid decay, under stress of facts, of the conception of an all-sufficient imperial market both for the mother-country and for the Dominions. As early as 1934 New Zealanders had discovered that "we must abandon our traditional view of the United Kingdom as a bottomless market". The Australian wool trade could not be cribbed and confined within imperial frontiers. "We must keep our foreign connexions as well as our British or jettison half our production. In bargaining with Britain with the preference bait for the minor products of Australia, we are filching from the wool trade our main support, that foreign reciprocity which is essential to its existence." It was this need of "foreign reciprocity", as well as the development of industry in the Dominions, which rendered illusory the vision of an unlimited imperial

[1] W. K. Hancock, *Survey of British Commonwealth Affairs*, ii, Pt. 1, pp. 230-67. All the quotations in the present paragraph are taken from this section.

market for British exports. The tide was ebbing fast from the
Ottawa high-water mark of economic imperialism. It was a matter of statistics that in the post-Ottawa years British trade with
the Scandinavian and Baltic countries grew more rapidly than
British trade with the Dominions. The trade of Canada with
the United States and of Australia with Japan grew more rapidly
than their trade with Britain. "We are reaching a point in economic history", said the future Australian Prime Minister Mr.
Menzies in 1937, "when a rigid insistence upon the fullest
measures of Empire preference may prevent the British countries from taking their proper part in a great movement of world
appeasement through a revival of trade." In November 1938,
Great Britain, Canada and Australia concluded with the United
States commercial agreements which may be said to have
brought the Ottawa period in its narrowest sense to an end.
"By 1938", Mr. Hancock sums up, "the nations of the British
Commonwealth had begun a new attempt to shape and adjust
the imperial pattern of their trade policies to a wider world
order".

There is therefore a fundamental fallacy in the view that
Britain can afford to neglect Europe because of the unlimited
overseas market to which she has preferential access. Such a
policy is impracticable and undesirable from the imperial standpoint. It is still more undesirable from the European standpoint.
Even the limited step in this direction taken at Ottawa was
seriously detrimental to Britain's position in Europe. Germany,
as the result of the Ottawa Agreements, faced new obstacles
in the Dominions markets and some of the weaker European
countries faced new obstacles in the British market. Germany
took advantage of these obstacles to build up a trading group
of her own, which was consciously and explicitly designed as a
rival of the British imperial group; and since the war this plan
has further developed into the grandiose conception of a continental European order dominated by Germany. Whatever
the train of circumstances which led up to them, these would-be

closed systems are economically as well as politically unhealthy. It would have been better if, in the nineteen-thirties, Germany had done more trade with the British Dominions and Britain more trade with Eastern and South-Eastern Europe; and the same principle will be equally valid after the present war. It would be just as fatal for Britain to abandon Europe and concentrate solely on her overseas economic interests as it would be for her to concentrate on European markets to the exclusion of those elsewhere. It may well be that after the war a shattered and disorganised Europe will offer more openings than any other market in the world for a development of British trade.[1] A well-balanced economic policy requires Great Britain to maintain and develop her European interests and to refrain from any policy elsewhere which would be incompatible with this aim.

Britain's Rôle in Europe

Both military and economic factors therefore render untenable the doctrine of splendid isolation and compel Great Britain to play an active rôle in Europe. But this rôle will be subject to limitations which we should accept and recognise. These limitations arise from three principal factors: (a) the necessity of reconciling Great Britain's obligations in Europe with her still more important relationship to the English-speaking world overseas, (b) the necessity of close cooperation with Soviet Russia, whose views and interests must have preponderant weight in Eastern Europe, and (c) the limitations of available power.

(a) Rejection of isolation from Europe as an admissible policy

---

[1] An analogous situation may soon develop in the financial sphere. Great Britain embarked on her career as a creditor Power by lending to Europe. During the latter part of the nineteenth century she lent predominantly to the Americas and to the Far East. More recently she has lent mainly to the Dominions and to the colonial Empire. But this third phase may also be drawing to a close. At the end of this war, Canada will probably have become a creditor of Britain, and other Dominions may be moving in the same direction. It may be time for Britain to become once more the banker of Europe.

should not lead us to embrace the opposite heresy of supposing that Great Britain can ever become a predominantly European Power and relegate to a secondary place her overseas interests Such a course is indeed not often openly advocated. But it has been implicit in the francophil policies advocated in the past twenty years in certain influential quarters; and it reappears from time to time in the conception of a world divided into regional or continental blocs, with the principal rôle in a European bloc assigned to Great Britain. It is, however, not difficult to show that for Great Britain's rôle in Europe the formula of a European regional group is both inadequate and inappropriate. Britain's position as a European Power is almost wholly dependent on her position as an overseas Power. Her policy in Europe must be more and more influenced by the attitude of overseas countries whose goodwill and cooperation are essential to her; and she cannot pull her weight in any European combination in which they have no place. Just as it is impossible for Great Britain to isolate herself from Europe, so it is impossible for her to immerse herself in Europe. Her rôle must be to serve as a bridge between the "Western civilisation" of Europe and the same "Western civilisation" in its new homes in other continents.

(*b*) The second limitation on Great Britain's rôle in Europe arises from the need of coordinating her policy with that of Soviet Russia whose cooperation, invaluable in the winning of the war, will be equally essential in the establishment of peace. Detailed discussion of the future rôle of Russia in a new European order may still be premature. But it is imperative to recognise that the Anglo-Russia alliance cannot remain one-sided in its terms and implications. In the first place, association between the two countries will inevitably tend to produce modifications in the outlook and policy of both in the direction of a common view as to the future ordering of European affairs. Secondly, just as preponderant weight will properly be given in Western Europe to the views and interests of Great Britain, the same preponderant weight must be given to the views and interests of Russia in Eastern Europe. The gravest weakness of the Eastern European part of the 1919 settlement was that it was concluded in the absence both of Germany and of Russia and, by ignoring the interests and susceptibilities of both, incurred their common hostility. With this disastrous experience in mind, it is unthinkable that Great Britain or the United States should, at the end of the present war, attempt to promote a solution of Eastern European problems which did not take full account of the wishes and policy of Soviet Russia.

(c) The third limitation, already partly implicit in the other two, is the limitation of available power. This limitation operates in terms both of time and of space. An essential condition of any kind of "order" is that there should be a permanent and virtually complete monopoly of power over the area involved. It is easy, and may be legitimate, to assume that the United States, Great Britain and Soviet Russia will at the end of the war have a preponderance of power, so great as to amount almost to a monopoly, over a considerable part of the world, and certainly over Europe. But it would be extremely foolish to assume without the most careful scrutiny that these countries will be both able and willing for a prolonged period to exercise that preponderant power over a wide area. Can we suppose that the United States will show the same eagerness to use power in Europe as in the Western hemisphere, or Great Britain the same readiness to use power in Eastern as in Western Europe? Can we suppose that Great Britain and the United States will be as willing and as able after twenty years of peace to use power to maintain the established order as they were to establish it at the close of the war? Or can we suppose that, if they relax their watchfulness, other Powers having perhaps less reason to be satisfied with the established order will take their place to defend it? These suppositions are so contrary to every lesson of experience that it would surely be rash to base our plans on them at the present stage.

In this respect, the Peace Conference of 1919 should serve as a warning rather than an example. By 1918 the opposition to Germany had taken the form of a world-wide coalition perhaps more inclusive than any which will be formed in the present war. Russia as well as Germany collapsed and was temporarily powerless. Japan, though restive, was unwilling to incur the displeasure of Great Britain and the United States and was therefore still amenable to persuasion. The victorious Powers assembled in Paris considered themselves, not altogether without reason, entitled and called upon to effect a settlement of a world-wide character. They wholly failed to count the cost. Great Britain and the United States who, with some minor concessions to France, virtually dictated the settlement, never once paused to ask whether in future years they would have the will and the power to uphold the kind of settlement they were making, when those whose acquiescence could now be taken for granted would rebel against it. In any settlement after the present war, this question should be asked and soberly answered, without indulgence in facile optimism, at every stage. If the English-speaking countries are not prepared to undertake, over a long period of years, a continuous responsibility for the exercise of power in all parts of the world, it is a dangerous illusion to suppose that they will find others willing to do so on their behalf. It will be highly imprudent of them to take the lead in establishing an order of their own designing beyond the limits of the area in which they are themselves prepared to act. If this area is restricted, then the area of the future order must be likewise restricted. We should at all costs avoid the fatal megalomania which overtook the peacemakers of 1919.

Our approach to the problem of Great Britain's future rôle in Europe must therefore be tentative and empirical. The demand which we are making on the Great Powers—and notably on Great Britain and the United States—to accept permanent military and economic responsibilities beyond their own borders is itself revolutionary in character. If the demand is pressed too far, it may well come to seem intolerable. The area of obligation must be determined, not theoretically, on the basis of neatly defined geographical divisions, but empirically, as action develops, on the basis of the power available to make cooperation effective and of the will to use that power. It will be important to remember that the durability of any European order will depend, in so far as it depends on power, not on the amount of power available to support it at the moment when it is established, but on the amount of power which will be available fifteen or twenty years later when it is most likely to be challenged and tested. No larger draft should be drawn on the next generation than the next generation can reasonably be expected to meet. Instead of setting out to dispense a uniform European or world order, it may be wiser to think of ourselves as making a modest clearing in the jungle of international relations and attempting within this clearing to apply those conceptions of political cooperation and international order which we are prepared if necessary to defend.

In these conditions, it is not possible at the present stage to do more than sketch the broadest outlines of a future Europe. But the whole situation is dominated by one central problem: Germany. Broadly speaking, the problem of Europe is the problem of Germany; and it is desirable to isolate this fundamental issue, and attempt to grapple with it, before we proceed to the wider question of European reconstruction.

CHAPTER 9

BRITAIN AND GERMANY

THE stubborn fact which we have to face is that the central part of Europe is occupied by an almost solid bloc of eighty million highly gifted and highly organised and highly self-conscious people, the majority of whom have a strong and apparenly ineradicable desire to be united together in a single country. There is, as we have seen, no other group or combination of peoples on the Continent capable of balancing the power of Germany. Great Britain has taken the responsibility of saying that Germany shall not exercise arbitrary and single-handed domination over Europe, and is enforcing this determination by military action. If she can thereafter devise some means of living peaceably with Germany, the peace of Europe seems reasonably assured for some time to come. If she cannot, then Europe—and Great Britain with it—faces final and irretrievable disaster.

Most British people are thoroughly uneasy, and even shamefaced, in their approach to this problem. They are conscious both of its critical importance and of its extreme complexity. They are painfully aware of the failure of the past twenty years, having the guilty feeling that coercion was applied to Germany at a time when a policy of reconciliation might have succeeded, and reconciliation attempted when nothing but coercion could any longer avail. They are desperately afraid of repeating the same mistake. They know that resentment was a bad counsellor in 1919, yet they find it difficult to resist the conclusion that the reiteration of the same experience within a single generation has justified that resentment. When they listen to those who argue that Germans are and always have been irreclaimably vicious, and that Germany must be treated for an indefinite period after the war as civilised society treats criminals and lunatics, they are embarrassed by an attitude which seems to stand in flagrant contradiction both to Christian and to humanitarian doctrine, and which offers no prospect for the future but unending repression and strife. When on the other hand they listen to those who preach reconciliation, they are uncomfortably sensitive to the charge of naïvety and of refusal to learn from experience; and they seek in vain for a convincing solution of an apparently insoluble problem. In moments of weariness or of righteous indignation, the temptation is strong to believe that the one path to safety lies, not in attempting to win the goodwill and co-operation of Germany in a future ordering of Europe and the world, but in keeping Germany permanently so weak that we can afford to ignore her inevitable ill-will. There is a serious danger that this mood of reckless and short-sighted cynicism may prevail in the immediate post-war period. The sin of certain propagandists is that they seek to perpetuate it by giving it a rational basis.

The Thesis of German Wickedness

The thesis of the inherent and irremediable wickedness of the German people, though often supported by an apparatus of somewhat dubious scholarship, is not really a reasoned case. It is the product of an emotional reaction, familiar in all periods of history, which has led men to brand their enemies as moral reprobates, particularly when it is desired to find a justification for treating them as inferiors and outcasts. In other words, it is propaganda for a certain policy. In the hands of some who use it, it may have, consciously or subconsciously, another and less avowable motive. International hatreds were long regarded by conservatives of many countries as an antidote against potential revolutionary trends. If the masses can be induced to attribute the evils of society to the malignity of a foreign devil, there is less chance of dangerous stresses arising within the fabric of the nation itself. Jingoism has often been fanned as a specific against social discontent and as a bar to social progress.[1] Nevertheless, there is no doubt that the degree of popular belief or unbelief in innate German wickedness will profoundly affect the policy adopted by this country towards Germany after the war; and though the sophisticated critic may recognise clearly enough that the allegation is not wholly disinterested or objective, it is important to investigate its historical basis, and to discover how much truth the impartial critic would be prepared to allow to it.

The precise character of the allegation varies. In order to sustain the hypothesis of innate German wickedness, some go back as far as Tacitus; others begin with Frederick the Great and regard German viciousness as a distinctively Prussian contribution, sometimes refining this theory with the argument that the Prussians were not German, or even Teutonic, in origin; others again are content to start with Bismarck. The recourse to the Germans of Tacitus need not perhaps be taken seriously. Their blood probably runs in most nations of Europe; and Tacitus did not form a notably more favourable opinion of the ancient Britons. This argument may suitably be left to Benito Mussolini, who appears to have invented it,[2] and to writers whose scholarship is of the same calibre. On the other hand, the third variant which begins with Bismarck seems rather in-

[1] This was the situation in Great Britain at the end of the nineteenth century. "A wave of imperialism was sweeping over the country and, as hatred of the foreigner—the German, the Russian, the Frenchman—prevailed over hatred of the domestic enemy, and race hatred thrust class hatred into the background, the situation became unfavourable to labour agitation" (E. Halévy, *A History of the English People in 1895-1914*, i, p. 259).

[2] "The Teuton has not changed his fundamental instincts. They are still the same men whom Tacitus described to perfection in his *Germania*" (*Scritti e Discorsi di Benito Mussolini*, i, p. 317). The date of this pronouncement is May 1918.

adequate; for it would be light-hearted to condemn a people as irredeemable on the evidence of seventy years of their history. The serious form of the indictment is the one which maintains, without embarking on foolish attempts to make a racial distinction between Prussians and other Germans, that Frederick the Great did import into Prussian, and thence into German, life an element of violence and aggressiveness which has become so deeply rooted in the national character that there is no reasonable hope of eradicating it in any predictable future.

The existence of this so-called "Prussian" tradition in modern German life must be freely admitted. Brutality, aggressiveness and what is rather invidiously called "militarism" have been exhibited by many other Powers besides Germany; but though they are not by any means the only qualities which Germany has displayed, it would be foolish to deny that they have emerged with especial prominence in Germany in many recent crises of history. The problem is, however, not illuminated, but obscured, by hasty and vulgar generalisations about the German or the Prussian character. The historical crux of the German problem resides not in any supposedly ineradicable national characteristics, whether German or Prussian, but in the late date at which Germany attained national unity and the plenitude of her power. In the great flowering of the Renaissance and the Reformation, France and England were already strong and united nations, able to absorb new elements into an already formed and coherent national tradition. In Germany, the new influences could never be fully assimilated and proved in the main disruptive. In the eighteenth century France was the strongest European Power—the home of the universalist traditions of the Enlightenment, of natural law and of the rights of man. German nationalism was moulded by the romantic historicism of the *Sturm und Drang* period reacting against eighteenth-century rationalism and eighteenth-century universalism. In the nineteenth century Great Britain was the strong world Power and the protagonist of economic universalism. Germany, having at length achieved national unity, was impelled to seek her economic place in the sun in rivalry with Great Britain, through monopoly and state-subsidised industry and commerce, in revolt against universalist *laissez-faire*.

The legacy of the past has thus given to modern German political development its two characteristic reactions—against individualism on the one hand and against internationalism on the other. The foundation of human society in the rights of individual men and the *laissez-faire* hypothesis of an economic world of independent individual units—these liberal nineteenth-century axioms were never really accepted as the basis of German life and thought. When it gradually became clear to the twentieth-century world that individualism was not enough—that the duties as well as the rights of the individual must be asserted as the necessary presupposition of an ordered society, that *laissez-faire* principles would not work precisely because individuals did not in fact any longer constitute the units of the economic system, that contemporary social and political problems were problems of the mass rather than of the individual—then it was almost inevitable that this challenge to nineteenth-century beliefs which she had never really shared should find in Germany one of its strongest protagonists. That acute critic of imperial Germany, Thorstein Veblen, writing in 1915, suggested that the "spirit of subservient alacrity on which the Prussian system of administrative efficiency rests is beneath the human dignity of a free man", but adds that it "has visibly been a source of strength to the German state, and presumably to the German people at large as an economic body".[1] To-day we may take still more strongly the view that the German tradition involves an intolerable challenge to our own conception of freedom. But it would be foolish to deny that the challenge is implicit in the nature of modern mass democracy, and still more foolish to pretend that it is the product

[1] T. Veblen, *Imperial Germany*, pp. 67-8.

of nothing more far-reaching than the perversity and wickedness of a single race of mankind. The problem is not solely and
specifically German. It is a universal problem, which awaits
solution from this generation, of the relation of the individual
to society.

In the same way, Germany has for historical reasons always
found her national development in opposition to the current
universalism or internationalism of the period. France and Great
Britain can look back to periods of history in which each was
everywhere recognised as the leading Power; and this period
was marked in each case by the growth of a strong cosmopolitan
or international tradition which rooted itself deeply in the national thought and culture. Germany has known no such period
—at any rate since the Middle Ages, when national consciousness in its modern form had not yet begun to dawn. Broadly
speaking, internationalism is attractive to the very strong Power
which can play a leading rôle in the international community
and to the weak Power which finds in it a vicarious bulwark
of defence.[1] Germany has never been quite strong enough to
enter the first category. The Germans are the most numerous,
the best organised and industrially the most richly endowed
of the peoples of Central and Western Europe. This entitles
them in their own judgment to recognition as leaders, if not of
the world, at any rate of the Continent of Europe. The policy
of "encirclement", which caused so much real bitterness in
Germany, consisted in German eyes in bolstering up a number
of weaker European states against Germany in order to deprive
Germany of her rightful position. Particularly after 1919, the
slogans of internationalism were used, in the League of Nations and elsewhere, to resist German claims; and this further

---

[1] An analogous situation exists among the Slav peoples. Pan-Slavism has its
attractions for Russia as the natural leader of a Slav family of nations. It has its
attractions for the small Slav nations to whom it would bring Russian protection. But it has few attractions for Poland, a country not strong enough to
aspire to the leadership of the Slavs and not normally weak enough to welcome
the protection of the pan-Slav umbrella.

increased German suspicions of internationalism in general. "By 'international' ", wrote a German resident in Great Britain not long before the war, "we have come to understand a conception that places other nations at an advantage over our own".[1] Much has been written and said in refutation of German arguments. But this does not help when the refutation is based on different and controversial premises, and when the arguments are not taken seriously enough to be understood. If we are to solve the German problem, we must at least understand the state of mind, not of a few Nazi fanatics, but of nearly all intelligent Germans who concern themselves with international politics; and instead of being content to attribute this state of mind to the innate perversity of the German character, we must trace it back to the historical conditions out of which it has grown.

If, moreover, we remain fully conscious of the darker shades in the German national tradition, it would still be an injustice to assess the place of Germany in modern history without taking equal account of her positive achievements. It is unfair to dwell on the aggressions of Frederick the Great and to ignore the honourable part played by Prussia in the defeat of the aggression of Napoleon. It should not be forgotten that the career of Bismarck, often depicted as an unvarying pattern of ruthlessness, contains the Treaty of Prague concluded with Austria after Sadowa in 1866, which ranks with the peace of Vereeniging as one of the wisest peaces of modern times imposed by a victor on a defeated state. Germans had a chief share in framing the doctrines and the organisation of modern socialism; and the modern system of state-controlled social services is almost wholly of German origin. The compulsory insurance of workers against accident, sickness and disablement, as well as old-age pensions, were introduced by Bismarck in Germany before any of them was heard of in any other civilised country. The

[1] *The Times*, November 5, 1938.

gradual adoption of similar provisions in Great Britain was largely due to the study and popularisation by the early Fabians of German models. German achievements in art, science and literature may be irrelevant for present purposes. But the striking capacity for large-scale organisation developed by Germans in the industrial conditions of the later nineteenth century is a quality whose value and importance in the modern world cannot be gainsaid. Nothing has occurred to reverse the accepted nineteenth-century judgment on Germans as a patient, thrifty and hard-working people. The modern world is not so richly endowed with ability and resourcefulness that it can light-heartedly cast out from its midst as irredeemably bad a nation possessing, in combination with many grave defects, so many valuable attributes. It is improbable that the future judgment of history on modern Germany will be painted all in one colour, and that colour black. The cool summing-up of a close student of the German people in the years after the last war holds good to-day:

They are not a lovable people; they even take a melancholy pride in the fact. But they are unmistakably and with all their faults a great people, and they can never remain a negligible factor in the future of Europe.[1]

The Policy of Repression

We may now turn to the policy which this hypothesis of irredeemable German wickedness is intended to justify. The principal instruments for the repression of Germany designed in 1919 were disarmament, military occupation, and the handing over to other countries of strips of predominantly German territory. These should, according to most supporters of this policy, be employed at the end of the present war in an intensified form, and should be supplemented by the further method,

[1] J. H. Morgan, *The Present State of Germany* (1924), p. 25.

not adopted at Versailles except in the limited case of the prohibition on the union of German-speaking Austria with the Reich, of breaking up Germany into two or more independent states. It is also held that whatever measures of repression are invoked should be maintained permanently, or at any rate for an indefinite period. This policy, plausible as it may appear, encounters several objections.

The first kind of objection is based on *moral* grounds. Attemps to indict and penalise a whole race or nation have long been repugnant to the moral sense of most progressive people. At a time when racial discrimination is coming to be widely recognised as an unscientific as well as a reactionary principle, it is doubtful whether opinion in the English-speaking countries —to speak only of them—would tolerate it for any length of time as a basis for their future relations with Germany. Such a policy would in the long run appear too inconsistent with the principles in whose name the war had been fought—principles which include the right of the individual to be regarded as an end in himself, not as a mere unit in a mass. The trouble is that, while for purposes of international relations we have to think in terms of abstractions like "Germany", and while we find it easy, especially in time of war, to believe in the guilt of "Germany", we can in fact only penalise "Germany" by penalising Germans; and once we re-establish relations with individual Germans after the war, we shall be incapable of believing in their wholesale personal guilt. If we wished permanently to destroy German power, the only sure and infallible way of doing so would be to exterminate 50,000,000 Germans either by slaughtering them or by transporting them to remote deserts or uninhabited islands to die of starvation or live as savages. The fact that even the strongest advocates of the policy of weakening Germany shrink from the only method which would make their policy really effective shows that the policy itself is incompatible with principles which we recognise as valid and from which, in normal times, we are not prepared to depart. After the last war, the milder method of keeping "Germany" in subjection by allowing individual Germans to go hungry proved unacceptable for the same reasons. Everyone remembers Mr. Churchill's story of the circumstances which finally compelled the Allied Governments to remove the blockade from Germany in March 1919:

> Lord Plumer, who commanded the British Army of Occupation in Germany, sent a telegram to the War Office, forwarded to the Supreme Council, urging that food should be supplied to the suffering population in order to prevent the spread of disorder as well as on humanitarian grounds. He emphasized the bad effect produced upon the British Army by the spectacle of suffering which surrounded them. From him and through other channels we learned that the British soldiers would certainly share their rations with the women and children among whom they were living, and that the physical efficiency of the troops was already being affected.[1]

The politician and the intellectual, breathing out vengeance against an abstract "Germany", stand reproached by the ordinary British soldier face to face with the individual German as innocent as himself of responsibility for the common disaster. Moreover, this reaction is cumulative. Years pass; a new generation grows up; and the conscience of ordinary people rebels more and more against the injustice of visiting the consequences of a so-called "national" crime on individuals who were innocent children or still unborn when it was committed.

Indeed, even if we remain on the ground of abstraction and ignore the moral difficulty of punishing innocent individual Germans for the crimes of a guilty Germany, the precedent of the last war makes it doubtful whether we shall, for any length of time, feel morally satisfied to adopt towards Germany a political attitude fundamentally different from that adopted

[1] Winston Churchill, *The World Crisis: The Aftermath*, p. 67.

towards other states. In 1918, feeling against Germany and against Germans, and an emotional conviction of their "war-guilt", had risen in most Allied countries to an even higher pitch than has been reached in the present war. The conception of a penal peace was almost universally accepted. Yet within a few months of the armistice the moral climate began to undergo a rapid change. It was perceived that other collective entities besides "Germany" were sometimes guilty of unreasonable or aggressive or cruel behaviour, and that it was not possible in all issues arising between them to regard them as morally right and Germany as morally wrong. The rough and ready war-time assumption of the guilt of Germany and the innocence of the Allies became repugnant to our more fastidious peace-time consciences. The weak attitude adopted towards Germany in Great Britain from 1935 onwards was in part the product of widespread remorse felt for the treatment of Germany at Versailles and after. There is every reason to suppose that similar treatment would provoke a similar reaction after the present war, particularly if the German people themselves take an active part in the overthrow of the Nazi régime. Those who now conduct propaganda for a peace which would aim at permanently reducing Germany to an inferior status incur a grave responsibility. The serious danger exists that, under the influence of such propaganda, a peace may be imposed which will eventually prove repugnant to the moral sense of the victorious Powers and which, having created the maximum of bitterness in Germany, will for that reason become a dead letter.

The certainty of a reaction against a policy of permanent coercion is reinforced by another argument. Belief in such a policy involves a fundamental moral pessimism which is unlikely to have a lasting appeal. The protagonists of this view are for the most part men already in middle or advanced life, whose minds were formed before or during the last war. They can count on a substantial measure of popular support so long as emotions are deeply stirred by the horrors of the war, and by

the peculiar ruthlessness of the Nazi régime. But it is doubtful
for how long they will exercise any influence on the rising generation—including active combatants in the war—who will feel
the need for a faith carrying within it the seed of a better world.
Idealism will regain its ascendancy. The final moral objection
to a policy of holding in permanent subjection the largest and
most powerful nation in Europe is that it offers no hope of a
true peace founded on reconciliation and consent, and actually
rejects the possibility of such a peace. After the war the need for
reconciliation with an emancipated Germany as the one conceivable way to European peace will gradually assert itself, and
will in the end become so strong as to preclude the pursuit of
any policy incompatible with it. The younger generation will
not be deterred from making the attempt; for in the long run it
is better to fail through the excessive faith which attempts the
difficult and hazardous task of turning an enemy into a friend
than through the excessive cynicism which offers no prospect
but the perpetuation of mutual hate. No policy ultimately incompatible with reconciliation can endure, for it will be found
morally unbearable. The danger is that it may be pursued long
enough to destroy the chance of reconciliation.

The next objection to the policy of permanent coercion is
the *practical* one. The proposal is not only that Germany shall
be subject to lasting disabilities not imposed on other European
countries, but that German territory—apart from such fringes
of it as may be ceded to other countries—shall be divided into
two or more separate states. It is difficult to gauge the extent
and strength of the fissiparous tendencies which have from time
to time been apparent in Germany since the creation of the
Reich in 1871. But they were probably exaggerated by wishful
foreign thinking; and they have progressively declined in in-
tensity. "C'est nous qui l'avons faite", exclaimed Thiers of German unity in 1871; and French policy played exactly the same
rôle of fortifying German unity after 1918. To-day any at-

tempt from without to break up Germany into two or more parts would merely have the effect of further strengthening national cohesion and would be resisted more pertinaciously than ever. In January 1919 Max Weber predicted that a penal peace would "turn the most politically radical German worker —not now, but in a year and a day, when the present tumult and the succeeding weariness are past—into a chauvinist".[1] This prophecy was fulfilled; and it would be fulfilled again. In other words the political dismemberment of Germany could be carried out only by force, and would be effective only so long as a powerful military force remained in occupation of the country to maintain it.

It is even less clear how a policy of economic dismemberment could be imposed. The world has plenty of experience of the difficulty of removing economic barriers, but little experience of the probably still more difficult problem of forcibly erecting and maintaining such barriers between people who desire to constitute an economic unit. Any form of permanent penalisation of Germany would involve permanent occupation and permanent administrative control in the teeth of persistent hostility and sabotage; and the burden of this would fall mainly on Great Britain—the only European country possessing the resources to sustain it over a long period. It seems scarcely necessary to propound such a solution in order to reject it. Nothing is more certain than that the British people would be unwilling, if indeed they were able, to undertake responsibilities involving a permanent British military occupation of Germany and permanent British control of the German administration. Here again forethought may save us from the mistake committed in 1919 of creating a situation which could be maintained only by the permanent and continuous application of force. If it is dangerous, immediately after the war, to embark on a course which, when a calmer mood sets in, will seem morally repugnant, it is

---

[1] Max Weber, *Gesammelte Politische Schriften*, p. 383.

equally dangerous to initiate a policy which, when the cost is soberly counted, will be recognised as impracticable. The policy of the dismemberment of Germany is open to both these objections.

The third objection is *economic*. The multiplication of economic units is directly contrary to the trend of contemporary economic development which calls imperatively for economic agglomeration, not disintegration. It seems difficult to imagine any effective policy for the dismemberment of Germany which would not involve the break-up of the economic unity of Central Europe; and such a break-up would be wholly retrograde and would repeat one of the worst blunders of the Versailles settlement. Europe cannot maintain—much less increase —her present standard of living without German productive power. Though powerful sectional interests might derive a passing advantage from the elimination of German competition, it is not possible to weaken Germany economically without producing a serious setback to the prosperity of Europe as a whole. Not one of the smaller countries of Western Europe could look forward with equanimity to the loss of their German markets;[1] and for those of Central and South-Eastern Europe such a contingency would mean a complete, and probably catastrophic, reorientation of their whole economic life. Above all, British interest in European trade means interest in German trade which must always constitute a substantial part of it. If Great Britain and her present allies, misled by what they have suffered at the hands of Nazi Germany, were to embark on a policy which broke up German productive capacity and destroyed the flow of German trade, the repercussion on their own heads would be prompt and severe. It may suffice to recall

[1] In 1938, Germany took 14·9 per cent of the exports of Holland, 12·2 per cent of those of Belgium, 19·7 per cent of those of Denmark, 15·3 per cent of those of Norway and 18·1 per cent of those of Sweden, Germany coming second to the United Kingdom as a customer of these countries. On the other hand, she took only 6 per cent of French exports.

the unheeded warning penned by Mr. Keynes in the autumn of 1919:

> If we aim deliberately at the impoverishment of Central Europe, vengeance, I dare predict, will not limp. Nothing can then delay for very long that final civil war between the forces of reaction and the despairing convulsions of revolution, before which the horrors of the late German war will fade into nothing, and which will destroy, whoever is victor, the civilisation and progress of our generation.[1]

If this prophecy was fulfilled in the loosely integrated Europe of the nineteen-twenties, the far more closely knit economic structure of contemporary Europe would reel still more heavily under a similar blow. This does not mean that the pre-war German economic unit was from any point of view an ideal or even a desirable one. But we must frankly accept, as part of the revolutionary process which underlies the war, the process of economic integration which has long been in progress, and which has been intensified by the pressure of war. We cannot put back the clock by breaking up the economic unity of Germany: we must help to build up the German economic system into a larger unit under different forms of control.

We may sum up the main objections to the proposed policy of penalisation, dismemberment and permanent coercion of Germany by saying that such a policy would prove in the long run morally repugnant, physically impracticable and economically retrograde. In the first flush of victory it could be imposed by force. But it could not be maintained except by the permanent use of force on a scale which Great Britain and the United States would be unwilling, and no other Power or group of Powers would be able, to apply; and it would bring economic disaster to Central Europe, which would have damaging repercussions elsewhere. The discussion leaves us, however, with the

[1] J. M. Keynes, *The Economic Consequences of the Peace*, p. 251.

necessity of finding a more positive solution. If our conception of a post-war settlement must be based on recognition of Germany's present and future strength, we have to find a way of reconciling this fact with some prospect other than that of either accepting German domination in Europe or fighting a war once a generation to prevent it. There is no guaranteed solution of any political problem, for nothing is proof against human folly and human wickedness. But the elements of the only conceivable solution have already begun to emerge. The German dilemma can be resolved, not by destroying Germany or by diminishing her, but by making her a partner in a larger unit in which Great Britain will also have her place. Germany's belated nationalism can be overcome only by making internationalism worth her while. Like all lasting political ends, this result can be achieved only by a combination of power and consent. But it is essential that these two processes should be pursued together, and that coercion should not be so applied as to destroy the chance of ultimate reconciliation.

Measures of Coercion

Coercion is implicit in any revolutionary process. Force of arms has been required to prevent the realisation of the German plan to dominate the continent of Europe and exclude Great Britain from any lot or part in it. The defeat of Germany is bound to be followed by an extensive military occupation. But this occupation should be effected as an operation of war, and should take place before the conclusion of any armistice—if indeed an armistice of the old-fashioned kind is required at all. Not all the arguments commonly advanced in support of a military occupation are equally convincing. It is sometimes said that failure to occupy German territory other than the Rhineland after 1918 enabled Germany to pretend and believe that she had not suffered military defeat. This is surely nonsense. Rarely in history has a people been so morbidly conscious of the humiliation of defeat as the German people at that time. That the army tried to save its face by attributing defeat to a breakdown in civilian morale is a comparatively minor point; and this could not have been avoided by any action of the Allies. An army of occupation in the winter of 1918-19 could, however, have performed a function of inestimable importance if it had conducted itself impartially and without vindictiveness. It could, without much difficulty, have enabled the new German Government, which at that time enjoyed considerable popular support, to maintain order. The first fatal, though unavoidable, step was taken when the Ebert régime was compelled to call in the old army to keep it in power. Thus the immediate dependence of the administration on the military authorities which existed under the old order was prolonged into the new.

At the end of the present war chaos is likely to be graver and more widespread than in 1918. Military occupation may well be necessary for the restoration of authority, and must in any case be maintained to bridge the transition from the old order to the new. It may be assumed that, in the event of a German defeat, the Nazi party—or at any rate its leaders and principal agents—will be swept away in the collapse, leaving a void behind. It is one of the characteristics of totalitarianism that, by drawing every form of social activity into the orbit of a centralised state or party machine, it makes any breakdown of government all the more devastating in its effects. Moreover, the Nazi régime has been particularly successful in eradicating potential leaders of an opposition; and it would be folly to attempt to construct an alternative government round a nucleus of German refugees abroad. But here we have an excellent opportunity of transforming the restrictive into the constructive, and of making the functions of military occupation not so much coercive as creative. A British occupying force will in all probability be widely welcomed in Germany for the purpose of restoring and maintaining order. The function of such a force would be to support any reasonable and effective administration, whether national or regional in scope, which might establish itself in Germany. This does not mean that democratic or any other specific forms of government should be dictated or required. The mistake of attempting to impose a constitution by pressure or by inducements from without should not be repeated. The sole purpose should be to allow and encourage the development of the form of government best suited to the wishes and the aptitudes of the German people. The traditions of communal and other forms of local government are extremely strong in Germany; and the occupying authorities need insist only on the condition that the administration should have local support and that its actions should not be oppressive or flagrantly unjust. This condition should be designed to secure the recognition of a necessary minimum of civic rights, reasonable freedom of speech and association, respect for the processes of law, and absence of racial discrimination. If the occupying forces in Western Germany are predominantly British (perhaps with Dominion or American reinforcements), there should be no difficulty in securing a common-sense interpretation of these requirements. If Russian forces occupy Eastern Germany, there is reason to hope that they will observe a similar restraint.

It is therefore essential that the presence of foreign troops on German soil should be treated not merely—and, after the first weeks, not primarily—as a measure for the coercion of Germany, but as part of the preparation for the establishment of a new European order in which Germans must ultimately be called on to participate. The German masses must be given from the outset the reasonable conviction that the new order will bring them not new privations and humiliations, but a higher measure of spiritual, social and physical well-being than the old. As a first instalment of this policy, military occupation should be accompanied by relief in the form of food, clothing and medical supplies. It may be that there will be no serious shortages of essential supplies, and that organisation of distribution rather than import will be the primary need. But in any case the error of 1919, when the blockade was retained for some months after the close of hostilities, must not be repeated. "The German people on November 11th", wrote Mr. Churchill of that time, "had not only been defeated in the field, they had been vanquished by world opinion. These bitter experiences [*i.e.* the maintenance of the blockade] stripped their conquerors in their eyes of all credentials except those of force." [1] It is important to defeat Germany by overwhelming force. But it is also important to convince Germans at the earliest possible moment that we have credentials other than force for the reorganization of Europe. Cooperation between Germans and the occupying authorities in the distribution of supplies should pave the way for other forms of cooperation. If the primary business of the occupying forces will be to keep order on German soil, this is a task which Germans can and must be called on to share. If a secondary function of the occupation will be to defend German territory against the unwarrantable incursions of organised or unorganised marauders, this too is a task in which German services can be enrolled. If therefore we can conceive the occupation not so much on the old lines of pure repression, but as the starting-point for German cooperation in creating a framework of European order, the right beginning will have been made. In this as in other respects it is psychologically vital to convince Germans that they have a part to play in the new order, and are not merely subjects or victims of it. Military occupation will be a failure in the long run if it provides nothing more than a deterrent against breaches of the peace: it must also provide positive incentives to Germans to keep the peace and opportunities to cooperate in maintaining it.

Military occupation must be completed by some immediate measures of disarmament. Disarmament requires to be placed in a new perspective and, instead of being regarded as mainly

[1] Winston Churchill, *The World Crisis: The Aftermath*, p. 67.

punitive and destructive, must become the starting-point of a process of construction. The obsolescence of engines of war is now so rapid that the surplus of one great war is hardly likely to prove serviceable in another. Of all the German material surrendered or destroyed after 1918, hardly anything—except perhaps a few naval units—could have played any effective rôle in the present war. Indeed it has already been noted that the absence of large stocks of obsolete and obsolescent material was one of the factors enabling Germany in recent years to build up a new and modern war machine at the shortest notice. At the end of this war some initial surrender or destruction of important material may be desirable. But the process should be limited to what can be achieved within a year of the laying-down of arms. The prolonged inquisition for arms in post-1918 Germany, provoking an elaborate and effective machinery of concealment, and poisoning relations between Germany and her conquerors for many years, was simply not worth the candle, and should not be repeated. The limitation of man-power is a still more dubious proposition; for there is little doubt that the restrictions imposed by the Versailles Treaty contributed in the long run to German military efficiency. The two really decisive factors in preparations for modern warfare are industrial capacity (sometimes dubbed "war potential" in discussions about disarmament) and the supply of raw materials. The key to what used to be called the disarmament problem is to be found not in the destruction or restriction of stocks of armaments, but in the international organisation and control of industrial production and of raw materials. The approach to the problem is not so much through coercive action taken immediately after the war as through the whole policy of international economic reconstruction, which will be discussed in the next chapter.

Another aspect of coercive action—the imposition of penalties—excites more public interest than it intrinsically deserves, and is responsible for a great deal of confused and highly emotional thinking. At the end of any war the victors evince a natural eagerness to exact retribution from the losers. In Europe this eagerness appears to have been gradually intensified throughout the nineteenth century, reaching its culmination in 1918. Ten years after the Versailles Treaty there was no part of that instrument whose futility was more widely condemned, or whose harmful results were more widely recognised, than the clauses relating to penalties. Yet so deeply rooted in human nature is the desire for vengeance, and so strong the impulse to personify the forces of evil, that it is impossible to feel confidence that the error will not be repeated in perhaps some slightly different form. The desire for revenge has, however, on occasions been restrained; and these occasions have generally produced the most satisfactory and durable peace. The Vienna settlement of 1815, the Prague Treaty of 1866 and the Vereeniging Treaty of 1902 are the most familiar modern examples. The settlement of 1919 may serve as an equally effective warning of what to avoid. Nobody will repeat the folly of piling up huge reparation accounts to be discharged over more than a generation. It would be reasonable enough to demand German participation in the reconstruction of devastated countries. But if these countries count on reconstruction to ease for them the problem of employment in the difficult transition period between war and peace, it seems unlikely that they will be any more willing than France after 1919 to employ German labour. It is doubtful whether they will be any more desirous of dislocating international trade by importing large quantities of material from Germany without countervailing exports. In any case, these problems should be treated under the head not of penalties, but of economic reconstruction, in which all will cooperate in their own interest. The experience of 1919 seems equally decisive against the imposition of personal penalties. Hitler, Mussolini and many of the other Nazi and Fascist leaders may suffer vengeance at the hands of the German and Italian peoples. If they escape, they should be subjected to no indictment save that of history and suffer no penalty save that of permanent isolation in some remote and secure place.

Reconciliation by Cooperation

Like other current political problems, the long-term problem of reconciliation and cooperation with Germany must be approached both on the economic and on the moral plane. The recent aggressive policy of Germany had psychological as well as economic causes. The dependence of future peace on prosperity and of a psychology of cooperation on material well-being is not absolute. But the link between them is far too substantial to be ignored; and the material problem must be tackled first.

The dominant factor of the economic situation is that the Germans cannot maintain—and still less increase—the standard of living to which they are accustomed except by extensive trade with areas outside those which constituted the German Reich in 1914 or even in 1939. The question is not one of "access to raw materials". Neither Germany nor any other country was in time of peace ever denied access to raw materials which she could afford to buy. The question is one of finding for German trade a sufficiently extensive market to provide her with the means of payment. The war of 1914-18 and the subsequent peace deprived Germany of this market. It has been said that those who cannot afford to buy must beg, borrow or steal, and that Germany, having begged from 1920 to 1925 and borrowed from 1925 to 1930, thereafter turned to stealing. The comment is not inapposite. It was only when Germany found herself in a position to put military pressure on her neighbours that German export trade began to revive and approached, though it never reached, its pre-war level. *Grossraumwirtschaft* and the military methods used to make it effective were in part, at any rate, a reply to the attempt to exclude German trade from world markets after 1919.

The war has enabled Hitler to carry *Grossraumwirtschaft* several steps further, thereby illustrating the dictum that war is merely the continuation of policy by other means. The European frontiers of 1939 no longer exist as economic frontiers. At the present time Germany has taken virtually the whole of European industry under her direct control and is operating it, for all practical purposes, as a single unit serving a single purpose. Alsace-Lorraine, Luxemburg, Bohemia and Moravia and the industrial sector of Poland, including the textile manufacturing centre Lodz, have all been annexed under one guise or another to the Reich. German forces occupy Belgium, Holland and Denmark, the industrial area of France and, in all probability, Northern Italy. Except perhaps in Sweden and Switzerland, there is scarcely an industrial enterprise of any importance on the Continent of Europe west of Russia which is not subject to instructions from Berlin. Germany herself has in fact abandoned the old economic unit of the Reich. In so doing, she has obeyed not only the immediate exigencies of war, but more fundamental economic trends which cannot be reversed. Hitler's policy has constituted a clear admission that Germany cannot live without foreign trade and that Germans will not in the long run be content with the standard of living which autarky can give them.

The solution which Hitler has found for this problem breaks down in two ways. In the first place, it is a one-sided solution imposed by force of arms, and confers exclusive benefits on Germany at the expense of the rest of Europe. Secondly, it rests on the hypothesis of a self-sufficient Europe which is in the long run almost as untenable as the hypothesis of a self-sufficient Germany. But the effectiveness of these criticisms of Hitler's New Order does not excuse us from the necessity of finding an answer to the problem of Germany's place in a future economic organisation of Europe. It would be an anachronism—of the kind which proved so fatal in 1919—for the victors in this war to attempt, first of all, to reconstitute the pre-war economic unit of the Reich, and then to break up this unit into still smaller units. In so far as smaller groups or units are required, the natural economic divisions conspicuously fail to coincide with former national frontiers. The industries of Upper Silesia on one side, and of the Ruhr and Lorraine on the other, are natural economic units. It would be futile to break up these units on grounds of self-determination, and equally futile to attempt to exclude Germans from an effective share in their management and exploitation. The problem remains insoluble until we recognise the necessity of placing it in a larger framework. It has already been observed that it would have been better if, in the ten years before the war, Germany had done more trade with the British Dominions and Great Britain more trade with South-Eastern Europe. It is unthinkable, however, that this return to a more dispersed and generalised world trade can be achieved by a "removal of trade barriers" or by a resuscitation of the *laissez-faire* principles of the nineteenth century. The results which we desire can be won only by a deliberate reorganisation of European economic life such as Hitler has in fact undertaken, but on different premises and for different purposes, and by the deliberate forging of new links between the economic life of Europe and the outside world, such as Hitler is not in a position to undertake. The opportunity to do these things in a radical way and on an extensive scale will occur at the end of the war, and must be promptly seized if it is not to be missed altogether. Some kind of European economic unit, whatever its precise scope and dimensions, has become imperative. If Great Britain wishes to provide for her own future well-being and security and to solve the German problem, she must be ready to take the lead in building this new Europe.

But the issue cannot be faced exclusively in material terms. It will be necessary to give the German people, not only a common interest in the building of the new Europe, but also the sense of a common moral purpose; and before we can hope to inspire this sense, we must first acquire it ourselves. The problem is sometimes described as that of the "re-education" of Germany; and the description is not a bad one if we realise the importance of applying the results of modern psychological science, which shows that neither penalty nor precept, but example and confidence are the most potent instruments of education. We can "re-educate" the Germans only if we are prepared, in the course of the same process, to re-educate ourselves. The suggestion is often heard that the German people, and particularly the German youth, have been so successfully inoculated with Nazi doctrine that some special action will have to be taken to convince them of the error of their ways. The Nazi and Fascist régimes have undoubtedly subjected their people, from their earliest youth up, to a particularly narrow and intensive form of propaganda. But there are several considerations which should be borne in mind in any rational approach to this question. The period of time during which this influence has been exercised is extremely short. Sudden and strong impulses are commonly followed by sudden and strong reactions. Defeat in war commonly provokes such a reaction. Most people would have said that loyalty to the Hohenzollern Empire in Germany, loyalty to Tsar and Orthodox Church in Russia in 1917 and loyalty to the Third Republic in France in 1940 were far more deeply ingrained than the present loyalty of the German and Italian peoples to the Nazi and Fascist régimes. Yet these loyalties collapsed utterly and irrevocably within weeks or days under the stress of military defeat. The problem most likely to confront us at the end of the war is not a German people clinging passionately to Nazi doctrines and ideals, but a German people which, having reacted violently against a system which has led it to defeat and humiliation, finds itself in a state of moral and intellectual exhaustion and chaos. In this respect the German state of mind may be less far removed than most people now imagine from that of other European countries, where consciousness of victory and deliverance

may soon be tempered by the anxieties of the problem of recon-
structing a broken civilisation.

The post-war German mind may well, as happened after
1918, become a potential prey to many aberrations. But it will
also be accessible, as it was after 1918, to nobler inspirations;
and it is by stimulating such inspirations that the victorious
nations can contribute to Germany's re-education. "Part of the
problem of undoing an abnormal history", an English writer has
said in another context, "is to restore the self-respect and inner
integrity of the victim of that history." [1] This cannot be
achieved by propaganda, and still less by force. The satirical
German couplet

> Und möcht'st Du nicht Bruder sein,
> So schlag' ich Dir den Schädel ein

has been frequently, and not unaptly, quoted to describe Nazi
policy towards some weaker countries. It is essential that the
same description should not be applicable to British policy
towards a defeated Germany at the end of the war. The future
of Europe will be determined not merely by force of arms, but
by the example and by the exertions of those who are able to
provide not so much a ready-made solution of the ills of mankind as the sense of a common purpose for which mankind can
work. Internationally as well as nationally the discovery of a
common purpose to replace the bankrupt ideology of a natural
and automatic harmony of interests is the cardinal need of our
generation. The German problem is but one facet of the broader
problem of European and world civilisation.

Indeed the more the problem of the rehabilitation of Germany is studied, the clearer does it become that it remains insoluble until it is transplanted into a broader setting. We cannot
solve it by treating Germans as Germans and nothing more. If
the problem of Europe is the problem of Germany, it can be

---

[1] J. W. Parkes, *The Jewish Question* (Oxford Pamphlet on World Affairs),
p. 31.

settled only within a European framework in which Germans can become not merely objects of policy but partners in carrying it out. Much has been written of the difficulty of collaboration between people who are not "like-minded" and of the necessity of creating a "psychology of cooperation". But neither "like-mindedness" nor a "psychology of cooperation" are fixed attributes. People become like-minded by doing things together and by sharing the same experiences; and the way to create a psychology of cooperation is not to preach cooperation, but to cooperate. This is particularly true of the younger generation. The only way to make young Germans into good Europeans is to give them a rôle to play in the reorganisation of Germany and of Europe which will restore and enhance their self-respect. Hitler appealed to the youth of Germany by demanding service to a narrowly national cause. Anyone who is to sway the destinies of Europe after the war must have the imagination to make an equally cogent appeal to the youth of Europe for service to a larger cause.

CHAPTER 10

THE NEW EUROPE

If then we are satisfied that Great Britain must undertake after the war a large programme of social and economic reconstruction, national and international; that she must readapt her relations with the United States of America to wholly changed conditions; that she cannot disinterest herself in the affairs of Europe and, in particular, of Germany; and that the German problem can be solved only as part of a general problem of European or world reconstruction; can we now take a further step and sketch the outlines of a concrete programme, however provisional, of post-war policy? Can we see the shape, however vague and unformed, of the institutions necessary to create a new order?

The Procedure of Peace-making

The first essential is clearly to dissociate measures designed to create a lasting international order from immediate measures specifically concerned with the termination of hostilities. Everyone is familiar with the discredit brought on the League of Nations in after years by the incorporation of its Covenant in the Versailles Treaty; and this was the inevitable result of attempting to combine in a single operation two distinct processes—the process of ending the war and the process of building the durable framework of an international society. These processes differ in character and in method. The first necessarily and rightly involves dictation by the victors to the vanquished. The second can be satisfactorily achieved only when dictation is relegated to the background and a real basis of cooperation established between former enemies. The latter aspect of peace-making is so much the more important that its needs ought not to be sacrificed to the exigences of the former.[1]

This difference in character between the two processes may also imply a separation in time. The measures taken to end hostilities must be prompt, drastic and makeshift. The building of a new order is a process to be undertaken slowly and cautiously; and there may be some delay before it can be profitably given anything like its final shape. There are many advantages to gain by this delay. The end of a great war leaves the balance of political forces violently disturbed or held in an artificial and temporary equilibrium which cannot long be maintained. The Versailles Treaty was based on the hypothesis—valid for the moment, but only for the moment—of the complete impotence of Germany and of Russia. A few years later so gross a miscalculation of the more permanent realities could scarcely have been made. Political conditions within the nation are equally subject to abnormal disturbance. This will be particularly true after the present war in countries which have been subject for months or years to enemy occupation, to partition and to the stifling of all ordinary modes of expression. These experiences, even more than the experiences of countries which have not actually suffered hostile invasion, are likely to bring about revolutionary changes in political life and thought. The character and extent of these changes cannot be gauged at the moment of the cessation of hostilities; and it will be some time before governments of these countries which have spent the greater part of the war on foreign soil can be confirmed in their mandates or be replaced by others. No peace claiming to represent anything like

[1] It will be recollected that the original intention of the victors of 1918 was to hold a preliminary conference of the victorious Powers to draw up a preliminary peace treaty, followed by a conference between victors and vanquished to draw up a final treaty. As things turned out, the final treaty was drawn up by what had been designed as the preliminary conference.

a consensus of European opinion can be established until there has been full time to study and assess the new and perhaps wholly unfamiliar trends resulting from the war.

Economic factors point the same moral. Modern war rudely dislocates the economic structure of every important industry in every important country, whether belligerent or not. It would require superhuman sagacity to discern, within a few months of the end of a war, which of these dislocations will be reversed by the coming peace, and which will lead to permanent modifications of the economic system. In 1919 the settlement was rushed through, and new frontiers were fixed, in the midst of the post-war economic chaos, and future economic trends were left to adapt themselves to dispositions made without regard to them. It is not surprising that they failed to do so. Such an error could be excused only on the ground of the survival of a *laissez-faire* belief in the divorce of politics from economics. Next time, if we wish to avoid the same failure of adaptation, it will be prudent to let the work of economic reconstruction proceed a long way before attempting to create the rigid political forms of a lasting settlement.

A third and extremely cogent reason for delay is psychological. The conduct of modern war of the totalitarian kind breeds—and indeed demands—an abnormal frame of mind in the populations affected by it. Under the stress of the sacrifices it requires and of the sufferings it imposes, large numbers of people do and believe and desire things which they would be quite incapable of doing or believing or desiring in ordinary conditions. Normal peace-time values are eclipsed or openly despised. The result is two-sided. The answer to the question whether war brings out the best or the worst in human nature is that it does both. Credulity and idealism, self-sacrifice and vindictiveness are all characteristic symptoms of war-time exaltation; and the intermingling of these qualities as well as the swift alternation of hopes and anxieties produces a general atmosphere of emotional instability. These abnormal psychological conditions are likely to persist in some measure for many months after the end of hostilities. The peace settlement of 1919 was marked by precisely this characteristic war-time blend of stupidity and vindictiveness with high idealism and unbounded faith in a near approach of the millennium.[1] A similar frame of mind, or perhaps some more extreme form of mass hysteria induced by the unparalleled sufferings and anxieties of the civilian population in all belligerent countries, seems likely to prevail at the end of the present war. If this prognostication is fulfilled, it provides a most cogent reason for delaying any comprehensive attempt to solve the problem of world order. "Those who can win a war well", wrote Mr. Churchill a few years ago, "can rarely make a good peace, and those who could make a good peace would never have won the war."[2] It may be suggested that the important factor is not so much the difference in different people's aptitudes for war-making and peace-making (though this no doubt exists), but rather the difference in the state of mind of people in general at different times and under different conditions. It took the people of this country a long time to discard their peace-time values and adapt themselves psychologically to the preparation and to the conduct of totalitarian war. The process of psychological readaptation to the needs of peace may prove equally difficult. Yet it should be axiomatic that a peace likely to endure will not be made by people who are still the victims of war-time psychosis. There must be time to prepare for the effective making of peace just as time was necessary to prepare for the effective waging of war.

Translated into concrete terms, this might mean that a considerable interval should be allowed to elapse between armistice

[1] The instability of political life in many countries after 1919 may be regarded—at any rate in part—as the psychological aftermath of the war. In Great Britain, millions who would have mobbed Ramsay MacDonald as a pacifist in 1918 voted for him as Prime Minister in 1924 and hailed him as the national saviour in 1931. In Germany, many who sincerely accepted the Wilsonian ideals of 1919 became the equally sincere Nazis of 1933.

[2] Winston Churchill, My Early Life, p. 346.

and peace conference.[1] But at this point one should perhaps enter a caveat against the traditional conception of the way in which wars are brought to a close. The end of the present war may be not so much a single event as a series of disintegrations— a gradual transformation of organised warfare into local fighting by armed bands. Armistices are concluded between armies. If the war in 1918 had been carried on for a few weeks longer, there might have been no German army with which to conclude an armistice; and it is not certain that this would have been a disadvantage. It should not be assumed without question that an armistice at the end of the present war will be either possible or desirable. It would be still rasher to make the same assumption about a peace conference. In 1919 the conception prevailed of peace-making as a single historical event limited in time and place—the drafting and signing of a diplomatic instrument or series of instruments—which would settle the destinies of the world for half a century or for all time; and impatience was expressed that the performance of these necessary acts had not been completed within six months of the armistice. After the present war it will be wise to recognise that peace-making is not an event, but a continuous process which must be pursued in many places, under varying conditions, by many different methods and over a prolonged period of time; and anyone who supposes that it will be complete within six years should be regarded with the utmost suspicion.

If therefore we wish to consider the procedure of peace-making, we should do well to envisage the complete military collapse and disintegration of the defeated; the establishment of effective control over the territory of the defeated by the victors; the setting on foot of a process of European reconstruction, beginning with immediate measures of relief and going on to the general rehabilitation of the industry, agriculture and

---

[1] M. Denis Saurat, writing before the French collapse, advocated, for example, a "congress for the reorganisation of Europe" five years after the conclusion of hostilities (*French War Aims*, p. 23).

trade of Europe and to the establishment of economic relations between Europe and the rest of the world; and finally, when this process is well under way and something like a new order is already shaping itself, an attempt to give political form to this new cooperation between peoples and continents. This arrangement of the agenda takes account of the fact that the fundamental problems of the world to-day express themselves in economic terms, and that a political settlement will have little chance of lasting unless it emerges as the crown and coping-stone of a successful economic reconstruction. This reconstruction must necessarily be slow and gradual. Its course should be guided by practical needs rather than by preconceived theories; and this course should in turn dictate the lines of a political settlement.

In particular, this principle must be applied to the vexed question of frontiers. The tradition which makes the drawing of frontiers the primary and most spectacular part of peace-making has outlived its validity. The idea that peace can be established by shifting frontiers in conformity with some fixed principle or set of principles did duty at Versailles, and has failed. To repeat the same process once more on the basis of the same or of other principles would be futile and hopeless. The urgent need now is to alter not the location, but the meaning, of frontiers. The drawing of frontiers thus becomes a secondary process, not only in importance, but in time; for it is impossible to have an intelligent opinion on the question how many frontiers can be tolerated, and where they shall run, until we have first obtained a clear view what frontiers are going to mean. We must first achieve a general picture of the new Europe before we can fill in the lines which will constitute its internal pattern. The pressure to take hasty political decisions as to the future territorial partition of Europe may be heavy, and will be based on the plausible ground of curtailing the uncertainty. But uncertainty is a lesser evil than the taking of wrong and irrevocable decisions. Resistance to such pressure is necessary if there is to be any chance of an eventual settlement on a firm and durable basis.[1]

A European Unit

The situation confronting us at the end of the war, while it cannot be foreseen in any detail, will certainly be baffling and anomalous. Effective military and economic control over Europe will probably be concentrated for the time being in the hands of two or three Powers, not all of them European. Some temporary provision must be made for carrying on the business of government in the countries released from months or years of Nazi domination. Yet in all these countries the utmost confusion will prevail. The eviction of intriguers and traitors, the resettlement of refugees, the administration of relief and the restoration of economic life will be the preoccupations of the moment. In such conditions, it would be folly to suppose that the will of the people can express itself through any normal electoral process. It would be more dangerous still to suppose that it can express itself through a group of men who have perforce been separated from the great mass of their compatriots throughout the whole of this epoch-making experience. In countries where the monarchical tradition holds, continuity of constitution is at least partially assured, though this does not necessarily involve continuity of policy. In what is perhaps the most difficult case of all, will anyone be rash enough to count on the emergence within, say, twelve months of the act of liberation of any government or body of men really qualified to speak in the name of France as a whole? In former enemy countries chaos may be even more complete. The conditions in which the war is likely to end will impose all over Europe a sort of interregnum in which there will be nobody properly entitled to take far-reaching decisions of policy on behalf of the countries

---

[1] A symptom of the prevailing trend of opinion is the general agreement that war aims must be defined at the present stage in social and economic terms, not in terms of frontiers.

which have passed through the cauldron of war. In this inter-regnum, imperfectly filled by local administrations possessing no real mandate, the existence of some effective authority of wider scope may almost everywhere be recognised as not merely desirable but imperative.

The measures taken after the end of hostilities in 1918 were planned almost exclusively in terms of the national unit. Sir Arthur Salter speaks of "the immense centrifugal force of national separatism" which made itself felt at that time and of the disastrous results of the encouragement given to it.[1] This time, if the same results are to be avoided, the need will be imperative to create from the outset some form of wider provisional authority or framework strong enough to hold centrifugal forces in check until the critical period is past. For purposes of convenience it may be useful in the first instance to call our framework "Europe". The term should not be taken to imply acceptance of the attractive but fallacious doctrine of "continental blocs". It need not be interpreted with much attention to geographical precision, and may well prove both too inclusive and too exclusive. We may perhaps provisionally limit it to the area which has participated, voluntarily or involuntarily, in the war and been directly subject to its ravages. The implication of the policy is that we should begin by treating our hypothetical "Europe" as a unit for the relief of its distress, and by ministering in the first instance to the needs of "Europeans", who are also in another (though for the moment less urgent) sense Frenchmen or Germans or Norwegians. The programme will be both empirical and experimental. In the words of an unofficial American group,

> Assuming a British victory, there will be a superior Anglo-American power in the world. The thesis is that this power should be used in the armistice period to provide real leadership in reconstruction; and that this reconstruction should be

[1] A. Salter, *Allied Shipping Control*, p. 266.

based immediately on economic coordination in a limited area which should gradually be extended outward.[1]

If this is the right line of advance, then we must avoid another error of 1919—neglect of the necessary continuity between the conditions and institutions of war and the conditions and institutions of peace. Some groundwork of the right kind had been done shortly before the armistice of 1918, when an Inter-Allied Conference on Enemy Propaganda referred in one of its resolutions to that "economic cooperation which is to-day a powerful instrument of war, and which may, after the war, serve as a basis for the systematic organisation of the resources of the world".[2] But when in the last days of the war the British Government, supported by various American officials in Europe, put forward tentative proposals to the American Government at Washington for the maintenance of economic cooperation during the reconstruction period, the reply of Mr. Hoover, then Secretary of Commerce, was "emphatically and indeed brutally negative, or perhaps it would be more correct to say, self-regarding".[3] The prompt withdrawal of American delegates caused the break-up of the most important existing organs of international cooperation and control just at the moment when enthusiasm for a League of Nations was reaching its peak and when initial drafts of the Covenant were being widely canvassed. Nobody seems to have remarked at the time on this incongruity. War was one thing and peace another; and what was relevant for the purposes of war was supposed to be irrelevant for the purposes of peace. Yet in retrospect it seems clear enough that, had these existing organs of cooperation been maintained and extended, and had the League of Nations never been heard of, the substance of an international order would have been far

[1] *The Eighth Fortune Round Table: Peace Aims* (Princeton, February 1941), p. 8.
[2] Campbell Stuart, *Secrets of Crewe House*, p. 183.
[3] A. Zimmern, *The League of Nations and the Rule of Law*, p. 157, where the most convenient account of the whole transaction will be found.

nearer realisation. In the light of this experience it has become easier to understand that clear-cut theories about future forms of international cooperation and control are far less valuable than a firm determination to carry forward unimpaired into the period of peace those forms of cooperation and control which have already been created.

This determination must be applied first of all to the military sphere. In the last war the principle of the single command in military operations conducted by the forces of more than one nation was gradually established. But no attempt was made to perpetuate this principle. Such unity of direction as existed was quickly dissolved. Within six months of the armistice, Polish forces equipped and financed by the Allies and conveyed to Poland under Allied protection and in Allied ships were openly resisting decisions of the Allied Supreme Council in East Galicia; and shortly afterwards there was fighting between Polish and Czech armies, both equipped with Allied arms and munitions. A firm hand will be required to prevent the recurrence of similar anarchy at the conclusion of the present war. Difficult as the problem appears, however, many new and valuable precedents have been created since the outbreak of the present war. A great deal of "mixing up together" has occurred not only between the United States and Great Britain, but between Great Britain and the smaller countries whose forces are now operating from Great Britain with British and American material and equipment, and under the British supreme command. Increasingly effective American cooperation will bring more direct American participation in these arrangements. Subsequent history has furnished cogent grounds for the Russian demand for naval and air bases on the northern and southern shores of the Baltic in the winter of 1939-40. A more valuable precedent may be found in the Russo-Polish agreement of July 30, 1941, which provides for the creation of a Polish army on Russian soil under the direction of the Russian High Command, but carrying with it the condition of Polish representation on that Command. Such arrangements must in one form or another be prolonged after the war. There is no reason why the armed forces of the Allies should not retain their present rights and status on British soil, or why British forces should not enjoy similar rights and status in other countries; and the principle of bases in the territory of one Power being leased to the forces of another Power admits of wide extension. It is, for instance, clear that British units occupying Germany will require bases in countries lying between Great Britain and Germany, and Russian units in countries between Russia and Germany, if such bases have not already been established before hostilities end. Such practical methods of military cooperation are far more promising than any formal attempt to create an international army. If the concentration of military power is a condition of the preservation of peace, this is far more likely to come about through the maintenance and progressive extension to other countries of an established framework of inter-Allied organisation than through the attempt to set up some new and theoretically more perfect system.

Equally important, and perhaps less difficult, will be the maintenance and development of existing organs of economic cooperation and control. These include machinery for the pooling of raw materials, for joint purchasing arrangements, for the standardisation of certain essential forms of production, for the joint control of shipping, for the financing of common needs and for the correlation of currencies. It is on this machinery that we must principally rely to bridge the transition from war to peace. The economic problems of peace will be substantially different from those of war, and different types of organisation will no doubt be required. But these must be allowed to emerge from existing organisations—just as the conditions of peace must be allowed to emerge from the conditions of war—not by an abrupt switch-over, but by a process of gradual evolution. This evolution will be the task of the reconstruction period, in which we may distinguish three different phases, logically interdependent and certainly to some extent overlapping in time: the phase of relief, the phase of reconstruction and rebuilding, and the phase of economic planning for the future.

Relief and Transport

The phase of relief will be theoretically the simplest. It will arise directly out of the war; it will be concerned with a problem whose reality and whose urgency nobody will deny; and it will raise no acute controversies of economic policy or motive. Difficulties of finance will be overcome by appeals, in part to philanthropy, in part also to self-interest. To leave some countries of Europe a prey to widespread famine and disease would expose those which remain to imminent risk of physical and moral contamination. Moreover the producing interests in overseas countries where surpluses of foodstuffs have accumulated will exercise strong pressure in favour of any relief programme which will provide them with a market. There may, it is true, be a demand for obeisance to economic orthodoxy in the form of "relief loans" to the recipient countries to finance these supplies. If so, such loans will be granted and received with the tongue in the cheek; for nobody will pin much faith to the prospects of repayment. It would be wiser—if such wisdom can be hoped for—frankly to recognise that these measures, which must be applied immediately after the war if civilisation is not to founder utterly, lie outside the normal organisation and practice of international trading and require special treatment. They should be regarded rather as an insurance premium paid by those countries which have the largest stake in the survival of civilisation.

The provision of relief provides an excellent starting-point from which to apply the principle of dealing rather with human beings or with "Europeans" than with nationals of particular countries. What kind of organisation will be set up to direct relief work cannot yet be foreseen. But the predominant influence is likely to be exercised by overseas representatives whose countries are providing major supplies and who may well be intolerant of discrimination between different national categories of recipients. The area under relief will have for practical reasons to be considered as a whole; and in discharging this humanitarian mission, priority must be given rather to those whose need is greatest than to those whose luck has placed at their disposal the largest resources in foreign exchange and shipping.[1] The shortages in non-German countries which have been under German occupation will be more marked than in Germany; and this will provide a sound reason for attending first to their needs. But no principle of discrimination against former enemies should be established. This would be universally recognised in the case of medical supplies to meet an epidemic or threatened epidemic; and the case of essential food and clothing is not really different. Where occupation of enemy territory takes place, it is important that it should be accompanied by relief officers to organise the distribution of vital supplies, so that the emphasis should fall on reconstruction rather than on repression—on the building of the new order rather than on the destruction of the old. The way to induce people to regard themselves as Europeans or as citizens of the world is to treat them as such, not to discriminate against them (or, indeed, in their favour) on the ground that they are members of a particular nation.

It is not improbable that want and distress in the weeks immediately following the end of active hostilities may be due less to actual shortages than to a general breakdown of transport and of normal agencies of distribution. This was the condition of Central Europe when an American observer visited it in January 1919. "One community may be starving while another has plenty of food, but the embargoes and seizure of railway transportation by the different governments prevent the food from being distributed. . . . He did not see a single potato

[1] The people of Great Britain will not refuse to set an example of self-sacrifice if the case for it is properly put to them.

on the market or on the table at Vienna, though millions of bushels of them were to be obtained in Hungary. . . . There is absolute and universal social disintegration." [1] In Russia at a slightly later date, according to those who worked there, "the way, first of all, to attack the famine would have been through the transport".[2] After the present war the destruction of ports and port installations, as well as of railway installations and material, may be a serious hindrance to the rapid distribution of supplies. The problem of relief thus brings us automatically and necessarily to the problem of transport; and here the case for international or "European" organisation is overwhelmingly strong. International control in one form or another has been established during the war over the shipping of a considerable part of the world. The needs of the immediate post-war period will be different in kind from those of the war, but scarcely less urgent; and the same control will have to be maintained for some time after the war if these needs are to be promptly and efficiently met. Centralised control of the principal European ports, and of transport on the European continent, by rail, by road and by air, as well as of coastal and inland shipping, will be no less essential for the regular and orderly distribution of supplies once they have arrived in Europe. How far such control may already have been established under Hitler's New Order is not exactly known. But it seems probable that before the end of the war something like a ready-made organisation will have come into being which the victorious Powers can take over and adapt to their purposes. There is no single field in which the old national unit has become more intolerably restrictive, or where there is more patent need for treating "Europe" as a whole, than in that of communications. There is also no field in which practical international cooperation, within certain preconceived limits, has in the past worked more satisfactorily. This is clearly therefore one of the fields in which an

---

[1] Quoted in A. Zimmern, *The League of Nations and the Rule of Law*, p. 159.
[2] A. Ruth Fry, *A Quaker Adventure*, p. 168.

immediate advance may be attempted with most confidence of success.

Here and everywhere else, however, it is of the utmost importance not to misunderstand or to underestimate the forces of resistance. The notion still entertained by the peacemakers of 1919 that any solution which seemed to them manifestly rational, and which commended itself to all independent "experts", would be voluntarily adopted by those concerned was a fruitful source of failure and confusion. The breakdown of international railway transport in Europe after the last war through the detention of rolling stock and other forms of non-cooperation was not due to any intellectual failure to grasp the common-sense advantages of an international system. It was due in part to the practical consideration that any railway administration which allowed rolling stock to pass out of its control had no guarantee of its eventual return, and in part to the psychological consideration that the exercise of power always brings both moral satisfactions and pecuniary advantages to those exercising it. Even in a field where the necessity and utility of centralised control are so widely recognised, power from without will be needed to establish it. Power will be required both to afford the guarantee of reciprocity and fair treatment which is a condition of any international system, and to check the inclination of local interests to exploit chaos for short-term advantages.

The needs of relief and transport are thus seen to involve, by a natural and unavoidable process, the need for some kind of international or "European" control and administration, established for the time being on a purely provisional basis and for certain limited ends. The amount of power required to establish this control will be in all probability extremely small, except perhaps in contested areas of mixed population where the presence of impartial military forces will be necessary in any event if order is to be upheld. The armies of occupation in former enemy territory should serve as an adequate nucleus of power; and in maintaining their own communications these forces will to all intents and purposes guarantee, and if necessary control, the transport system of Europe. No difficulty need be anticipated in utilising local administrations and local officials. Once the centralised control is established, and is known to have power behind it, the problem becomes predominantly technical. Goods will move expeditiously because people will want them and because there will be a power concerned to see that people get them.

Reconstruction and Public Works

The problem of organisation cannot for any but the briefest period be confined within the framework of relief and of the means of transport for its distribution. Once the immediate threat of famine and pestilence is staved off, the reconstitution of ordinary ways of life and the obliteration of the ravages of war become the primary need. Thus we reach the group of problems bearing the familiar label "reconstruction", which includes the physical rebuilding of objects destroyed, the reabsorption into the normal productive process of man-power drawn by the war into the armed forces or into emergency occupations such as munition-making, and the diversion of material and plant from war-time to peace-time production. Here we find ourselves at once in the realm of long-term economic planning. Reconstruction cannot in fact consist either in setting up again the "normal" economic structure destroyed by the war, or in maintaining, with some slight adaptations, the abnormal economic structure created by the war. Both these conceptions—the one looking back to the immediate, the other to a more remote, past—prevailed with disastrous results after 1918. They may prevail again unless the problem is promptly faced. Side by side with a European Relief Commission and a European Transport Corporation we shall need, hardly less urgently, a European Reconstruction and Public Works Corporation, whose task will be to set on foot such major works of construction or reconstruction as are too extensive or cover too wide an area to be handled by local initiative; and a European Planning Authority, whose mission will be nothing less than the reorganisation of the economic life of "Europe" as a coherent whole.

The European Reconstruction Corporation will have an immediate appeal because it will be dealing with things tangible, obvious and important. There has been devastation and there must be reconstruction. In the first place, therefore, the Corporation will absorb into its sphere the problems of "reparation", which can be solved only on the basis of work to be done, not of money to be paid. But it may prove expedient as well as generous to treat the task of physical reconstruction as one shared by all the European nations involved in the war rather than imposed as a penalty on certain responsible nations—the more so since the rapid progress of the work will probably depend in part on the voluntary cooperation and support of non-European countries. The psychological importance of introducing at an early stage the conception of cooperation in a common task rather than of burdens imposed by one group of nations on another can hardly be exaggerated. It may not be too much to say that the victorious peoples will be called on in the post-war period to make a fateful and irrevocable choice between the immediate pleasures of indulging in vengeance, however just, and the more remote but more lasting benefits of future peace. The two may well prove incompatible.

Secondly, since reconstruction cannot merely mean the replacing of what has been destroyed, the European Reconstruction and Public Works Corporation will necessarily and rightly find itself involved from the earliest moment in large-scale plans of building and development. International public works have in the past few years entered the public consciousness as something calculated not merely to remedy unemployment but to promote practical international cooperation as a psychological substitute for war.

> All over the world [wrote an American publicist recently] there are tools to be made and installed, roads to be built, swamps to be drained, rivers to be controlled, waterfalls to be harnessed. It is probably in concerted efforts to do this job that the peoples of the world stand the best chance of finding what William James called "a moral equivalent of war".[1]

The widespread prevalence of this belief in the efficacy of international public works is in itself a factor of importance. The essence of international cooperation is to find some immediate and concrete task which people think it worth while cooperating about, even at some sacrifice to themselves; and it seems likely that after the war important and far-reaching schemes of international public works can be made sufficiently striking and dramatic to capture the imagination and to receive popular support.

In this case there should be little opposition to the creation of an international investment fund to finance such enterprises.[2] Such a fund, though it might have prospects and hopes of becoming one day self-supporting, would of course be dependent for its initial operations on government subsidies. But the subsidising of employment and of export trade has become so familiar that the task of inducing well-to-do governments to finance public works lying outside their own territories, but likely to create indirect employment for their citizens, can hardly be regarded as a novel departure. We can have more hope of laying the foundation of an international financial institution on these lines than by attempting to impose something in the nature of international taxation upon governments.

[1] E. Staley in *International Conciliation*, No. 369 (April 1941), p. 400.
[2] The operations of the American Reconstruction Finance Corporation deserve study as a useful precedent.

A European Planning Authority

The most ambitious body of all—the European Planning Authority—will be called into existence at an early stage through the necessity of reaching decisions beyond the competence of any other organ on long-term issues arising out of the immediate problems of reconstruction; and from this it should be encouraged to develop into the ultimate authority responsible for vital decisions on "European" economic policies.

The European Planning Authority should therefore be regarded as the master-key to the problem of post-war settlement. If such an authority can be established and made effective, there is hope for the future of Europe. If it cannot, the prospect is almost unrelievedly dark; for the constitution of some such authority seems the only alternative to a recrudescence of the economic nationalism of the past twenty years—the inevitable outcome in modern conditions of providing no alternative to the pursuit by national units of independent, and therefore self-defeating, economic policies.[1] A certain qualified optimism may be justified by the experience of both combatants in the present war. On the one side Hitler has, through his very ruthlessness, established some sort of centralised European authority, and has created bonds some of which it might well prove difficult to destroy even if we wished. On the other side, the war has placed in the hands of the English-speaking countries and their associates an enormous concentration of economic power and has created some at least of the organs through which that power can be exercised. The European Planning Authority will in practice find itself the heir of two going concerns; the cen-

---

[1] "It will be our wish", said Mr. Eden in his Mansion House speech on peace aims of May 29, 1941, "to work with others to prevent . . . the currency disorders throughout Europe and the wide fluctuations of employment, markets and prices which were the cause of so much misery in the twenty years between the two wars." The experience of that period shows that such an end cannot be achieved without the establishment of some effective central authority.

tralised economic machinery of Hitler's New Order and the machinery of Allied war-time controls. Both these organisations will prove in different ways unsuitable for adoption as they stand. But unless—as happened in 1919—the advantage of building on existing organisations is recklessly and wantonly squandered, the rough foundations of an effective European Planning Authority will have already been laid before the end of hostilities. We must build on them, and perhaps recast them in the process of building.

Whatever may be the precise constitution of a European Planning Authority or of other "European" institutions in the immediate post-war period, they must from the outset represent, and be felt to represent, the interests of "Europe" as a whole and not of any one section of it. The needs can perhaps be most clearly defined by way of opposition to the defects of Hitler's New Order; and this contrast will incidentally provide that basis for British propaganda in European countries which is at present so lamentably and conspicuously lacking. The nature of Hitler's bid for European support and sympathy should not be misunderstood. He offers—at a price—order, security and unification. But his scheme is based on the hypothesis of German predominance; and it aims at securing exclusive advantages for Germany. In both these respects, the European Planning Authority must stand for a different principle.

In the first place, the European Planning Authority must enshrine the principle of equal cooperation between peoples, not of national or racial predominance. Hitler's New Order presupposes a German *Herrenvolk* ruling over inferior subjects. The nucleus of power on which the European Planning Authority will depend will no doubt be drawn in the first instance from the English-speaking countries and from Russia; and the economic as well as military strength of these countries will necessarily give them a powerful voice in its decisions, at any rate in the first years. But there can be no branding of those of different nation or race as inferiors and no exclusion of them from the councils of the Authority. The conception of an international organisation cannot be reconciled with the permanent and predetermined supremacy of a single nation.

Secondly, the European Planning Authority must not aim at securing exclusive advantages for the country or countries possessing the maximum power and resources. Hitler's New Order is admittedly designed to concentrate in Germany the most highly skilled and therefore most lucrative forms of production, and to reserve less lucrative forms of production—especially agriculture—to satellite countries. Even within Germany, according to some versions of the plan, foreign labour will continue to be employed after the war on menial, unskilled and ill-paid work. The machinery of currency and price control will continue to be used to secure for Germany the maximum profit from exchanges of goods with neighbouring countries. The principal economic purpose and result of the New Order will thus be to maintain for Germans a permanently higher standard of living than for other peoples brought within its scope. The European Planning Authority must from the outset reject the principle of differentiated standards of living. Living standards have become one of the most crucial issues in international politics and will constitute what Woodrow Wilson called the acid test of our sincerity. It must be the guiding aim of the European Planning Authority to raise the standard of living throughout the area in which it operates to the highest level prevailing within that area. This is one of the first essentials in any process of peace-making; for no real sense of community between countries is compatible with the maintenance of conspicuous and permanent discrepancies in the standard of living. In a period in which the natural flow of immigration from lower to higher standard countries is almost everywhere dammed back, the perpetuation of marked discrepancies between countries of comparable capacity carries with it the eternal menace of war.

Production, Trade and Finance

The full development of the functions of a European Planning Authority, and of the various organisations which will spring up under its aegis, must be a gradual and continuing process. Its primary function will clearly be to intervene in those fields of economic life where the misconceived and unqualified independence of the national unit has proved so fatal to peace and prosperity in the past twenty years: (1) production and marketing, (2) international trade, and (3) international finance.

(1) There is nothing novel about the idea of the international control of production. It has existed for many years on an extensive scale in the form of international cartels for particular industries or groups of industries. In agriculture, where the producing units were smaller and more difficult to organise, governments stepped in and established international control of production through an International Wheat Conference and an International Sugar Council. In raw materials, international rubber and tin controls have been more or less successful in organising production under a single authority. There are, or have been, control schemes for tea, coffee, copper and aluminium. The trend of all forms of production towards monopoly has conduced to the same end by a natural process of concentration. The International Nickel Company of Canada exercises what is virtually a world-wide control over the production of nickel. If the European Planning Authority began by concerning itself only with commodities which have been subject to some form of control, official or non-official, before 1939, there would already be a substantial basis for its operations. If it adds to these a majority of the commodities in which the British Government has been directly dealing during the war, the scope of its activities will be fully established. The need is not to create fresh controls, but to organise old ones. The question now at issue is not really whether there shall be international

control of the major branches of production, but what form
that control shall take and in what interests it shall be exercised.

The pre-war system of control exhibited two main shortcomings. In the first place, the control was exercised, openly and
admittedly, by producers in the interest of producers—a fatal
inversion, as has already been shown, of the process which
should govern production. Secondly, the control was exercised
on the basis of particular industries or forms of production and
without, in the nature of things, any serious attempt to determine the proper relation between different forms of production
—except perhaps on a basis of potential rivalry or conflict of
interests. The war has introduced new kinds of international
control of production, from which these shortcomings are
eliminated (whatever others may be involved). Control is exercised in the interests of the consumer, *i.e.* the war machine; and
relations between the different branches of production are, or
by common consent should be, determined by the order of priority of the consumer's needs. This is equally true of the international control of production established in Europe under Hitler's New Order and of the more rudimentary forms of international control of production set up by agreements between
Great Britain and other countries associated with her in the war.
The European Planning Authority will therefore find, super-
imposed on an untidy and unsatisfactory pre-war system of
controls, cartels and monopolies, a substantial number of new
war-time international precedents and a certain amount of war-
time international machinery. The transformation of these and
their application to a system of peace-time production will
be the first task of the Authority.

For some months after the war, needs will be almost as acute
as they were during hostilities. The problems of matching production to consumption will be similar in kind to those which
we are now experiencing, though perhaps less formidable in extent. This period will be prolonged by the necessary absorption
of resources and man-power in rebuilding and in public works.

But it would be fatal if the conditions of "post-war boom" which may be induced by these operations were to create the impression that a permanent remedy for our economic troubles had been found, and that no further organised or coordinated exertions were needed. The period of reconstruction in the narrower sense should be regarded as at best a short respite; and it should be utilised to plan and organise the future expansion of consumption—and through consumption, of production—when the immediate impulse of reconstruction has exhausted itself. This is perhaps in the long run the essential function of the European Planning Authority. It is also the crucial point where the ultimate possibility of creating some kind of international society will be tried and tested. The issue is neither constitutional nor, strictly speaking, economic. It will be found to turn mainly on the question whether we are prepared to accept it as an imperative moral purpose, worthy of some necessary self-sacrifice on our own part, to raise the standards of living of other human beings, not merely within the boundaries of our own national unit, but beyond them.

At this as at every other point of our enquiry, precision is rendered difficult by uncertainty as to many conditions likely to prevail after the war, including the uncertainty as to the area over which our "European" Authority will operate. It does not seem unduly optimistic to count on close American collaboration. But it would be rash at the present stage to expect full participation, including the direct extension of the scope of the Authority to the Western hemisphere. The same may be said of the relations to the Authority of the British Dominions and of Soviet Russia. If full participation is rejected, their approval and goodwill, as well as the closest collaboration, will none the less be essential; and it is easy to imagine joint organs for specific purposes, so that collaboration would be more complete and more intimate in some spheres than in others. On the other hand, it may be assumed that the overseas colonies of the European Powers will be brought within the full scope of the

Authority. A way will thus be open to treat the administration and management of colonial territories as a matter of international concern, and to ensure that the development of their resources and the reciprocal advantages of trade with them should lose their purely national character.

(2) These considerations are particularly apposite to the problem of international trade both within the area of the Authority and beyond it. The international control of production is closely bound up with the organisation of international exchanges of goods. Throughout the world—and especially in Europe, and most of all in Great Britain—international trade is a condition of economic well-being and a substantial part of production must be directed to foreign markets. But here we are faced with a psychological difficulty. For whereas there is a broad consensus of opinion that some organised and centralised control over production has become unavoidable, no such general agreement exists—at any rate in Great Britain and the United States—that any control or organisation of international exchanges is necessary or desirable. In Great Britain, belief in free trade has behind it the strength of a long tradition of rapidly expanding prosperity and of theoretical cogency. Economists have never had the slightest difficulty in demonstrating that in pure theory—and in practice, if non-economic motives were eliminated from human behaviour—restrictions on trade militate against maximum production. But the demonstration becomes largely irrelevant when considerations of social well-being override those of maximum production.

This is what has now happened internationally as well as within individual countries. Distribution has become a more burning issue than production. It is less important to achieve the maximum world production of iron and steel, of motor-cars and of cotton piece goods, than to provide for the more widespread and more equitable distribution both of the commodities themselves and of the benefits which accrue from the processes of production. It may be that the concentration of the manufacturing resources of the world in a few favoured areas—the corollary in modern conditions of the absence of barriers and regulations—would conduce to the maximum production of manufactured goods. But the world at large is not prepared to tolerate the overwhelming concentration of wealth and privilege and military power which such concentration of industry would involve. It may be true that the maximum production of grain crops at the minimum cost can be achieved by mechanised agriculture working in prairie conditions. But the world at large is not prepared for the social upheaval which the concentration of production in such conditions—the probable result of a removal of trade barriers—would involve. *Laissez-faire* and free competition, which tend to make the strong stronger and to eliminate the weak, are incompatible with what we have been led to regard as one of the primary aims of our policy and the sole method of averting future conflicts—the increasing equalisation of standards of living, and a wider distribution of the processes of production, between the more privileged and less privileged countries.[1]

This conclusion has an important bearing on the planning of our European economic system. We have already suggested that this system must rest in two respects on opposite principles to those of Hitler's New Order: it must reject the doctrine of the military and economic domination of a single Power, and it must aim at an equalisation of standards of living. These ends are wholly incompatible with *laissez-faire*. In the interests of

[1] Some remarks of the Yugoslav Delegate at Geneva, made in 1931, and already quoted in E. H. Carr, *The Twenty Years' Crisis*, p. 74, are apposite here: "The fact is that apart from economic considerations there are also political and social considerations. The old 'things-will-right-themselves' school of economists argued that if nothing were done and events were allowed to follow their natural course from an economic point of view, economic equilibrium would come about of its own accord. That is probably true (I do not propose to discuss the point). But how would that equilibrium come about? At the expense of the weakest. Now, as you are aware, for more than seventy years there has been a powerful and growing reaction against this theory of economics. All the socialist parties of Europe and the world are merely the expression of the opposition to this way of looking at economic problems."

military security, it must be one of our purposes to break up the virtual monopoly of heavy industry which has been gradually concentrated in German hands and to encourage regional industrial groupings which cut across national frontiers. In the interests of social welfare it may be desirable to introduce some measure of industrialisation into the low-standard countries of South-Eastern Europe. These are examples of aims which cannot be achieved unless we are prepared to control the flow of trade both within the European continent and between it and the overseas world. To promote international exchanges of goods will be one of the main instruments of our policy. But these exchanges will have to be deliberately organised in such a way as to serve the end in view. Economic policies broke down in the twenty years between the two wars not because we failed to translate our ideals into practice, but because we pursued the wrong ideals. If we wish to clear our minds on this subject, we must cease to regard the mere removal of trade restrictions as an ideal—even as an impracticable ideal—and recognise that organised trading is an essential condition of the fulfilment of our purposes.

The European Planning Authority will therefore have to establish, preferably though not necessarily in a single centre, clearing-houses for all the staple commodities which it takes under its control. Just as the British Government has found it convenient to trade, not in its own name, but in that of the United Kingdom Commercial Corporation, so the European Authority should probably set up a trading corporation to act on its behalf. Through this corporation it will organise the supply of commodities in urgent demand, and endeavour to find markets for commodities in abundant supply. It may do this to some extent by price regulation. Its aim will, generally speaking, be to maintain sufficient reserves to keep prices stable over short periods, but to use the price weapon where necessary in order to stimulate or curtail production over a long period. Price will thus be used, as it is already being used almost everywhere to-day, partly as a test of supply and demand and of the relative value to the consumer of different commodities, and partly as the instrument of a definite policy. Hitherto such control has been exercised internationally for single commodities, and nationally, in time of war, for virtually all essential commodities. The only novelty will be the combination of these two methods of control under a single authority; and even this has been to some extent anticipated in handling supplies for the Allies during the war. The crux of the problem is not to overcome technical difficulties, but to maintain in time of peace the common impulses and spirit of cooperation which have been established for the purposes of war.

(3) The problem of finance is in all essentials analogous to the same problem as it arises in the national sphere. The answer to the question, How can we afford it? or, How much can we afford? is the same, *i.e.* that we can probably afford a good deal more than we think, but that we cannot judge exactly how much till we try. The limits of our capacity lie, not in any mysteries of international finance, but in the extent of the resources in man-power and material which will be available and in the extent of our will and power to organise and use them. Above all, perhaps, they will depend on the limits of our readiness to recognise an obligation to people of other countries as well as of our own. If we take the view that Great Britain is unconcerned with the well-being and the standards of living of Belgian workers or Danish farmers or Norwegian fishermen, then no financial ingenuity will make any international society work. If we take the opposite view and are prepared to act on it, then financial difficulties are not insuperable, provided we face squarely the fact that financial risks have to be taken. The international financial system which flourished until 1914 is often spoken of as if it had operated to the profit and advantage of everyone concerned. This system, in fact, involved a continuous flow of loans from Great Britain and certain other countries (especially France), the repayment of which was provided for when

the time came by further loans; and when this cumulative process came to an end, default was the inevitable result. The advantages of the pre-1914 international financial system were paid for in the end by the British and French investors who lost their millions in South America or in Russia. The system seemed profitable to all only because those who benefited from it succeeded in unloading the cost on posterity. The process by which Germany was enabled to pay reparations between 1924 and 1930 was no novel phenomenon, but a repetition on a small and short-term scale of the process by which nineteenth-century borrower countries had regularly been enabled to pay their debts. It is not certain that the same confidence trick can be played again. If it cannot, it seems probable that those who occupy the most privileged position within any international financial system will be obliged from time to time to make deliberate sacrifices in order to make the system work; and these liabilities, like money spent on relief, must be regarded either as the discharge of a moral obligation or an insurance premium for the maintenance of civilisation.

If our European Planning Authority is to become effective, it must clearly have a "Bank of Europe" as one of its departments. The functions of such a bank may perhaps be grouped under four heads: (*a*) investment, (*b*) the financing of trade, (*c*) the liquidation of claims and (*d*) the control of currency.

(*a*) It has already been suggested that the urgent needs of reconstruction should be financed by an international investment fund. The capital required for the re-starting of industry is also unlikely to be available from private sources, and it may in any case be undesirable that private interests should be allowed to obtain control of staple industries through financial intervention. But here an important proviso must be made. The experience of the war has taught us much; and we have learned —or should have learned—to think of loans and investment in terms, not of money lent and money repaid, but of goods or services supplied or surrendered on a promise of goods or services to be returned at a later date. In other words, "money" should not be lent through or by the Bank of Europe for the establishment of an industry or for the mechanisation of agriculture without consideration, first, of the nature of the goods and services on which it will be spent and, secondly, and more important, of the nature of the products in which repayment will be made and of the market available for them. It is only by restoring consumption to its proper place as the determinant of production, and by seeing that those goods are produced for which consumers can be found, that we can hope to avoid that accumulation of unpaid and unpayable debts which brought the world to financial chaos and to war. Finance will become once more the agent, not the controller, of production; and the investment policy of the Bank of Europe will be a part, and an instrument, of the general economic policy of the European Planning Authority.

(b) The technical problems of financing international trade turn largely on the extent of the area over which the operations of the European Planning Authority will extend and on the precise nature of its relations with other important trading centres. But the essential principle which must be kept in sight is that all exchanges are ultimately exchanges of goods and services, not of money, and that all trade, whether bilateral or multilateral, ultimately partakes of the nature of barter. Just as pre-war instability in monetary exchange rates was not a specific disease susceptible of a financial remedy, but merely the symptom of a deranged balance of trade, so the establishment of stability in exchange rates is not a financial problem at all and can be achieved only by the establishment of a healthy balance of trade. What is needed, in the words of Mr. Eden's Mansion House speech of May 29, 1941, is "the development of a system of international exchanges in which the trading of goods and services will be the essential feature". The vital decisions of policy in this field must be taken by the European Planning Authority, working through its clearing houses. The function of the Bank of Europe will be essentially one of accountancy.

(c) The war will leave behind it all over Europe a mass of financial claims, public and private, of whose payment there will be not the smallest prospect, and whose authenticity and reasonableness will be difficult to test. Probably the largest item among them, though by no means the only item, will consist of claims against the German Government, German banks, and German trading or other institutions. Most of these obligations should be promptly wiped off as irrecoverable. Apart from any other obstacles to their recovery, the dislocation to the international economic system resulting from the attempt to collect them would be comparable with that caused by the attempt to collect reparations after 1919. But just as the small investor will probably be exempt from the inevitable scaling-down of national debts everywhere after the war, so it would be highly desirable, however difficult such discrimination may prove in practice, to make an exception in favour of the trifling international claims of the "little man"—the private citizen and the small trader. It would be no bad thing for the Bank of Europe to take over responsibility for these minor claims, undertaking to pay them in small instalments to the creditor and collecting them from the governments or the official or semi-official institutions responsible. Such a scheme would give considerable numbers of people in many countries a vested interest, however small, in the stability and continuance of European institutions, and would bring these institutions, in however trivial a way, within the range of consciousness of ordinary people. From this point of view, the admission of minor German claims to the same benefit as those of other countries would have a psychological value quite incommensurate with its intrinsic importance.

(d) The problem of currency management is more beset with the prejudice of preconceived notions than any other aspect of finance. The existence before 1914, of an international money, based on a gold standard and enjoying almost universal recognition, has done more than anything else to encourage the fatal belief in money as an independent entity obeying laws of its own. Much of the opposition to the only kind of financial expedient which will save us from disaster springs from a belated faith in a return to the rigid gold standard— to a conception of money as something imposed on us from without, not as an instrument to be controlled, modified and made use of by ourselves in the pursuit of a policy or purpose. It is therefore necessary to consider briefly the two main reasons why a return to the gold standard or to any single international currency standard is impracticable at present.

In the first place, as has already been noted,[1] the international gold standard currency of the nineteenth century was, like all other currencies, a "managed" currency. Thanks to the supremacy of the London money market, which financed a considerable proportion of international trade, and was a frequent and lavish lender to overseas countries, this international currency was "managed" by the bankers and bill-brokers of London. The gold standard was the symbol and the instrument of British financial hegemony: it was, in fact, just as much a sterling as a gold standard. Since 1914 there has been no single money market in the world strong enough to perform the functions of management exercised by Lombard Street in the nineteenth century. No single authority is now in a position to play that preponderant part in financing world trade and world indebtedness which the London market played down to 1914, if only because capacity and willingness to lend abroad on a large scale are an essential condition of making the system work. The valiant, if misguided, attempt to resuscitate an international gold standard in 1925 broke down as soon as the United States, the largest creditor country, ceased to lend freely to Germany, the largest debtor country. The Tripartite Monetary Agree-

[1] See pp. 176-7.

ment of 1936 between Great Britain, the United States and France was regarded by some as an initial step toward the revival of a single international standard. It never looked like achieving this result, not because one of the partners was too weak to have any right or claim to participate, and not because of the division of authority between London and New York, but because London and New York no longer in fact enjoyed anything like a monopoly in the financing of world trade, and above all because neither London nor New York had the will or the capacity to make extensive loans to foreign countries. So long as these conditions are not realised, it is useless to dream of a return to the nineteenth-century system which was wholly dependent on them.

The second and more fundamental reason why it is impracticable to restore the gold standard or any other single international currency standard is that the existence of such a standard presupposes an unrestricted flow of international trade. It is impossible to maintain a stable currency level between two countries unless a fairly free flow of goods and services from one to another is allowed to relieve the pressures arising from discrepancies in price-levels or from other variations due to conditions of labour or other factors of production. The naïve suggestion is sometimes made that, if at the end of the war the United States would share out among other countries in equitable proportions the gold now buried in Kentucky, the gold standard could thereafter be expected to resume its prosperous and uneventful career. This is sheer delusion. The same conditions which have attracted so much of the gold of the world to Kentucky would continue to operate with increasing force, so long as the United States, like other countries, are unwilling to admit freely to their territory either goods or immigrants from countries with lower standards of living. So long as barriers to trade and immigration are maintained, the same pressures will produce the same results, and neither the gold standard nor any other single international currency standard can be established. Money can never be given an independent existence of its own. It is an instrument and a measuring-rod for exchanges of goods. The authority which regulates these exchanges will also regulate the currency in terms of which the exchanges are conducted. Regulated international trade and an unregulated international currency standard cannot exist side by side. This does not mean either that gold may not serve a useful purpose as a convenient standard of measurement or that no importance attaches to the stability of relations between different currencies. But it does mean that this stability can be achieved only by deliberate regulation, which will be a function of the regulation of exchanges of goods.

It will therefore be the task of a Bank of Europe to manage and organise a "European" currency system. Whether it proves possible to realise the more ambitious project of a European currency, or whether each country will maintain its own currency, is a point of symbolical rather than practical importance, provided the different currencies are centrally controlled and stand in a fixed relation to some known standard. In other words, there is no practical drawback in having separate currencies circulating in, say, France and Holland under the name of francs and gulden so long as they can be exchanged at a fixed rate for sterling or for one another. But it is essential that this fixed relation should be maintained by a single central authority; and this authority must in the last resort be the authority empowered to control the flow of trade, since it is the flow of trade which ultimately determines rates of exchange.

The question of currency control raises, however, the far more problematical issue of the relation of a European currency or currency standard to the rest of the world. Since no European standard could be maintained without, at any rate, the support of Great Britain, it may be assumed that it would have a fixed relation to sterling; and the question of its relation to the rest of the world is therefore in the main a question of the relation of sterling to the dollar. This is once more not really a monetary problem, and can be treated only as a function of the problem of trade relations between the United States, Great Britain and Europe, including Russia. It seems improbable that the domestic policy of the United States will permit of the maintenance of a fixed and permanent relation between the dollar and gold. In any case gold cannot usefully be allowed to enter into the determination of the relation between sterling and the dollar. The issue depends partly on the extent to which the United States will participate in the setting up of a European Planning Authority or other European organisations, and partly on the character of trade relations established after the war by the United States with Great Britain and Europe. It is difficult to pursue our speculations any further on this subject in the absence of any clear indication of future American policy.

The New Europe

It is not until these provisional arrangements have been long enough in operation to demonstrate their value and their indispensability that we may hope to create out of them something like a new political and economic order. If our provisional "European" organisations have succeeded in maintaining some sort of *de facto* international military control for the preservation of order and in establishing some sort of international economic control which promises a substantial measure of prosperity and security to the people of Europe, they will have so far justified their existence that no serious question will arise of their abrogation. Habit will have insensibly created new and necessary institutions. In this provisional period, two conditions are above all necessary. The first is that Great Britain and the United States, together with Soviet Russia, should place their overwhelming military and economic power and resources behind the new Authority and make it effective over the area in which it operates. The second is that the power should be used, not for political ends, but primarily in order to restore economic prosperity and to raise standards of living all over Europe. If these conditions are fulfilled, it should not be difficult to convince a large majority of the people of Europe that these organisations fulfil a vital need, and that they contain at any rate the seeds of a truly representative European or international order.

Nothing has yet been said—and nothing precise can well be said in advance—of the procedure by which our European Relief Commission, our European Transport Corporation, our European Reconstruction and Public Works Corporation and our European Planning Authority will be created. Assuming that some or all of these bodies will be called into existence at the end of hostilities, or shortly afterwards, the method of their appointment—like everything else done at that time—must necessarily be provisional, makeshift and somewhat rough-and-ready. There can at that moment be no means other than guesswork of making them even approximately representative, in any formal sense, of those in whose interest they are to work. The constitution of these bodies will naturally vary according to function. On the European Relief Commission, the representation of the countries furnishing and organising supplies will be as important as representation of the beneficiaries. In the European Planning Authority some form of combined representation of countries and interests, such as the ingenious plan of the International Labour Organisation, might prove effective. Other devices may be tried to make these bodies representative of as many interests and as many parties as possible, pending the time when more regular methods of selection become practicable. It may be appropriate to begin by regarding these various "European" authorities and institutions as representing for the time being, not so much the governments or the nations or even the peoples, but simply the people, of "Europe". If this view is right, it is by some such direct appeal to the people themselves, to the "little men" of all countries, rather than through any constitutional process of league or federation, that a European order, and ultimately perhaps a world order, may come into being.[1]

If we have proceeded so far, we shall realise that, half consciously and half unconsciously, in adopting new methods of procedure, we have made a vital departure from the underlying philosophy of the 1919 settlement. In 1919 the consciously or unconsciously accepted view of an international society was that it should be constructed by the piecing together of national units. Each nation-state, based on the principle of national self-determination, should be encouraged and assisted to build up its own military and economic structure with primary regard to its own national interest; and each national unit, by asserting its own interest to the full, would be induced by that very interest to cooperate with other units actuated by similar motives. Consistently with this philosophy, the Allied leaders gave full rein to the centrifugal tendencies of national self-determination and, having allowed and encouraged these forces to assert themselves, thought to counteract their dangers by the device of a League of Nations. Having proclaimed unqualified independence for all nations as a principal Allied war aim, and having fostered the growth of a maximum number of independent national units, they sincerely believed that these dispersed fragments could be induced by their own interest to re-unite into a unit of common obligation. It was, as the sequel showed, a policy of self-contradiction and self-frustration. What the peacemakers of 1919 in fact did was to create, by one part of their policy, conditions which made the other part wholly impracticable. Next time the best hope lies in a reversal of this process. Instead of basing our settlement on a recognition of the unrestricted right of national self-determination, and then seeking to build up an international system out of independent

---

[1] It is worth nothing that Ministers and officials, like company directors, have a certain vested interest in resisting any form of cooperation or fusion which may limit their own importance. This resistance is not necessarily based either on the will or on the interests of those for whom they claim to speak.

national units, we must begin by creating the framework of an international order and then, as a necessary corollary, encourage national independence to develop and maintain itself within the limitations of that framework. The settlement of 1919 was planned in terms of the national unit. Our task must be to plan from the first in terms of the wider framework.

We are passing through the greatest revolution of modern times, and to describe a policy as revolutionary is merely to indicate that, at any rate in this respect, it is appropriate to the age for which it is designed. New institutions can be made effective only on the basis of new loyalties arising out of newly felt needs: yet to create these new loyalties new institutions are required. This dilemma can be resolved only in revolutionary times and by revolutionary action. It has been suggested elsewhere in this book [1] that one key to the problem of national self-determination is to recollect that there are no rights of nations, but only of men and women, and that the so-called claims of Ruritania are nothing more or less than the claims of people who happen to be Ruritanians. If this be true, it cannot be assumed as a matter of course that we have in the past been right in beginning with the nation in order to construct our international order. It may well prove that the traditional specifics for promoting international unity—the League of Nations, the United States of Europe, Federal Union—started, so to speak, at the wrong end. It may be that we should build our international framework on different principles and on other foundations if we wish to make it strong enough to resist the disintegrating forces of nationalism contained within it. If at the conclusion of the present war we can create such a provisional framework of collaboration over a limited area of the world most directly affected by the ravages, we may find that we have constructed something which mankind will come gradually to recognise as indispensable to its future well-being

[1] See pp. 49-50.

and which can some day be given both a wider geographical
extension and appropriate constitutional forms. When this stage
has been reached, it will be time to think of formal agreements,
of definitions of functions, and of constitutional rules. These
agreements, definitions and rules will then be determined, not
theoretically according to some *a priori* conception of league,
alliance or federation, but empirically as the outcome and expression of a practical working arrangement.

The building up of such a European order is in no sense a
derogation from the principle of self-determination. It is an
application of the principle suggested in an earlier chapter of
this book that, if a durable international order is to be realised,
men must be induced to determine themselves into different
units for different purposes and that, for the control of military
and economic policy, the national unit has become visibly too
small. Moreover the more solidly a wider European or international framework can be forged, the more perfect can be the
realisation within it of national self-determination. Just as democracy flourishes most where national cohesion is most assured, and liberty where authority is most deeply rooted, so
self-determination can be most real when the international order
is most firmly established. Once military and economic power
have been centralised and made common, an important limitation on the principle of self-determination is removed; and
we shall be spared the embarrassments familiar in 1919 of forc-
ing recalcitrant people into the wrong national unit, or joining
together on strategic or economic grounds those who would
have preferred to remain asunder. It is the only method by
which true self-determination can be made compatible with
military and economic security. Only where international order
has been assured can national aspirations for independence and
self-government, for the development and maintenance of national institutions and national culture, receive their full and
unrestricted expression.

The most serious ground of anxiety about the making of

peace is the same which has handicapped our waging of war: complacency and an ingrained disposition to minimise the exacting nature of the task. Few things are more dangerous to the future welfare and prestige of Great Britain than the common inclination to assume that, once Hitler is defeated and Germany rendered helpless, the world can with relatively little trouble be re-settled on familiar and comfortable lines. Two things will be urgently required; and if this country means to play a leading rôle hereafter in world affairs, they will be required of this country. The first is the exercise of power. It is necessary to dispel once for all from our minds the pleasant illusion that, once victory is achieved, unreserved goodwill and reasonableness will prevail among the victorious Powers and will induce individuals and nations to combine spontaneously together for the common good. No durable peace can be made unless those who have the power have also the will in the last resort, after having tried all methods of persuasion, to take and enforce with vigour and impartiality the decisions which they think right. The second and still more important requisite is that those who have the power should recognise the moral obligation which alone makes its exercise tolerable to others. Neither the will to take the initiative nor the will to sacrifice which such a course entails can be achieved without a high sense of moral purpose. If after the war is won British power and British prestige are not to be either frittered away in apathy and reaction or swept away in the uncontrollable current of revolution, British democracy must find leaders inspired by such a purpose in their attitude both to national and to international affairs.

The old world is dead. The future lies with those who can resolutely turn their back on it and face the new world with understanding, courage and imagination. This book is a call for such leadership.

INDEX